Praise for *When We Were Free to Be*

"A moving reminder that the women's movement
was and is ardently pro-child. These fascinating reminiscences
and timely essays about what still needs doing to make our children
truly 'free to be' will have you singing the songs again—
or discovering the joy of learning them."

STEPHANIE COONTZ, author of *A Strange Stirring: The Feminine
Mystique and American Women at the Dawn of the 1960s*

"*Free to Be* was a declaration of independence for children's dreams.
. . . That it is seen by some today as obvious or naive is because it so
utterly supplanted the previous mindset. This marvelous collection
reminds us of that paradigm shift, still gently iconoclastic,
while reminding us how far we have yet to go."

MICHAEL KIMMEL, author of *Guyland:
The Perilous World Where Boys Become Men*

"Finally, a book that takes seriously the kids' record that
altered the way a generation saw the world and itself. . . .
The story it tells is of a remarkable moment in which children
were entrusted to shape the future. An exhilarating book about
an exhilarating (and catchy!) piece of our popular culture."

REBECCA TRAISTER, author of *Big Girls Don't Cry:
The Election That Changed Everything for American Women*

"*Free to Be* showed my daughters they had the power to
lead their own dreams. . . . *When We Were Free to Be* shows how
profoundly this one book has empowered an entire generation."

GLORIA FELDT, author of *No Excuses: 9 Ways Women
Can Change How We Think about Power*

When We Were Free to Be

To Suzie,

It's a pleasure to sign
this book for you!
Enjoy! All best,
Lori

EDITED BY

Lori Rotskoff & Laura L. Lovett

When We Were
Free to Be

Looking Back at a Children's Classic
and the Difference It Made

THE UNIVERSITY OF NORTH CAROLINA PRESS   *Chapel Hill*

© 2012 THE UNIVERSITY OF NORTH CAROLINA PRESS
Copyright notices for contributions to the book appear on pp. 311–12.

The illustrations on pp. 20, 26, 33, 34, 39, 53, 54, 213, and 258 are from
the personal collection of Marlo Thomas. Used with permission.

All rights reserved. Designed by Sally Fry.
Set in Caecilia and Font-on-a-Stick by Rebecca Evans.
Manufactured in the United States of America

The paper in this book meets the guidelines for permanence
and durability of the Committee on Production Guidelines for
Book Longevity of the Council on Library Resources.

The University of North Carolina Press has been a
member of the Green Press Initiative since 2003.

Library of Congress Cataloging-in-Publication Data
When we were free to be : looking back at a children's classic and the
difference it made/edited by Lori Rotskoff and Laura L. Lovett.
p. cm.
Includes bibliographical references and index.
ISBN 978-0-8078-3723-8 (cloth : alk. paper)
1. Children—Conduct of life—History. 2. Self-acceptance—History.
I. Rotskoff, Lori. II. Lovett, Laura L.
BJ1631.W48 2012
305.230973—dc23
2012021752

"We and They" by Lucille Clifton is quoted in full
in the essay by Gloria Steinem. © 1972 Lucille Clifton.
Used by permission of the Free to Be Foundation.

16 15 14 13 12   5 4 3 2 1

To Benji and Eli
Lydia and Arlena

Contents

Illustrations

When We Were Free to Be

Introduction

LORI ROTSKOFF & LAURA L. LOVETT

If you grew up or raised children during the days of pet rocks, mood rings, and lava lamps, there's a good chance that you remember *Free to Be . . . You and Me*, the groundbreaking children's record, book, and television special that debuted in 1972. Yet unlike other relics from the recent past, the messages and melodies from *Free to Be . . . You and Me* still resonate for many children, parents, and teachers today. Even if you're younger than the generation that first came of age with it during the 1970s, you've probably heard some of the album's songs or stories before.

Free to Be . . . You and Me still stirs up a heady mix of memories for adults who once belted out the words to "William's Doll" and "Parents Are People" in second-grade classrooms or wood-paneled dens with orange shag carpet. If it's nostalgia that led you to this volume, you'll find plenty of recollections here to take you back. You'll rediscover how *Free to Be . . . You and Me* encouraged children to confront the world with a spirit of unfettered possibility and imagination.

But this book isn't just a cozy trip down memory lane. And *Free to Be . . . You and Me* wasn't merely an entertaining novelty for the primary-school set. It also offered kids a fresh alternative to rigid gender and racial stereotypes that had long prevailed in American society. Featuring a mélange of songs, skits, stories, and poems recorded by celebrated musicians, actors, and singers, *Free to Be . . . You and Me* dramatically changed the way in which parents and children thought (and continue to think) about gender roles and social equality. Conceived by actress and children's welfare activist Marlo Thomas, and coproduced with Carole Hart, this unique compilation taught children to value cooperation and resist blind conformity to social expectations. Infused with positive messages endorsing freedom of expression, fairness, and respect for diversity, *Free to Be . . . You and Me* taught young people to resist prejudice and transcend prevailing norms of acceptable "boy" or "girl" behavior. Using popular media as a vehicle to inspire and influence children—as well as the adults who taught and cared for them—*Free to Be* combined entertainment and education to animate a particular vision of social change rooted in the civil rights and women's liberation movements of the 1960s.

Today, when the landscape of childhood harkens back to the sharply divided sex roles of the *Leave It to Beaver* era, the vision of gender neutrality and equality that infused *Free to Be* can seem not just quaint but almost utopian. And so we wonder: What happened to the ideals that inspired *Free to Be . . . You and Me?* Just walk into any local toy store (if you can find one still in business) and notice how the playthings are segregated. One realm beckons girls with Cinderella daydreams, while the other bombards boys with fantasies of manly bravado. When crass commercialism shows its true colors, pink and blue don't make purple, they make green, multiplying profits every time parents buy into the premise that boys and girls require different playthings, books, websites, and computer games.[1]

This exaggeration of children's gender differences is far from a benign predicament. From birth, baby girls are swathed in pink stroller blankets, while boys receive totems expressing the normative power of boyhood sports. For every girl who downplays her interest in asteroids in favor of lip gloss, there's a boy who skips auditions for the school musical because his friends will tease him for doing something "girly." Too often, when youth don't fit the standard-issue gender scripts, they suffer from ridicule and ostracism, cruel reminders that we have a long way to go when it comes to respecting human diversity. Children of both sexes—as well as those who resist conformity to a single gender category—lose out when they hide their true interests because they don't fit prevailing norms.[2] The continuing need for feminist, antiracist, gay rights, and transgender activism speaks to the reality that countless people are not yet "free to be."

Free to Be . . . You and Me was part of a broader set of liberal feminist efforts focused specifically on children. Advocates for equal rights worked tirelessly to level the playing field—literally and figuratively—for the youngsters in their midst. They urged toy companies to make puzzles depicting black female police officers and airplane pilots. They bought macramé kits for boys and chemistry sets for girls. Hammering away at stifling stereotypes, they ushered in a new historical moment when gender equality was for children, too.[3]

We know this because we lived it ourselves. In 1974, the year the *Free to Be . . . You and Me* book was published and the television special hit the airwaves, we were five and eleven years old, respectively, and attending our local elementary schools. We grew up in middle-class communities far removed from the hotbeds of progressive politics: Lori in the suburbs of St. Louis, and Laura in Virginia Beach and later San Diego. While neither of our mothers was politically active in the women's movement, they raised us to embrace—and even to expect—equality between the sexes.

We rediscovered *Free to Be . . . You and Me* when we had children of our own. As soon as our toddlers grew tired of lullabies and Elmo songs, we slotted *Free to Be* into our stereos and smiled when they hummed and drummed to the soundtrack so indelibly etched in our brains.

But our rediscovery of *Free to Be* was academic as well as personal. Trained to analyze artifacts of popular culture as documents rich with social meaning, we couldn't help but approach *Free to Be* as primary source material. Years ago, when we began teaching college courses in American history, we included *Free to Be* in our assigned readings on the feminist movement, along with books such as Betty Friedan's *The Feminine Mystique* and Robin Morgan's *Sisterhood Is Powerful*. On campuses ranging from the University of Tennessee to Sarah Lawrence College, some of our students knew *Free to Be . . . You and Me* intimately, while others had never heard of it before. Some thought the songs were radical, while others critiqued what they perceived to be heterosexist assumptions of family life. Given these varied reactions by our students, we knew that *Free to Be* was ripe for historical analysis.

Looking back, we realize what a profound impact *Free to Be* had on our own values and aspirations. The message from "Parents Are People"—that mothers can "be almost anything they want to be" *and* be "busy with children and things that they do"—rang through loud and clear. In hindsight, of course, we know that combining work and family life isn't so simple. Structural barriers in the workplace, the ongoing demands of child rearing, difficulties in securing child care, and often economic insecurity make it far more challenging for parents to live out the song's sunny, "have-it-all" vision. But that fact doesn't discount *Free to Be*'s impact on the expectations it helped set for the children who grew up with it. Rather, it makes *Free to Be* all the more relevant in retrospect: as an artifact that registered concerns unique to the moment that produced it, and as a cultural landmark that still generates new meanings today.

As we mark *Free to Be . . . You and Me*'s fortieth anniversary, the moment is right for a retrospective account of its history and legacy. This collection explores the creation, popular reception, and social impact of *Free to Be . . . You and Me* over the past four decades. Our contributors combine original research, personal reflections, and pointed insights to explore *Free to Be*'s significance from different generational vantage points. As editors, we reached out to more than thirty people with strong personal or professional connections to *Free to Be*, including musicians, actors, television producers, teachers, sociologists, historians, choreographers, activists, and of course, seasoned writers and journalists. Collectively, we honor the creative work that brought *Free to Be . . . You and Me* to fruition, but we also address some of the blind spots and backlashes that have limited its impact along the way.

Our book begins with a lively and informative prologue by Marlo Thomas, who conceived and coproduced this landmark trio of children's literature and popular culture. And given that Marlo was inspired to invent *Free to Be . . . You and Me* by her young niece, Dionne, it is fitting that Dionne Kirschner—now a television producer and mother of two—offers here a loving tribute to the starring role that *Free to Be* has played throughout her life and for many others of her generation.

Part 1, "Creating a World for Free Children," takes us behind the scenes into the brainstorming sessions, recording studios, and Manhattan set locations where Marlo Thomas and her collaborators produced the three incarnations of *Free to Be . . . You and Me*. As historians, we know how important it is to access the voices of people who have shaped our culture, so we asked *Free to Be*'s creators as well as other educators involved in nonsexist child rearing to record their own stories. While producer Carole Hart offers a thoughtful overview of *Free to Be*'s creation, songwriter Carol Hall wryly notes the origins of her renowned lyrics. Composer and musical director Stephen Lawrence sheds light on *Free to Be*'s musical arrangement, while Alan Alda muses on how his childhood and later political activism informed his contributions as an actor and director. In addition, Letty Cottin Pogrebin, Gloria Steinem, Francine Klagsbrun, and Barbara Sprung explore the many ties between *Free to Be* and the wider women's movement, social activism, early childhood education, and the pioneering journalism of *Ms.* magazine.[4]

The essays in Part 2 situate *Free to Be . . . You and Me* in a broader historical context. Here, we sketch a more complete history of second-wave feminism than has been previously recognized, one in which children and childhood mattered in significant ways. One of the most misleading myths about feminists is that they ignored children and sought to free women from maternal obligations. It is true that motherhood and child rearing were fraught issues for feminists, many of whom chose not to bear children. Other feminists, exposed to women's liberation after they became mothers, struggled (sometimes painfully) to differentiate between the love they felt toward their children and the social ideologies that exalted motherhood to the exclusion of careers, paid work, and other public roles.[5] But feminists' social critique of "patriarchal motherhood" did not prevent them from focusing on early childhood education, subsidized child care, children's health, and other programs designed to improve young people's well-being.

Indeed, *Free to Be* was part of a broader nonsexist child rearing movement that engaged radical and liberal feminists alike. Just as they fought to ensure equality in the workplace, the government, the university, and the sports arena, so too did they advocate equal rights for the nation's youngest citizens. From toy stores and television sets to preschools and playgrounds, from local libraries and Little Leagues to dancing schools and day camps, feminists reshaped the material world of childhood to enact their progressive vision of fairness and freedom. Across the nation, PTA committees, consciousness-raising groups, and other local coalitions made progress in the playroom—and in the classroom, too.

The campaign to create a sexually egalitarian environment for children was as germane to second-wave feminism as the crusade for reproductive freedom, the passage of antidiscrimination laws, or the struggle for equity in the workplace. From the earliest stirrings of the women's liberation movement, child rearing emerged as a vital arena in which feminists enacted their essential claim that the personal is political. Placing *Free to Be . . . You and Me* at the center of this history reframes how we understand the achievements of second-wave feminism in the United States and underscores the significance of children and childhood to its development.[6]

During the years of *Free to Be*'s production, sweeping legal and political changes paved the way for many children to participate in feminism. In 1971, partly in response to student activism against the Vietnam War, Congress lowered the voting age to eighteen; consequently, more youth began to see themselves as participants in the life of the nation. And in 1972, the U.S. Congress passed Title IX, an overarching piece of legislation that prohibits sex discrimination within any educational program or athletic activity that receives federal funding. After the passage of Title IX, children learned that gender discrimination in public settings was not just a matter of social custom or moral concern, it was against the law.

In this context, *Free to Be* invited children to experiment with social roles and to contemplate the future with a spirited sense of optimism. Although most young listeners during 1970s were not literally "free" from adult control in a general sense, the album fostered strong feelings of independence and autonomy. By creating an imaginary middle ground between adult-imposed expectations and unfettered free will, *Free to Be* enabled children to experience momentary feelings of liberation and acquire values necessary to resist the more conservative dictates of the dominant culture. This is not to suggest that *Free to Be* didn't instruct children in particular ways of feeling, thinking, or acting toward others. Didactic lessons abound in these tales and tunes. Nonetheless, most young fans had no trouble discerning an empowering message of self-discovery.

From the first bright notes of the title track, children entered an imaginary "land" that was freer and more equitable than the world they actually inhabited. This place was a fantasy, of course. But isn't that what many inspiring works of children's literature do? Invite children into a make-believe world where so much seems possible? Where the narrative puts *them* at the center of the moral universe it constructs? As Alan Alda notes in his piece, the album created a rich soundscape of impressions that allowed children to project themselves into the drama, to take their places among characters who sprang to life from the vinyl disc.

That's quite an accomplishment for a children's record. Equally inspiring, though in different ways, were the book and television versions. Forty years later, *Free to Be . . . You and Me* remains a beloved, complex, and sometimes contested collection of literature, art, and entertainment. It even bears hallmarks of a children's classic. Some readers might ask if it isn't premature to proclaim *Free to Be* a classic. Does it deserve to be listed among even recent "classics" like *The Little Engine That Could*, *Harold and the Purple Crayon*, or *Pippi Longstocking?*

We think there's a good case to be made for calling *Free to Be* a "clas-

sic" forty years after it appeared. We're living in a different historical moment, so audiences encountering it today will absorb different
meanings from it than did earlier generations of children. But that's
the case with all enduring children's works: characters say and do
things that seem "old-fashioned," antiquated, or just plain weird. Yet
certain kernels of emotion and experience continue to resonate with
later generations. *Free to Be*'s creators didn't talk down to children but
instead took them seriously, inspired their curiosity, and made the
world seem like a more welcoming place. That sounds pretty "classic"
to us.

But classic doesn't mean "universal" in that all listeners or readers
have identified seamlessly with its representations of childhood. In
line with *Free to Be*'s own insistence that children learn to question the
status quo, many contributors to this volume challenge conventional
wisdom, point out inconsistencies, and critique aspects of popular
media from the standpoint of issues that matter most to them now.

In Part 3 of this book, "Parents Are Still People: Gender and Child
Rearing across Generations," contributors explore the extent to which
Free to Be still speaks to them as thoughtful parents today. Blending a
new mother's bleary-eyed wonder with the probing analysis of a feminist bibliophile, Deborah Siegel explores how her twin infants were
inducted from birth into a highly gender-differentiated world. With
refreshing candor, Robin Pogrebin lays bare the conflicting desires she
feels as a working mother, while Abigail Pogrebin pens some sharply
observed lyrics of her own—a song that will strike a chord with many
grown-up "Free to Be" daughters still determined to "do it all." Jeremy
Adam Smith revisits his connection to "William's Doll" for clues to the
slowly shifting contours of normative masculinity he now encounters
as a father; Laura Briggs relates legacies of nonsexist child rearing to
her sensibilities and strategies as a lesbian parent; Nancy Gruver and
Joe Kelly chronicle their long-standing commitment to equally shared
parenting; and Karin A. Martin explores the influence of *Free to Be* in
parenting advice manuals decades after Dr. Spock first took up his
pen.

Finally, the essays in Part 4, "How Free Are We to Be?: Legacies and
Critiques," deepen our investigation of *Free to Be*'s cultural impact and
social limits. What's a mother to do, asks Peggy Orenstein, when her
daughter is dazzled by Disney princesses at every turn? What ensues
after Deesha Philyaw, a teacher and writer on antiracist parenting,

curls up on the couch to watch Michael Jackson sing "When We Grow Up" with her middle-school children? How did Marlo Thomas's iconic role on *That Girl* inspire Becky Friedman, a preschool teacher turned television writer, to create a new show for children today? How does choreographer Trey McIntyre draw on memories of his progressive midwestern childhood to create a new modern dance performance to the original *Free to Be* music?

In this section, contributors ponder these and other probing questions about gender difference, media representation, and social equality. How have children and adults of different races, economic classes, religions, sexualities, and gender identities responded to *Free to Be*'s joyful call for freedom? What if you loved the song proclaiming that "daddies are people," but your best friend's father left the scene? What if you're a girl who just wants to wear a frilly pink dress? What if you're a boy who wants to do so? What happens when, as an adult, you can no longer reconcile the expectations of your church with the ideas enshrined in your favorite childhood songs? While recognizing *Free to Be*'s singular achievements, the authors in our book's final section add complexity and nuance to our project of historical assessment. As they reveal how much has (or hasn't) changed over the past several decades, they also speak to the power of *Free to Be*'s original message: You matter, and what makes you different also makes you who you are.

Free to Be was a remarkably bold, forward-thinking project during its time. Social change doesn't happen progressively or consistently. It happens in fits and starts, and even when it lurches forward, there are glitches—and sometimes full-blown backlashes—along the way. Even the most visionary reform policies or the most cutting-edge works of popular culture don't solve all of our problems all at once. They don't speak to everyone or address every kind of social injustice at one time.

Furthermore, the meanings and emotional connections that people attach to these songs and tales vary considerably—and these responses have shifted, too, as political debates and cultural priorities regarding gender and sexuality have changed over time. The intentions of *Free to Be*'s creators arose within a specific historical context. But as is true of audiences for any work of popular culture, *Free to Be*'s listeners, readers, and viewers have made sense of these stories and images through different interpretive lenses. While this book includes a colorful array of perspectives, the voices in it represent only

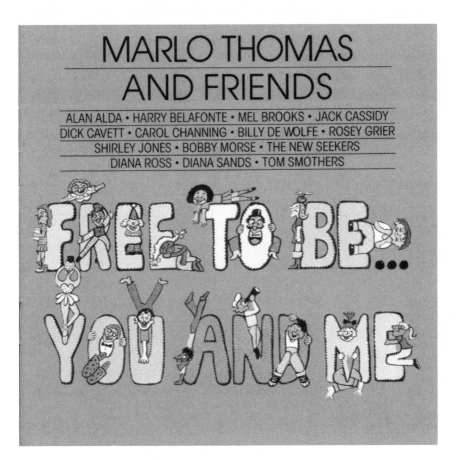

Original *Free to Be . . . You and Me* album cover, 1972.
Used with permission of the Free to Be Foundation.

a fraction of potential interpretations. No single document offers a complete or "representative" account of *Free to Be*'s creation or legacy. Collectively, however, the essays in this book suggest how complex the social impact of progressive children's culture has proven to be. Our hope is to spark continued reflection and debate—and to inspire readers to contemplate their own personal histories.

The 1970s are history. But despite how far we've traveled from our parents' or grandparents' generations, as Gloria Steinem put it in her original preface to the *Free to Be* book, "The children we once were are inside us still." *Free to Be . . . You and Me* still speaks to adults today for this reason: it summons the children still within us—those dormant, youthful parts of ourselves that that once looked out toward a horizon

Free to Be . . . You and Me book cover, 1974.
Used with permission of the Free to Be Foundation.

of open possibility. That momentary feeling of boundless potential was always a fantasy, an idealistic, necessary illusion that encouraged children to imagine a fulfilling future. As we explore the messages and the merriment of this childhood classic, we rediscover anew a place and time when we were free to be.

Inspiration

Prologue

MARLO THOMAS

Honestly, I was just trying to do something for one little girl. That it would grow to become a cultural phenomenon was never a part of the plan. Then again, can something like that ever be planned?

It has been forty years since *Free to Be . . . You and Me* first arrived in homes across America as an entertainment for children. And though its journey since then has been, to say the least, remarkable, I've never been able to pinpoint precisely how it took root as a cross-generational touchstone. But what I have had is an enormous amount of anecdotal evidence.

"I counted the days until my daughter was old enough to begin listening to records," a woman once told me in line at an airport, "so I could finally introduce her to those wonderful stories and songs in *Free to Be . . . You and Me.* They were such a huge part of my childhood."

"When I was eight years old," a man once whispered to me in a restaurant, "my mom used to have this ritual on Friday nights. We'd put on *Free to Be* and dance to all the songs. It's one of my favorite memories of my mom."

"I still have my original pink copy of the book," I've been told by more people than I can possibly count. "Every time I move, it goes with me—the very same book that sat on my childhood night table!"

And from innumerable gay men: "'William's Doll' and 'It's All Right to Cry' were the first inklings that I was going to be okay."

And from educators everywhere: "I taught from *Free to Be* when it was first released, and I still teach from it today."

That last comment is something I have experienced firsthand, as I've traveled from city to city performing in plays and raising funds for St. Jude Children's Research Hospital. In every town I visit, I receive letters from teachers inviting me to see their classes' stage productions of *Free to Be.* Or their *Free to Be* May Days. Or *Free to Be* Graduations. And as often as I could, I've attended them, and I've always been knocked out by the spirit of the children and their complete grasp of the material. It is so touching to me that it's become part of their young lives.

Witnessing this passionate embrace of *Free to Be . . . You and Me* over the course of four decades has been undeniably satisfying—as well as confounding. Those of us who gave our hearts and hopes to this project wanted it to be received enthusiastically—wanted it to make a difference—but that it exceeded even our wildest expectations has always made me wonder: Where did we go right? What was it about *Free to Be* that would compel children to memorize—then recite, line by line—a funny little sketch about two newborn babies discovering their gender? Why did the story of a little boy and his favorite doll land with such a profound and lasting impact? How is it that a simple song about crying could make children sing away their fears about their feelings?

It had all begun quite small, with a little girl and her auntie. The year was 1971, and my sister Terre's daughter, Dionne, was in nursery school. The first of a new generation of Thomases, Dionne drew the adoring attention of the entire family, and I was among those enthusiastic admirers. I especially enjoyed telling her bedtime stories. Watching her eyes widen and hearing her small gasps as the story took an unexpected turn never failed to touch me. Instead, it would take me back to the days when Terre and I were children ourselves, and we'd play story records on our portable pink phonograph. Loretta Young reading *The Littlest Angel*. Bing Crosby's *The Happy Prince*. *Bozo the Clown*, *Cinderella*, *Snow White*. We'd lie on our backs and look up at the ceiling and see all the pictures in our heads.

But as Dionne moved from picture books to storybooks, I began to realize how outdated the material was. The books all told the same old stories, starring the same old prince, promising the same old happy ending. None of them had any new ideas that would encourage Dionne to dream her own dreams.

"I can't believe you're reading her the same books we grew up with," I said to Terre. "Didn't it take us half our lives to get over these stories?"

"That's all I've been able to find," Terre said. "Why don't you try?"

Obviously, I thought, my sister hadn't looked hard enough. So off I went to the bookstore, confident that I would return with an armful of inspiration. But Auntie Marlo had a lot to learn. Not only had nothing changed, but in some cases things had gotten worse. One book I'll never forget was called *I'm Glad I'm a Boy! I'm Glad I'm a Girl!* The pictures were cute, but the captions were appalling.

"Boys are pilots, girls are stewardesses."

"Boys are doctors, girls are nurses."

"Boys can eat, girls can cook."

"Boys invent things, girls use what boys invent."

I almost had a heart attack in the children's book section.

How could this be? After all the marches, the consciousness-raising, the literature? I thought back to Terre's and my old records and wondered, *How hard could it be to create an album for Dionne, with stories and songs that she could lie on the floor and listen to, and see pictures in her head that would awaken her imagination instead of putting her mind to sleep?*

Girls use what boys invent, indeed!

I wanted to create something that would make fun of all the old stories and outmoded ideas that I grew up with—the ones that told us what girls and boys could and couldn't do. At the suggestion of my friend, author-illustrator Shel Silverstein, I met with Harper and Row's great children's book editor, Ursula Nordstrom, and told her my idea. But after working with a few of her authors, I realized that using conventional children's story writers on the album was not the way to go. This was not the *Littlest Angel* generation that I wanted to get to—these kids had rock concerts blaring from the TVs in their living rooms. The material couldn't be preachy. It would have to be entertaining and have some razzmatazz. And it would have to make kids laugh. That's the only way they'd get it—and *remember* it. Who was it who said, "What is learned with laughter is learned well"?

So I decided I'd approach my friends in show business about creating the songs and stories—people like Carl Reiner, Mel Brooks, Sheldon Harnick, Herb Gardner, and of course Shel.

But first, I needed a terrific coproducer, someone who understood humor and music—and children—instinctively. After a long search, I found that someone in Carole Hart, who had been a contributor to *Sesame Street*. Carole's intuition about the nuances of children's entertainment was unerring, and when I sent her a few of the pieces that Ursula's writers had given me, she agreed that, with the exception of Charlotte Zolotow's *William's Doll*—which had the perfect message— we needed something different, something more daring.

So we began to develop the album, sitting around with our writer friends and talking about our own childhoods and what we wished we had learned when we were kids. Those all-night sessions at my New York apartment were really the seed of the project.

I remember those conversations vividly.

"I'd like to have heard that it wasn't a sissy thing for a boy to show his feelings," Herb Gardner said. And the gifted Carol Hall wrote the terrific song, "It's All Right to Cry."

"I'd like to have read one story about a princess who wasn't blond and who didn't get married to the prince at the end," I said. And Betty Miles updated the ancient myth of Atalanta—only in her version, it's up to the princess (now a *brunette*) to decide for herself whether she will marry the prince in the end. I always loved the last line: "Perhaps someday they will be married, and perhaps they will not. In any case, it is certain, they are both living happily ever after."

And the ever irreverent Shel wrote a piece called "Ladies First," about a spoiled little girl who is eaten by tigers. It was Shel's conviction that children didn't need to be protected from life's sharp corners—and kids adored him for that.

As confident as we were about the material we were assembling, we wanted to be sure that we were on solid ground with respect to the messages we were sending to children. Gloria Steinem introduced me to Letty Cottin Pogrebin, who was one of the founding editors of *Ms.* magazine. Letty had written extensively about the sexism in children's books, which made her a perfect fit for our project. She was a fountain of knowledge and quickly became a true and passionate guide on our journey. And Letty led us to other experts—thinkers at the Carnegie Council, child development specialist Marian Wright Edelman (who would go on to found the Children's Defense Fund), and a host of child psychologists. All of them provided invaluable information and support.

Because most of the material came out of our own experiences, it didn't take us long to realize that we were, in effect, rewriting our own childhoods. But it was lyricist Bruce Hart, Carole's husband, who came up with the timeless words, "Free to Be . . . You and Me"—and his title song, written with composer Stephen Lawrence, brilliantly captured a child's passionate desire for freedom, with its striking images of rolling rivers and galloping horses. The first time Bruce and Stephen played the song for us, we knew we had our anthem.

As the record album began taking shape, we wanted to test it out. So I began dropping by schools in New York City—like Hunter Elementary, Bank Street and P.S. 6—to see if the songs and stories resonated with the kids. And I did the same in Los Angeles at my alma mater, Marymount. And, of course, I invited Dionne and her young friends—both girls and boys—to give us a listen. Getting their feedback was vital to the project's development. Children famously don't beat around the bush, and they weren't the slightest bit shy about telling us what they liked and what they didn't.

Just before we went into the recording studio, I contacted my good friend, Alan Alda, about directing us, and he eagerly agreed. Alan was perfect. Not only was he the devoted father of three small girls, but with his flawless sense of comedy and musical background, he was right in our groove.

By now, our creative team was in a zone. We were on a mission, all of us, obsessed with changing the world one five-year-old at a time.

And that heartfelt conscientiousness paid off. Almost from the first day, the *Free to Be . . . You and Me* album became a life force, exploding like a firecracker in the public consciousness. The record went gold, and its success emboldened us to keep going. I'd always imagined it living on children's bookshelves, so our team quickly regrouped and began mapping out a print version. We found a terrific and forward-thinking publisher in McGraw-Hill, and were lucky enough to enlist the great Sam Antupit to supervise the book's art direction.

Like the album, the print version of *Free to Be* was received enthusiastically, and the book quickly became a staple in classrooms across the country, as teachers used it to encourage their students to take a deeper look at their lives and to provide enlightenment about the boundlessness of their dreams. More than anyone, I believe, these educators were responsible for turning Dionne's little record and book into something much, much bigger.

All of us on the creative team were thrilled by *Free to Be*'s overwhelmingly positive reception, and it didn't take us long to see what our next exciting step could be: turning it into a television special. Up until now, our team had worked autonomously, so we went about creating our teleplay in the same headstrong way. Having produced my own TV show, *That Girl*, which had broken new ground for women, I was already seasoned in the politics of tearing down old barriers. But it's one thing to introduce audiences to an unmarried girl living on her own and chasing her dreams. It's a whole other thing to target a generation of children, tackling the all-encompassing issues of gender and racial stereotypes.

Once we finished editing the special, I proudly took it to ABC Television and screened it for the top brass. When the lights came up afterward, I could immediately tell by the looks on their faces that they were conflicted. They'd liked what they'd seen—they just didn't like some of what we were saying.

"William's Doll," they insisted, would have to go. "You're going to turn boys into little sissies," one executive worriedly told me. Then there was that other matter of Harry Belafonte and me portraying various mommies and daddies in the song "Parents Are People." In one sequence, Harry and I cheerfully pushed our baby carriages through the park, side by side. That particular clip brought a carefully worded response: "It looks like you and Harry are married. That just doesn't belong in a children's special. And they'll never play it in the South."

Yes, the visuals had made our more controversial material that much stronger and possibly more inflammatory. But we were not going to back down. And we didn't. And to its credit, ABC aired our complete version of *Free to Be . . . You and Me*—in prime time. And guess what. The sky did not fall down.

In a review the day before the show aired, John Leonard of the *New York Times* raved "Free to Be! Hooray!" in his headline, then promised to watch the show with his entire family the following evening, "whether or not our children deserve to enjoy themselves as much as [this] one reviewer did."

But not everyone agreed with Leonard. "Keep your children away from the set tonight," wrote the *Boston Globe* TV critic the morning of the show's airing. The world wasn't changing as fast as we had hoped.

Thankfully, however, the *Free to Be* TV special was warmly received, scoring terrific ratings and going on to win an Emmy and a Peabody Award. Then came a demand for a stage version for kids to perform in schools and community theater, which we immediately put together. Hitting the bull's-eye in one entertainment medium is pretty difficult: *Free to Be* had done it in four.

Yet one question remained: How did all this happen? And why?

That's why I was so intrigued when Lori Rotskoff and Laura Lovett first approached me about compiling this book. Many wonderful and interesting things have been written about *Free to Be . . . You and Me* over the years, but what Lori and Laura proposed was something different: an academic curiosity that might just yield the answers to the very questions I've pondered over the years.

We all know, for instance, that *Free to Be* came of age in the 1970s, as girls and boys everywhere, and their families, began to emerge from the age-old constructs of previous generations—rethinking gender stereotypes, redefining the family, breaking down the barricades that had, until then, kept us all from realizing our own destinies. But what was it specifically about *Free to Be* that made it the perfect vehicle for such a seismic societal transformation? Was it a kind of potent alchemy of inspiration, collaborative chemistry, and cultural savvy that made it so important to its audience—or was it just a matter of solid material and good old-fashioned timing?

When I first read the essays in this anthology, I couldn't help but notice how each of the writers drew from their *Free to Be* experience their own customized lesson. For some, it would go on to shape their worldview as women, as they sought and explored the newfound liberties that the project had helped to unleash. For others, it would set the stage for their own parenthood, as they replayed the songs and stories in their heads, only now with a deeper understanding of how the material spoke to the beloved small person in their lives. For still others, it remained an uplifting entertainment—smart and tuneful and upbeat—that continues all these years later to give them warmth, like comfort food for the spirit.

The fact that all of these lessons are unique is the whole point of *Free to Be.* We created it as a colorful road map for children and the grownups in their lives but quite pointedly left the ultimate destination up to the listeners (and readers and viewers) to determine for themselves. And how wonderful it is to see the paths taken by the younger contributors to this book—the ones who were children when *Free to Be* was first released. Reading about their journeys delighted and inspired me.

But seeing Dionne's name there on the printed page is what really moved me. I was instantly transported back to that childhood bedroom of hers, its frilly quilt and army of stuffed animals swallowing us up as we talked about her hopes and dreams. And I recalled that piercing curiosity in her eyes, and that exquisite smile, both of which would inspire an aunt, and then a group of grownups, most of whom she didn't know, to create something for her and all the Dionnes and Donnys of the world.

And when I finished reading her essay, I thought: *Darling Dionne, it's not just that you were this little girl who brought such profound happiness into the lives of your mom and your dad and your Auntie Marlo and all of our*

Dionne and Auntie Marlo.

family. It's that you became the grown woman you wanted to be—a loving wife and mother, doing the work you love and living the life that makes you happy.

That's what I was hoping for. That's why I created *Free to Be . . . You and Me*. And it's why, I think, for forty years, moms and dads and grandmas and grandpas and aunties and uncles have eagerly brought it into the lives of the children they love—to sing its songs and tell its stories and then pass them down to their own children, so that they all might one day write their own happily ever afters.

Free to Be Memories

DIONNE GORDON KIRSCHNER

As a five-year-old girl, I had no idea what a meaningful gift my aunt had given me by dedicating *Free to Be . . . You and Me* to "her niece, Dionne." As I grew older, I was able to comprehend how this book and music had influenced not only me but so many other children of my generation. *Free to Be* was so special—it was like nothing else from its time. This collection of stories and music shaped the dreams and ambitions of millions of boys and girls. To this day, when a stranger or acquaintance somehow learns that I was "The Dionne" mentioned in the dedication at the beginning of the book or on the back of that pink record, a wonderful story always follows about what the book meant to them and their siblings as children. A lot of times, people will just break into song. Still.

My brother, Jason, and I listened to *Free to Be* almost every day of our childhood. During this time, we lived in Los Angeles with our mom, who raised us as a single, stay-at-home parent. We lived minutes from my Uncle Tony, my Auntie Marlo, and my grandparents. We were a very close family. My brother and I played together every day. We loved to play outside, but inside, we always played in our playroom. We would put our little record player on and listen to *Free to Be . . . You and Me* over and over again. I can still hear the scratchy sound of the needle when it first touched the vinyl record. That magical first song would start, "There's a land that I see/Where the children are free," and we would sing at the top of our lungs. Also in this playroom lived a spectacular gray rocking horse with a bright red saddle that my Auntie Marlo had given to me for my birthday. I would listen to the music on *Free to Be* and ride and ride and ride, galloping along to my favorite tunes. Whenever Auntie Marlo gave us a gift, it was always an exciting event at our house (and, by the way, it still is, even though I am now forty-two!) But the greatest gift she ever gave me was *Free to Be . . . You and Me* and all the lessons stored within its pages.

From as early as I can recall, I remember the strength and power of being a woman. There were no limitations in our home based on gender. My mom was an independent, single mother, raising us kids on her own. It was a home where a father was not present but also was never missed because that powerhouse of strength—my mother—could play both roles so well. We didn't realize anything was amiss. Both my mom and her sister, my Aunt Marlo, were role models of independence and strength for me as a child and a young woman. It made no difference to my mom that she wasn't married any longer, even though everyone was "supposed" to be. She was going to do the job of raising us regardless, and she was going to do it well. I also remember my aunt being unmarried, wildly independent, and very successful. In the 1970s, these traits were very uncharacteristic for a woman.

What I have always loved about my aunt is that she is fearless. She lives life to the fullest with never a dull moment. She does what she wants to do and what she thinks is right. She has always been "Free to Be" in my eyes. I grew up feeling that I wanted to attack life in the same way. I knew that whatever dreams I had would be my own and not a product of what others wanted for me. I was free to make my own decisions and be who I wanted to be without worrying about what others expected of me. I was raised to be smart, make my own decisions, and fight for what I believe in. I was also raised knowing that I was strong enough mentally to compete with a man in any field. Along with my mom and my aunt as role models, *Free to Be* empowered me in its one-of-a-kind, progressive, and skillful storytelling. As a young person, it left me feeling energized, transformed, and capable of taking on anything that might come my way.

Every time I put on *Free to Be* as a child, I felt comforted and reassured. I always loved "When We Grow Up," and it's still my favorite song today. It's about accepting and even embracing who you are. What a profound lesson to learn so young. It can shape your whole life. "Parents Are People" gave me the confidence to pursue my career and forge my own path with perseverance and without fear. Whenever I heard this, I thought of all the possibilities that were open to me to pursue. It was a very powerful message to hear repeatedly as a child. And "Glad to Have a Friend Like You" celebrates the enduring importance of friendship.

But the story that was most personal and had the greatest impact on me—and which I still think about regularly—is "Atalanta." Atalanta ran that race for herself, not for anybody else. I always secretly wanted to be Atalanta. I wanted to run the race as I wished and make my own decisions as she had done so bravely. I think this was the most important story in *Free to Be* for women of my generation. We no longer had to do exactly as our parents did or as they said we should. We could travel the world, experience life, meet plenty of people before we decided to settle down and get married, or we could decide not to marry at all. We had the power to make these decisions for ourselves when the time was right.

At the time, I had no concept that these ideas were groundbreaking. My aunt and her colleagues were pushing the boundaries of where women could go and manifesting these ideals in the record, book, and TV special. Many girls of my generation grew up thinking that the world was wide open to us. Amazingly, because of *Free to Be*, we didn't know that it had ever been otherwise.

With *Free to Be* in my life, I felt like my options were limitless. I felt that I could do it all—whatever "it all" would mean for me. As I look back, this book and record album undeniably shaped how the little girl I once was became the woman I am today.

Today, I am a television producer—a woman in what was once traditionally a man's world. (My aunt was one of the first female producers of her era.) I produce television comedies, shows that make people laugh and bring families together. I'm pleased that the shows I work on conclude with a positive message for kids and families. So whether viewers are eight or eighty, they come away feeling upbeat, lighter, and always laughing.

I have been married for seventeen years to a wonderful man who is committed to a marriage where each of us pursues our dreams at work and where we share the responsibilities and joys of parenting. For many years, I focused on achieving my career goals, and once I had done so, we decided the time was right for us to have a family. Ten years after getting into show business, I gave birth to our first child, Ryan Thomas Kirschner, who is now age nine. Three and a half years later, we had our second child, Jake Henry Kirschner, who is now five. Their births were the best moments of my life.

My husband and I work in television and raise our children at the same time. It's a challenge. Like all working moms, I am constantly juggling my family and my career. There are definitely times when I wish I could be in two places at once. I work hard to maintain the balance of being a fully present mother and a fully present producer. But I am doing both at the same time because that is what is most fulfilling for me, and I have no regrets. I think I have worked out the balance in the best way possible. My work schedule allows me to take my boys to school every day and attend their school functions. Also, I love bringing them to work with me so they can be involved in what I am producing. When they sit in the audience on show nights, it's an absolute delight for all of us. I hope they will have fond memories of being on the set with their mom and dad as kids, just like I did when I was little—and like my mom, aunt, and uncle did when they were growing up.

One of the thrills of my life is playing *Free to Be* for my kids. They can't believe their Auntie Marlo's voice is on the CD and that the book was dedicated to me—their mom! Having them sing the songs back to me is like life coming full circle. One of my favorite memories is when Ryan was in first grade. For his birthday, the teacher invited me to come and read to the class, and Ryan wanted me to read from *Free to Be*. When we recited "Boy Meets Girl," his teacher read the Mel Brooks part and I read the Marlo Thomas part. Ryan was beaming, and all the kids were laughing. The fact that this book is still influencing and delighting new generations is a huge testament to its power.

Decades later, my favorite baby gift to send to friends is a signed and personalized copy of *Free to Be* from my Aunt Marlo. She always writes the same beautiful note, "With the hope that you will always be free to be."

Thank you Auntie Marlo, from the bottom of my heart, for this precious, life-changing gift. I know that you already know that I am truly "Free to Be."

Part One

Creating a World for Free Children

Marlo Thomas and children in Central Park during the filming of the
Free to Be . . . You and Me television special, 1974.

The Foundations of
Free to Be . . . You and Me

LORI ROTSKOFF

Both before and after Marlo Thomas decided to create a new kind of children's entertainment, she was involved in the burgeoning women's movement, fully supportive of the Equal Rights Amendment and other liberal feminist goals. When she began to work on the *Free to Be* album, she surrounded herself with collaborators whose personal experiences, political inclinations, and intellectual backgrounds shaped their collective commitment to promoting equality and autonomy for girls and boys.

In an interview with a *New York Times* reporter in 1973, Thomas explained that both sets of her grandparents, who were of Lebanese and Italian descent, were set up in arranged marriages. "My grandfather and his sons would eat in the dining room while my grandmother and her daughter ate by themselves at the kitchen table," she recalled. And as she has explained more recently in her memoir, *Growing Up Laughing*, during her youth, within all of the marriages she witnessed among her relatives—including her parents'—"the husband was *numero uno*. There wasn't any abuse or that kind of thing. Just the everyday drip, drip of dissolving self-esteem." At the tender age of ten, Marlo's budding feminist instincts blossomed into a book she wrote, "Women Are People, Too." After graduating from high school, she had ambitions to become an actress but instead went to college to study education, as her father had encouraged. Throughout her young adulthood, Thomas remained famously unmarried—and so, too, did the character she played on the hit television show she conceived and produced, *That Girl*. "I knew I didn't want to give up my dreams for love and miss them for the rest of my life, like my mother," she has reflected.[1]

Thomas's objection to early marriage was personal, of course, but it also emerged in the context of broader social and demographic changes. Although many of *Free to Be*'s creators were born before the Baby Boom officially exploded in 1946, they came of age during a time when millions of Americans embraced a mode of privatized, nuclear family life that dovetailed with the construction of new suburbs (such as Levittown on Long Island, New York) enabled by the GI Bill of Rights. When World War II ended in 1945 and veterans returned from overseas, new federal benefits and guaranteed mortgages made homeownership and higher education increasingly affordable, allowing young white men to improve their prospects as breadwinners and embark on marriage and parenthood at an earlier age than any generational cohort before them.[2]

White women, for their part, were cast in the roles of homemakers, consumers, and family caretakers during the *Leave It to Beaver* era. Although the majority of women who worked for pay during the war had planned to keep their jobs after the war was over, by the mid-1940s, government policies and employers effectively privileged male workers, pushing millions of female employees out of the workplace and back into the home. These social changes were reinforced in nearly every arena of popular culture, including television shows, advertisements, movies, and magazines, as well in higher education and the mental health professions. From all corners, it seemed, women in postwar America were bombarded with messages exhorting them to marry young, forgo careers, and behave with deference toward men.[3]

This was the context in which most of *Free to Be*'s collaborators came of age, but several years before they started the project, they had already begun to chafe against the gender arrangements that prevailed in American society. Battling against barriers they faced in the workplace, they began to carve out lives as independent career women: Marlo Thomas became a prominent actress and producer, Carole Hart began writing acclaimed television shows, Letty Cottin Pogrebin worked as a book publicist, Gloria Steinem launched her career as a journalist, and Mary Rodgers composed songs for successful musicals. These women were pioneers in the public realm well before the women's movement gathered steam—and, indeed, before some of them emerged as leaders within it.

Another aspect of the postwar domestic consensus against which *Free to Be*'s creators later reacted lay in the racial and ethnic discrimination that had long defined it. Not only did depictions of the stereotypical *Leave It to Beaver* family cast American citizenship as a white, middle-class ideal, the financial and federal policies that underwrote the suburbs systematically excluded African Americans and many ethnic minorities from living there. Although white ethnic groups including Jews, Italian Americans, and Irish Americans were frequently able to enter suburban enclaves, government agencies and banks adopted restrictive racial covenants and "redlining" practices to exclude blacks, Hispanics, and other racial minorities.[4]

Although *Free to Be*'s principal creators did not personally experience this kind of racism, they objected to racial discrimination and the social injustice that resulted from it. Sympathetic to the civil rights movement and committed to offering an inclusive, multicultural vision, *Free to Be*'s producers and consultants sought to attract a racially and ethnically mixed audience of listeners. On the one hand, when commissioning writers to draft the stories and lyrics, with one exception they did not hire African American authors or songwriters. (The exception was Lucille Clifton, an acclaimed poet, whose story, "Three Wishes," was published in the *Free to Be* book and animated in the television special.) On the other hand, when hiring performers to sing, act, and dance on the album and small-screen segments, they enlisted more than a dozen African American artists and performance groups. In contrast to the white-bread sitcoms that mostly excluded black actors and characters from the prime-time airwaves well into the late 1960s, *Free to Be* made a concerted effort to depict racial harmony and integration in children's media and to showcase the talents of popular black performers.[5]

These social motivations also fueled the *Free to Be* team when they created the subsequent book. New selections for the printed page explored timely themes, including sibling rivalry in Judy Blume's "The Pain and the Great One"; war and pacifism in Anne Roiphe's "The Field"; the intersection of race, class, and friendship in Lucille Clifton's "Three Wishes"; and the effects of divorce on families in Linda Sitea's "Zachary's Divorce." Artists and photographers contributed colorful illustrations, woodcut prints, and expressive photographs to enhance the book's message and visual appeal. Reflecting the creators' desire to incorporate children's own perspectives, the youngest illustrator, seven-year-old Daniel Pinchbeck, penciled a steam engine and a spaceship to accompany Elaine Laron's poem "No One Else." Many pages were devoted to actual sheet music—a direct appeal to music teachers as well as older children or parents who had studied piano.

When the *Free to Be* team transformed the album into a one-hour ABC television special, they retained eleven of the tracks from the album and added four new pieces. Today DVDs, streaming media, and on-demand cable television allow us to watch programs whenever the mood strikes us. In the early 1970s, though, there were just three major commercial television networks, so a television special aimed at children really *was* special. Countless children who grew up at this time watched televised holiday specials, such as *It's the Great Pumpkin, Charlie Brown, Frosty the Snowman*, and *The Grinch Who Stole Christmas*, to name a few. ABC began its Afterschool Special series in 1972, preempting regular afternoon programs four or six times a year with made-for-television movies. While *Free to Be . . . You and Me* was a prime-time special with a variety-show format, it shared the social relevance that many of the Afterschool Specials also conveyed. After the show first aired, McGraw-Hill Films provided schools with copies of the film as well as a "learning module" complete with posters, educational games, craft projects, and teachers' guides.

In dramatizing children's literature through music and animation for the small screen, *Free to Be* shared features with another special that soon followed it. Author Maurice Sendak directed *Really Rosie*, a half-hour television production based on several of his previous books that aired on CBS in February 1975. The songs in this spirited animated musical featured lyrics by Sendak and music written and performed by singer-songwriter Carole King. (King also sang the vocals for the record album version of *Really Rosie* released by Ode Records the same year.) Many kids who loved *Free to Be* also enjoyed *Really Rosie*, which centered on the antics of an outspoken ten-year-old girl who dreamed of theatrical stardom. Like *Free to Be*, some of the tunes conveyed lessons on such matters as the value of expressing opinions, showing concern for others, and coping with difficult emotions. Moreover, the fact that the show featured a strong central female character—and one vocalized by a singer and lyricist whose performance style was already enmeshed with the cultural politics of the women's movement—lent *Really Rosie* an implicitly feminist air.

Yet among all children's media productions during the 1970s, *Free to Be . . . You and Me* was rooted most firmly in the soil of organized feminism. Indeed, the connections between the *Free to Be* projects, *Ms.* magazine, and the Ms. Foundation for Women ran deep. Several of the magazine's founding editors helped facilitate *Free to Be*'s creation, and when the album was complete, *Ms.* promoted it to a huge captive audience with frequent ads.[6]

Even before Marlo Thomas began recording the album, her plan was to channel all the monies raised through the sale of the *Free to*

Be materials into programs that would benefit women and children. When she contacted Gloria Steinem and explained her idea, Steinem responded enthusiastically, telling Thomas that the editors of *Ms.* were contemplating forming a new foundation for women. It was an ideal partnership, connecting Thomas and the *Free to Be* project with Steinem, Letty Cottin Pogrebin, and Pat Carbine, who together founded the Ms. Foundation for Women, which grants funds to grassroots organizations and public outreach agencies that serve racially and ethnically diverse populations. As Steinem wrote in her preface to the original *Free to Be* book, all royalties that would normally have gone to *Free to Be*'s contributors went instead to support "a variety of educational projects aimed at improving the skills, conditions, and status of women and children." As Steinem elaborated, this meant "developing new kinds of learning materials, child care centers, health care services, teaching techniques, information and referral centers and much more: all the concrete ways in which this book's message of freedom can be realized and all the practical changes that are necessary to get rid of old-fashioned systems based on sex and race."[7]

While *Ms.* magazine showed little sign of becoming profitable, the *Free to Be* project gathered steam, earning enough to support the foundation. By 1975 *Free to Be* generated sufficient royalties to allow the organization to hire directors and to begin doling out funds. Just a year later, the Ms. Foundation's grants totaled $87,175, a considerable sum for a budding philanthropic venture at the time.[8]

At first, the Ms. Foundation planned to focus on funding women in the arts, small businesses, education, and scholarship. But board members soon shifted their emphasis to "survival issues" and "action projects" to empower women across class, race, and age barriers. They began by making small grants, usually up to ten thousand dollars, to grassroots groups focused on issues such as health care, domestic violence, job advancement, migrant workers' needs, and legal services. Publicity materials explained the foundation's goal of supporting "changes in women's lives that are as practical, immediate and inclusive as possible."[9]

Free to Be's creators were also influenced by intellectual currents that flowed strongly during this period, including the field of humanistic psychology. In *Free to Be*'s conception of a "liberated" childhood, every child is endowed with an internal, true, or "authentic" self: a basic set of personality traits, interests, and inclinations. This notion is best summarized in the final stanza of Dan Greenburg's poem, "Don't Dress Your Cat in an Apron":

"A person should wear what he likes to
And not just what other folks say.
A person should do what he likes to
A person's a person that way."

Here, the freedom to act on one's internal motivations is figured as a basic entitlement in a liberal democratic society. This poem and other *Free to Be* vignettes encapsulated core ideas about human purpose and achievement central to humanistic psychology, a school of thought that developed during the mid–twentieth century as a third alternative to the reigning theories of behaviorism and Freudian psychoanalysis. Emphasizing people's conscious capacity as self-determining agents, humanistic psychologists focused on how people develop competence, accomplish goals, and engage effectively with others. Abraham Maslow, a major proponent of this theory, popularized the concept of a "hierarchy of human needs." At the bottom of the pyramid are basic survival needs such as food, clothing, and shelter. Once those needs are met, a person moves up to higher levels, which include social acceptance, love, and self-esteem. Perched at the top of the triangle is "self-actualization," the optimal expression of one's unique potential through productive engagement in society at large. Not to be confused with narcissism, those at the peak of human potential work intently to effect positive changes in the world *outside* the self.[10]

This last tenet, in fact, made ideas about self-actualization appealing to many activists at the time. Just three years before *That Girl* premiered on the airwaves, Betty Friedan incorporated humanistic psychology's dual emphasis on human freedom and human connection into her best-seller, *The Feminine Mystique*. Friedan, who had studied psychology at Smith College, was disturbed by the fact that relatively few women were able to achieve self-actualization as Maslow had described it. As she argued, the "cultural prescriptions requiring middle-class housewives to devote themselves exclusively to the needs of husbands and children also doomed them to a psychological hell, or at least a decidedly second-class emotional existence." She continued, "Our culture does not permit women to accept or gratify their basic need to grow and fulfill their potentialities as human beings."

Letty Cottin Pogrebin, Marlo Thomas, Gloria Steinem, Robin Morgan, and Pat Carbine. No date.

Significantly, Letty Cottin Pogrebin studied personally with Maslow during the late 1950s when she was a student at Brandeis University, and he had a "seismic influence" on her "intellectual and emotional development."[11]

Free to Be's social reach was limited, however, by the fact that these underlying ideas about human potential were forged in a context of relative economic security. Then as now, a person's ability to "be all he or she can be"—to capitalize creatively and ethically on empowering exhortations to "be free" or "follow your dreams"—is more readily achieved or even attempted by those who are socially and economically advantaged than by those who are not. Cultural narratives about the promise of self-actualization carry implicit assumptions about the attainment of middle-class identity. The ways in which children respond to messages about individual freedom—including the personal meanings they attach to those messages—are not entirely determined by social factors such as race and class but are, to varying degrees, shaped by the economic and cultural resources afforded to their families and communities.[12] Free to Be's creators and consultants were aware of this, which is why some of them also lobbied for policies to ensure essential services and a material safety net for families.

Gloria Steinem, Betty Friedan, and Marlo Thomas. No date.

It's also why they routed the profits back into the Ms. Foundation. Of course, no matter how empowering the message, songs and stories alone cannot remedy social inequalities and injustices.

With these social commitments and intellectual foundations in place, Marlo Thomas, Carole Hart, and their colleagues reached out to leading professionals in the realms of book publishing, Broadway theater, Hollywood, television, and the music industry to produce a landmark work of children's popular media. Combining their talents as musicians, songwriters, actors, directors, journalists, educators, editors, activists, and parents, they made a significant contribution to children's history. In the pieces that follow, they take us back to the production of *Free to Be . . . You and Me* and to the social movements and educational campaigns that nourished its creation.

In the Beginning

CAROLE HART

The following is a tale of magical connections and sublime collabora-
tions. It's a story about the creation of *Free to Be . . . You and Me*, but it
begins with a short prelude about *Sesame Street*.

My husband, Bruce Hart, and I had just received our first Emmy
Award for our work together as writers on *Sesame Street*. We joined the
project with the Children's Television Workshop before the show even
had a name. Once it did, my husband sat down with composer Joe
Raposo in a small room with a grand piano, where they wrote *Sesame
Street*'s title song.

That experience and the recognition we received from it brought
Marlo Thomas to me, through our agent at the William Morris Agency,
Scott Shukat. Bruce and I, songwriter Carol Hall, and Stephen Lawrence, who wrote three songs and produced the music with Bruce,
were all Scott's clients. He also secured the release of the *Free to Be*
album, with a small label called Bell Records, after it was turned down
by many of the larger music companies, who just couldn't get past its
gender liberation premise. In fact, one well-known music executive
rejected it with the words, "What would I want with a record produced
by a bunch of dykes?" I tell this story to remind us of the climate in the
music business and much of the country at the time.

But I'm getting ahead of myself.

Marlo was looking for a woman to develop and produce a children's
record album with her. While reading to her young niece, she became
distressed by traditional bedtime stories and how they limited options
in life for both girls and boys. This realization inspired her to collect
a number of nonsexist stories that were beginning to appear in the
publishing market. She also had a few pieces specially written. She
approached me at our first meeting with her powerful vision and copies of the material she'd amassed.

I was impressed with the idea for the album and with Marlo's passion and intelligence, but I can't say the same about the material that
had been collected so far. I told Marlo that I thought it was an exciting
and important project, but I also expressed my disappointment with

the material she'd found or commissioned. I said I didn't think she could get to where she wanted to go with these selections and that we would need to create our own original material. Not knowing Marlo as I do now, I wasn't prepared for the explosion of activity and creativity that followed. Soon, we were in touch with many talented writers and composers from the theater, movie, and book worlds. Many had no prior experience writing for children.

Along with a team of consultants Marlo had assembled, we examined gender stereotypes and identified other elements in our culture that prevented children from being and expressing their true selves. We also had wonderful late-night meetings at Marlo's apartment with Bruce; Herb Gardner, Marlo's beau at the time; and their close friend, Shel Silverstein, a beloved children's writer and illustrator (*The Giving Tree*). One of our guiding principles was that children are far more intelligent than many people think they are, and we didn't want to talk down to them. We also wanted the material to be clever enough to appeal to their parents as well.

Guided by this philosophy, we started to go to writers. We asked Shel, but he was concerned about writing anything for us because he didn't want to preach. When we told him that that was exactly why we wanted him, he came up with two perfectly wicked but perfectly on point pieces, a story titled "Ladies First," and a short, sly, and funny song called "Helping." Mary Rodgers adapted the story for performance on the album.

Marlo also found a newly published book called *William's Doll*, by Charlotte Zolotow. Its message was ideal, but its tone was a bit too earnest for our purposes, so we went to lyricist Sheldon Harnick, renowned for *Fiddler on the Roof*, and composer Mary Rodgers, a woman of many talents, and asked them to turn it into a song, which they did. Brilliantly.

There's a lot more to say about the creation of the material. Inspired by Mel Brooks's and Carl Reiner's popular *2000-Year-Old Man* comedy routine, Marlo came up with the idea for the album's signature piece: two newborns in the hospital trying to figure out which one was the boy and which one was the girl. We went to Broadway and movie comedy writer Peter Stone, who teamed with Carl Reiner, to bring this hilarious piece, "Boy Meets Girl," to life.

I found a lovely story about a boy, Dudley Pippin, who was reprimanded by his teacher and began to cry. He was very ashamed, but his principal told him it was good to cry. We showed that story to Carol Hall, and she came back with a great song to follow it, "It's All Right to Cry." It gave boys permission to express their emotions, which we hoped they would remember as they grew into men.

I could recall the provenance of every piece on the album, but I think it's enough to say that the songs and stories that we developed had some delightfully serendipitous connections with one another that made the assembly process delicious and made the album much more than the sum of its parts.

We were amassing all this wonder-filled material, but we still didn't have a title. Fortunately, being a lyricist, Bruce had a special gift for titles. Because he loved triple rhymes, the title came to him first as *Free to Be You and Me Jamboree*. I nixed the "Jamboree" part because I was so impressed with the power of the first six words. They captured the spirit of the album beautifully. We tested it on some of the people on our team who loved it, but Marlo worried that it was not child-friendly enough. I urged her to let Bruce write the lyric and Stephen Lawrence the music. When she read the lyric and heard the song, she was deeply moved and embraced it wholeheartedly. Those six simple words have now permeated our culture.

Confident of the material we were offering, it was now time to go out to performers. Our casting choices were ambitious. Mel Brooks just had to be the baby playing opposite Marlo in the opening comedy piece. Bruce, a devout New York Giants fan, came up with the idea of getting Rosey Grier to perform "It's All Right to Cry." Tom Smothers had just the right ironic approach for Shel Silverstein's "Helping." And we knew Marlo and Alan Alda would work well together in our "story theater" adaptation of Betty Miles's "Atalanta," a piece created in response to Marlo's pronounced aversion to having to get married. It was a dream list, and the dream came true. At this point, I began to feel like something was going on that was bigger than all of us. The divinely matched cast and material felt ideal.

Now all we had to do was record it! Since many of our artists were on the road or too busy to come to us, our music producers and I went to them. Harry Belafonte, who was singing a duet with Marlo, was on tour. We caught up with him in Las Vegas, without Marlo, who was on her own theater tour, and then recorded her separately when she returned, bringing their voices together through the magic of mixing.

Recording the Voices of East Harlem in New York City singing "Sisters and Brothers" was truly inspirational. They turned the song into a rousing gospel celebration of our unity. In the studio, the versatile Alan Alda graced us with his acting, his singing, and his skillful directing of many stories and poems.

It took us more than a month to edit the album, mixing the music tracks and adding sound effects and incidental music to the stories. Although the album was composed of independent pieces, each entertaining and meaningful, when we put it all together like a jigsaw puzzle, it gave us a picture of a whole world of new possibilities.

We completed the final editing touches during an all-night session so it would be ready for a listening party to be held at the Ms. magazine offices the next morning. Everyone on the staff and lots of guests who'd been involved with the process were there. I was so nervous that I couldn't stay in the room, so I sat outside in the hallway with the door slightly open. There was applause after the title song and lots of laughter during the baby piece, and both continued throughout the playing of the rest of the album, with major cheers at the end.

The album was released with a lot of fanfare and Marlo's devoted promotion. *Free to Be . . . You and Me* became an instant critical and commercial hit. Everyone was surprised, especially all the honchos in the music industry who'd turned it down.

It was a breakthrough of major cultural importance, affirmed by its subsequent incarnations as a book and then an ABC television special in 1974. Creating the television special was an exhilarating experience, as we adapted the existing materials that called out to be visualized and created new songs and stories to pull it all together, using New York City as our own beautiful back lot. Going onstage with Marlo to receive an Emmy for the year's best children's television special was the least of the rewards that it gave me.

For the television special, we turned the babies in "Boy Meets Girl" into puppets, created by a genius puppeteer named Wayland Flowers, and then put the puppets into a series of running pieces that introduced the themes of each act. The puppets also performed in a witty musical number, called "Let's Hear It for Babies," with music and lyrics by Ed Kleban. All the sets were created by Tony Walton, one of Broadway's most illustrious set designers.

The album had celebrated friendship between boys and girls. We built on that theme by animating Lucille Clifton's story, "Three Wishes," for television. We followed it with a new song, one of my

Marlo Thomas and Carole Hart receiving an Emmy Award for best children's television special, 1974.

personal favorites, by Bruce and Stephen, "Circle of Friends" which was cleverly written as a round and sung by Marlo, Kris Kristofferson, Rita Coolidge, and some other friends.

I believe the television special was the culmination of *Free to Be*'s highest expression of love, freedom, and equality. It ends with the consciousness-raising view from outer space of our Mother Earth. When the idea popped into my head of playing, over that image, the concluding words, "Sisters and Brothers" from the Voices of East Harlem's performance, I got chills.

Amazingly in our throwaway society, *Free to Be* has endured. In 2007 we published a thirty-fifth anniversary edition of the book. Designed by Peter Reynolds, it featured the original content with new illustrations attuned to kids' current sensibilities. I went to a book-signing event and noticed that people were entering the bookstore in groups of three: grandmothers, who were the first audience; their daughters, to whom they had passed it on; and their daughter's children—toddlers—many of whom could already sing the songs.

I leave it to other thoughtful writers to analyze the cultural and historical significance of *Free to Be . . . You and Me*. I am thankful now for this opportunity to look back at the extraordinary group of people who came together and created a work with such a strong and lasting impact. I am also grateful that it lives on as a tribute to the heart and soul and talent of my beloved Bruce Hart, who passed away in 2006.

Free to Be taught me that the right media projects at the right time *can* create great positive change in the world. That became the mantra for all my future work. With so much noise and distraction out there today, the challenge is how to create content that is heartfelt, distinctive, and powerful enough to break through and make the kind of changes in consciousness and awareness that *Free to Be . . . You and Me* was able to make. We need it now.

A Thousand Fond Memories
and a Few Regrets

LETTY COTTIN POGREBIN

It began in February 1972, with an offer I couldn't refuse: Gloria Steinem asked me to have lunch with Marlo Thomas. Are you kidding? What time?

In those days, Gloria was one of the few women doing serious advocacy journalism. She was also a nationally known spokesperson for the civil rights, antiwar, and women's movements. The previous summer, she had asked me to join her in starting a magazine that eventually would be called Ms., a feminist enterprise so committed to its egalitarian, nonhierarchical structure that I could never have admitted how thrilled I was to be working at a desk just feet away from hers. The truth is, I would have done anything she asked.

Not that meeting Marlo was exactly a hardship. In the early 1970s, she, too, occupied a top spot on my Most Admired list. Her popular TV series, *That Girl*, was the first mass entertainment that overtly acknowledged the autonomy and dignity of the single woman, a category in which I had counted myself for four years after I graduated from college and before I met my husband. Defying the then-current image of the unmarried woman as a pitiful spinster, Marlo's spunky character positively reflected my singlehood experience in that she earned her own money, didn't live with her parents, and had an active love life.

But on March 1, 1972, when we met for lunch, it turned out that Marlo didn't want to talk about Ms. or *That Girl*, magazines or television. She wanted to talk about books. She'd been searching for books about smart, brave, adventurous little girls and had been shocked by the proliferation of stories about princesses, nurses, moms, stewardesses, and demure goody-goodies. Being a can-do person, she channeled her frustration into action: She decided she would produce a long-playing record album of children's entertainment that would break the bonds of sex stereotypes and inspire girls *and* boys to become their best selves. To that end, she had asked Gloria to recommend some stories to be read on the album. Gloria, with no kids of her own and no reason to monitor the world of children's literature, had put Marlo in touch with me.

I was the "expert" in a field that barely existed. I had three children under the age of seven. I had written an article, "Down with Sexist Upbringing," published in the preview issue of Ms., that had addressed the corrosive effects of sex role stereotypes on the education and rearing of children. I had also created a special feature to run in every issue of Ms., "Stories for Free Children," that required me to comb through mountains of publishers' catalogs looking for books for youngsters that were nonsexist, nonracist, and multicultural. With those credentials, I had become by default the go-to editor at Ms. for anything relating to children and families.

While I dove into my french fries at the Ginger Man restaurant on the Upper West Side, Marlo asked for my help finding stories that could be adapted for her record. I told her I'd had trouble finding even *one* book a month suitable for "Stories for Free Children." In fact, I thought I might have to buy original stories written just for Ms. The two of us began commiserating over the sad, sexist state of American culture. We talked about how both genders suffer from conventional sex-typing and about the urgency of breaking down the walls between girl land and boy land. We talked about ourselves and our childhoods, what we'd dreamed of becoming, and the barriers we'd faced. We became BFF, or, as Marlo once described our first meeting, "It was instantly obvious that we were soul mates. We both wanted to save the world and agreed the place to start was with its children."

And so began my involvement in the rollicking, intoxicating journey that resulted in the record, book, and TV special *Free to Be . . . You and Me*, coproduced by Marlo Thomas and the television writer and producer Carole Hart.

On the back cover of the hot pink LP record album with the chubby, whimsical lettering, I am listed as "Consultant." This basically meant I was the feminist Jiminy Cricket who sat on Marlo's shoulder and occasionally whispered, "We need something affirmative about girl/boy friendships." Or "We need to challenge the sex-typing of both paid jobs and household chores." In other words, I tried to help Marlo and Carole frame our message, refine our subject matter, and clarify our goals. On my own, I talked with progressive psychologists and educators about child development and sex role socialization, challenging them to define what *really* constitutes femininity and masculinity. I asked librarians and teachers for their recommendations and invited a few top children's book writers to meet with us and give us guidance. I raided my kids' bookshelves and lugged piles of books to our meetings.

I vividly remember the brainstorming sessions in either my living room or Marlo's, mining our memories of how *we* had felt stymied or stultified when we were growing up, what we wished our parents or teachers had said or done—or *not* said or done—to enable us to be more comfortable with ourselves. We talked about how adults might encourage kids to vault barriers, resist conformity, explore a wider world, and pursue their dreams. We wanted stories about independence and self-fulfillment; love, sharing, and mutual assistance; creative, cooperative relationships among children and between kids and their parents, siblings, and friends. A tall order.

I thought of my twin daughters, Robin and Abigail, then seven, and son, David, four, as grass roots, canaries in the mine, our first focus group. I remember them listening to the tapes of the songs and stories that Marlo and Carole had commissioned. When my kids laughed at "Don't Dress Your Cat in an Apron," teared up at "It's All Right to Cry," and danced around the room to the title song, "Free to Be . . . You and Me," I knew we'd hit pay dirt.

The record was a roaring success from the start, partly due to the wonderful writing by prominent creative talents and partly due to the performers who spoke or sang their lines in the recording studio.

The following year, when we began working on the book version, veteran writer and book editor Francine Klagsbrun joined us, serving as editor and liaison with our publisher, McGraw-Hill. Francine kept the gears running smoothly as we reached out to more talent—writers *and* illustrators this time—and made more assignments. As each new submission came in, I vetted the manuscript and tested it out on my kids (and occasionally their friends, too). On the TV special, Carole and Marlo oversaw the creative work and produced the show; I functioned minimally in the background as the "issues person," making sure that the words and images were devoid of race and gender stereotypes and that each piece contributed to the project's overarching themes and goals.

In today's polarized world, the entire *Free to Be* enterprise, and certainly my role in it, might be caricatured as an exercise in "political correctness," a charge many of us have had to refute more times than we can count. The label is both insidiously manipulative and just plain bogus. To call someone "politically correct" is nothing more than a transparent attempt to silence those who have identified an injustice and tried to fix it. Obviously, there are extremists on the left, as there are on the right. But as commonly applied, the term insinuates that leftist ideology is somehow more prescriptive and coercive than rightist ideology. It accuses liberals and feminists of trying to dictate rigid rules of speech and behavior.

In fact, *Free to Be . . . You and Me* did exactly the opposite. Rather than impose "politically correct" behavior on children, we offered a social *corrective*, an antidote to society's toxic conventions about "proper" behavior for males and females. We showed the tyranny of femininity to be dysfunctional and ridiculous and the tyranny of masculinity to be soul-crushing. We flung open the windows of a closed, musty room, aired it out, yanked the boy/girl labels off the toy chest, balanced out the bookshelf, and gave kids permission to be who they are and who they want to be. The only voice we tried to silence was the judgmental one that says, "You can't, because boys shouldn't," or "You shouldn't, because girls can't." Rather than "Do this" or "Don't do that," our message was, "Give it a try," "Go for it."

The delights of *Free to Be* in all its incarnations quickly spread across the country from kid to kid, house to house, classroom to classroom. Children memorized every lyric and asked their parents and teachers play the record over and over again. When the book came out, it won awards, hit the best seller list, and flew off library shelves. When the TV special aired, it earned an Emmy, and the video has been selling ever since.

In sum, *Free to Be . . . You and Me* became not just a junior anthem of the women's movement but a lighthearted symbol of massive social change. Its ripple effect was felt everywhere—in altered family roles, school curricula, language usage, toy packaging, advertising copy, characters on TV shows, and so much more. It changed how kids viewed themselves, how parents treated their children, and how children treated one another. It challenged teachers to face up to their entrenched, often unacknowledged, gender biases and to cast a more critical eye on the books they were assigning, whom they called on most often in class, whom they allowed to dominate the block corner or the dress-up box. It made all of us laugh and think and dream of "a land where the children are free."

To a large extent, that land has materialized. Today, Marlo Thomas could find hundreds of marvelous children's books about strong, independent, enterprising female characters and male characters who express themselves in more venues than just the Western frontier, sports arena, or outer space. Mommies can be almost anything nowadays—doctors and welders, CEOs and Supreme Court justices. Daddies are more involved in the domestic sphere, especially in child care, and some even choose to stay home to raise their kids. Today, little girls don't just dream, they design plausible futures for themselves because, in fact, they *can* grow up and run for president or serve as secretary of state and Speaker of the House. And they know that women *have* been leaders of other countries (England, Germany, Liberia, Israel, and Argentina, among others), and women *are* astronauts and admirals, plumbers and police officers, wrestlers and race car drivers, architects and inventors.

My six grandchildren are the beneficiaries of these seismic social transformations, yet all of them love the forty-year-old *Free to Be . . . You and Me* because it still speaks to them. I choke up when I hear them belt out the songs my children sang four decades ago or when they watch the video and excitedly point out each of their parents—my children—who are seen in the opening number riding on the carousel in Central Park and then turning into cartoon characters who take off for the sky. My grandkids never tire of watching the puppet babies trying to figure out which is the boy and which is the girl, and they don't think there's anything peculiar about the lyrics of "Parents Are People." To them, the only thing on the video that's dated is Michael Jackson's face.

I feel enormous pride as I recall the genesis of our project—however, it's a pride tempered by reality. Back then, I thought that *Free to Be* and the values it represents would change the world for good. But, sadly, many of my generation's gains have been chipped away over the past few decades by various forces: the conservative backlash, the "political correctness" police, media ridicule of the equality agenda, a widespread disillusionment with the idea of a perfectible society, and people's general reluctance to speak out and make waves.

However, to my way of thinking, passivity is not an option because so much remains to be done. Yes, mommies can be anything. But they don't always get equal pay for equal work, and if both mom and dad work, guess which parent usually stays home if their child gets sick.

And when some daddies lose their jobs, as many have in the current economic downturn, they feel they've lost their manhood because masculinity is still associated with money and power. We've got to fix that.

Children in playgrounds are still being watched over by women. Kids in younger grades are still being taught by women. School principals mostly are still men. Moms still plan children's social lives, memorize their shoe sizes, take them for checkups, and supply the cupcakes for the PTA bake sale. We've got to fix that.

Toys are back in their old gender ghettos: Shop Target online and you'll find Lego under "Boys Toys," a toy sewing machine under "Girls Toys." Stroll down the color-coded aisles of any Wal-Mart or Toys R Us, and you'll see pint-sized vacuum cleaners with pictures of little girls on the box and train sets with all-boy illustrations. Tell the salesclerk you're looking for a toy for a nine-year-old and you won't be asked, "Is the child interested in science? Art? Action? Fantasy? Construction?" You'll be asked, "Boy or girl?" We've got to fix that.

Years ago, Barbie could only be a nurse, bride, babysitter, princess, or stewardess. Now you can get a Barbie TV news anchor—but her TV camera is pink. You can get a Barbie computer engineer—but her computer is pink. You can get "Share a Smile Becky," a doll in a wheelchair—but the wheelchair is pink (and it doesn't fit into the elevator of Barbie's Dream House). We've got to fix that.

Check out the online catalog for children's furnishings from Pottery Barn Kids: The "Girls Rooms," decked out in terminal pink fluff, are labeled "Paris Toile," "Pink Daisy," and "Lindsey Butterfly," while the "Boys Rooms," whose palette runs from blue to brown, sport names like "Junior Varsity," "Madras Shark," and "Super Star." Even *curtain rods* have a gender: for boys, they're decorated with airplanes or Rugby stripes; for girls, they're adorned with butterflies or polka dots. We've got to fix that.

In the gynecologist's office recently, I heard a pregnant woman say she hadn't wanted to know the gender of her baby, but it's doing a lot of kicking, so it must be a boy. People still respond to babies according to the color of their bunting. If it's blue, they say, "What a big buster!" If it's pink, "She's so adorable!"—even though *both* babies may be four months old, fifteen pounds, and bald. We've got to fix that.

Today, boys can still be ridiculed if they go out for drama club, kiss their fathers in public, or ride a bicycle without the right crossbar

Letty Cottin Pogrebin and her daughters, Robin and Abigail, at a march for women's rights, mid-1970s. Personal collection of Rita Waterman; used with permission.

(otherwise known as a "girl's bike"). Little League has been legally required to accept girls since 1973, but only one in seven current players is a girl. Walking in Central Park several times a week, I notice the playing fields are always dominated by men and boys. Title IX is supposed to ensure gender equality in school sports, yet I'm always reading about girls' high school teams getting less practice time or gym access than boys' teams. We've got to fix that.

Today too many girls hate their body images; some as young as eight already have eating disorders. Too many boys are becoming bullies or are being bullied. Very few gay teens feel free to be themselves. Too many kids are listening to rap songs, watching music videos, and playing computer games in which girls and women are demeaned, objectified, vilified, hypersexualized, beaten, and raped. Too many children are victims of violence, incest, and sexual abuse. Too many adolescents are committing suicide. This isn't the world we envisioned forty years ago. It wasn't supposed to turn out this way. We've got to fix it.

I'd like to close my eyes to all that backsliding, but I can't because the world my six grandchildren are inheriting contains those grim realities as well as the great advances of my era. I worry about their future and the future of all our children.

And I'll keep worrying until more adults are willing to do what Marlo Thomas did in 1972—recognize what's wrong and resolve to fix it. What's wrong today—what's harmful to children, unfair, inequitable, and intolerable—cannot be solved one kid at a time, one household at a time, or one teacher at a time. As has always been the case, it takes time and effort to galvanize a group. It takes a collective commitment and a huge amount of organizing to get things done. It takes outrage transmuted into action, passion harnessed to hard work, and vision translated into troublemaking.

Forty years ago, *Free to Be . . . You and Me* was fueled by one woman's outrage at injustice and inequality. I can't help wondering what you could accomplish—what problems you could fix, what projects you could initiate, what wrongs you could right—if you got going today. Why not start by calling a friend for lunch? America's children are waiting.

Mommies and Daddies

CAROL HALL

I was thrilled when I got the call. It was a call from my agent. I was brand-new to the experience of having a theatrical agent, not to mention one who made phone calls to me, so this was already good.

I was a young mother of two children, in my early thirties, recently separated from my husband as well as recently moved from Boston, the town I'd been a "married lady" in, to New York. I'd left New York City five years earlier, and it still held all my hopes of becoming a songwriter.

I'd come there with a clear-eyed dream of writing music and lyrics, and I'd had some encouraging modest success. A young singer by the name of Barbra Streisand had recorded a song of mine, a lullaby called "Jenny Rebecca," on her second album, *My Name is Barbra*. Her recording my song was probably the reason I was able to get the agent's attention. And now he was calling me, and it was about work.

Apparently, television star Marlo Thomas had conceived of a new project. She felt passionately about gathering together a group of writers who would create a new kind of album of songs and stories for children, the likes of which had never been done before. It was to be called *Free to Be . . . You and Me*.

It was the 1970s, and the rumble of feminism was being heard loud and clear across the land. *Ms.* magazine had burst onto the scene. The phrase "nonsexist child rearing" was a major issue on the feminist agenda. Marlo's album would break down gender-specific stereotypes and clichés of what defined girls' and boys' behavior. A girl could be an astronaut. A boy could sew.

The agent said they wanted a song about all the different kinds of jobs that mothers and fathers could have, and they were calling me. The song needed to reflect the idea that there was no work that was "man's work" or "woman's work." Work was work. Oh, and by the way, said the agent, this was not to be a polemic. It was for kids, and therefore it had to be funny and bright and clever and joyous and above all entertaining. Could I write this?

I was thrilled. Ever since I'd had my two children, Susannah and

49

Daniel, then eight and six years old, I'd thought constantly about my choice of profession and what it meant to give one's entire life over to being a writer. "Writer" could seem a vague sort of word for something one hoped to support her family by doing.

Whoever heard of a woman being a songwriter anyway? I had known of a few women who wrote lyrics, but they almost always wrote in partnership with men. And I had seldom heard of a woman who wrote music. I found the whole idea of a song in which parents do a variety of jobs deeply interesting, and I couldn't wait to begin.

I was calling it "Parents Are People."

It would be easy. I could just start with myself, start with "writer." But since writing could be a job for either of the parents, which one of those two to choose to give it to? Suddenly an odd moment from the past burned into my memory, a thought I hadn't remembered in years.

When I was about sixteen and in high school, I had been talking to my boyfriend one night about plans for the future. I had suddenly found the courage to confess all my songwriting dreams and secret ambitions and hopes to him. I would go to New York, I had told him. I would write music and lyrics, maybe hear the songs recorded by brilliantly talented people, perhaps see them being sung in the movies or even in a Broadway show.

When I finished sharing my triumphant fantasy, what did the boyfriend have to offer in return? He had said, "That's okay. You can write at home all day and still be there to cook dinner when your kids get in from school."

Hmmm. I imagined Richard Rodgers in the kitchen making sandwiches.

I decided to give the job of "writer" to the verse about daddies.

"Rancher" was the next profession that I thought of, mostly because I have a cousin who was the only child and only grandchild of a highly respected ranching family in Colorado. By the time she was ten years old, she could ride a horse, rope a calf, drive a tractor, repair a barbed-wire fence, and then come in and work on a dress she was sewing to enter at the county fair.

And now my cousin was a rancher, grown up, married, and the mother of three kids who were doing much the same things she had done. Talk about "nonsexist child rearing!" Everyone on a ranch knows how to feed the animals and how much.

So in honor of my cousin, the mommy verse got the "rancher."

My mother was a classically trained musician, a violinist who sometimes played in a local orchestra. When I was about five years old and she was in rehearsal, her idea of an easy babysitting arrangement was to let me sit in the brass section with my coloring book. I loved the horn players.

So I'd grown up with the idea that sometimes there were dads or moms who never went to an office for their work but instead sat in folding chairs, played tubas and trumpets and trombones, joked around with the other moms and dads there, made an enormous amount of noise, and were generally a lot more fun than a babysitter would have been. It never occurred to me that that was an actual job.

I thought about all this as I was writing. I had forgotten how much fun it had been to sit in the orchestra. I wondered if that had anything to do with my dream of writing music and lyrics. Is that where I had gotten the idea that making music could be a full-time, everyday joy?

By now I was having a very good time. Little ideas tickled my fancy. I thought of Marlo's father, world-renowned comedian Danny Thomas, and that gave me the inspiration for the daddy verse to have "a funny joke teller."

I also wanted to pay attention to those jobs that might not seem "glamorous" or even "important" but are crucial to every society. Ordinary things. Where does a tuna fish sandwich come from, for instance? Someone fished that tuna out of the water.

Hence, came the line "Some daddies . . . sail on the sea."

(By the way, I did not for one moment think that anyone listening to my song would wonder where their tuna sandwich came from. It was just my own subtext for the lyric.)

So now I had the daddy verse:

Some daddies are writers
Or grocery sellers
Or painters or welders
Or funny joke tellers
Some daddies play cello
Or sail on the sea
Yes, daddies can be
Almost anything they want to be

Next came the mommy verse:

Some mommies are ranchers
Or poetry makers
Or doctors or teachers
Or cleaners or bakers
Some mommies drive taxis
Or sing on TV
There are a lot of things
A lot of mommies can be

An odd thing occurred while I was working on the mommy verse. I had started with "Some mommies are ranchers" and was trying to add a phrase that would be simple but unexpected, like "mommies drive taxis," when my son, Daniel, leaned over my shoulder and said firmly, "That's wrong. Mommies can't be doctors. Mommies are the nurses."

What? Where had he gotten such an idea? How was this possible? *His pediatrician was a woman!!!!!*

Trying not to show how surprised I was, I asked him to tell me more about what he had said, and to my amazement, there wasn't much more. No, no one had ever told him about mommies not being able to be doctors, he just "heard it." No, he didn't know where he heard it. But mommies were definitely the nurses.

"Daniel," I said, "It's wonderful to be a nurse, but why can't mommies also be doctors if they want to?"

He didn't know. But they couldn't. That's just how it was.

In a house where a single parent was trying to make her way financially supporting her family as a writer (and where the children's pediatrician was a woman), the idea of a working woman having to be one thing and unable to be another had somehow taken hold.

How could this be?

A few days later, I was at the piano working, picking out notes and singing the chorus quietly to myself.

"Mommies are women, women with children . . ."

Susannah said to me, "There's one word you should change."

(I should mention at this point that in our house, everyone is allowed to be a friendly critic.)

"One word I should change?"

Marlo Thomas and Harry Belafonte during a recording session, 1974.

"Don't say 'Mommies are women, women with children.' Say mommies are 'ladies' with children."

I was astounded. "Why, honey?"

"Because," said Susannah, "'Ladies' sounds better. It's nicer."

That's how I became radicalized.

I was a woman with a mission.

Marlo Thomas appearing
as a taxi driver during the
filming of the *Free to Be*
television special, 1974.

Marlo Thomas appearing as
a welder during the filming
of the *Free to Be* television
special, 1974.

If my son thought a woman couldn't be a doctor and if my daughter thought "lady" was a "nicer" word than "woman" and if they hadn't heard that from me . . .

There was serious work to be done.

I called my agent and told him I had ideas for a lot more songs I could write.

I took great delight in doing the next two. The producers of the album wanted a song about how it was all right for a boy to cry. To research the idea, I went to Susannah and Daniel's school and interviewed a classroom full of five-year-olds. I asked everyone to tell me one sentence about how it feels to cry. One little girl said, "It's like raindrops from your eyes." A little boy said, "Crying gets the sad out of you."

I stole those lines and never looked back. The song is called "It's All Right to Cry."

The brilliance of Marlo and her producers is that the person they chose to sing it was Rosey Grier, a famous 230-pound football player, who felt passionately that this message was very important for boys to hear. His rendition of the song, in his warm and scratchy voice, has made it a classic.

I wrote my third song because I had never been able to find a single children's story in which girls and boys played happily together, plus, I wanted to write about games that didn't cost anything. It wasn't to be anything complicated. There was no technology! It was merely about what I remembered as the happiest times of my childhood—just very simple play—cooking, fishing, building a tree house, making "sugar-on-snow" with snow and maple syrup, inventing secret codes, maybe having a friend with whom you could even confess that you still need your teddy bear at night. Very old-fashioned.

The song is called "Glad to Have a Friend Like You."

I began to feel like the luckiest woman in America to have been asked to do this project. I became a woman on fire with the joy of working on something that I believed was actually important.

And now it's forty years later, and I'm still grateful. I have had many of my most fantastic dreams come true. Songs of mine have indeed been sung by amazing people, and I've heard my work performed both in the movies and on Broadway.

But *Free to Be . . . You and Me* has my heart. It was—and always will be—the thing I am most proud of having written.

Free to Be . . . the Music

STEPHEN LAWRENCE

It started one day when I sat in Marlo Thomas's living room on the Upper West Side of Manhattan, as a group of people brainstormed the ideas that would coalesce into *Free to Be . . . You and Me*. Bruce and Carole Hart had recently introduced me to Marlo and invited me to work on their new project. The energy in the room was palpable. I knew that whatever developed from this meeting, I wanted to be part of it. I don't think we would have predicted that a timeless phenomenon was germinating in the room at that moment, but I did have a feeling that we were embarking on something bigger than deciding what to have for lunch.

All of the themes resonated within me: gender stereotypes; the importance of friendship and love; the need to express emotions; and, of course, the freedom to be who you want to be. My job as musical director would be to compose music to express these ideas. I would also arrange and conduct my own music as well as the songs written by others.

Bruce Hart and I were given the job of writing a title song. Coming up with titles was among Bruce's special gifts. Within a few days he showed me a lyric. "There's a land that I see where the children are free" seemed just right, an invitation to a world filled with boundless possibility.

I composed the music in one day. I work best—and fastest—when fighting a deadline. Early on, I discovered that stalling leads to more stalling and composing leads to more composing. As a *Sesame Street* composer, I once composed the music for seven songs in ten days. I was pleased with all of them. I am motivated to work quickly so I have the luxury of throwing out early ideas if they don't pass the overnight test: I record a piece into my computer—for "Free to Be," of course, it was a tape recorder—and forget about it. The next morning, I hear it fresh, and if it's not good enough, out it goes and I start again. "Free to Be" passed the test. I knew that people of all ages would be able to hear it easily and sing it easily.

Music and lyrics from other songwriters began to appear, and performers were recruited and matched to them. Marlo and Harry Belafonte were a perfect fit for Carol Hall's wonderful song, "Parents Are People." The instrumental tracks for the album and television special were recorded on sixteen-track tape in New York City. Marlo's voice was recorded there, and we recorded Harry singing in Las Vegas. They were also shot lip-syncing in various locations around New York City. The rolls of tape, 2 inches wide and 10.5 inches in diameter, soon became too valuable to lose, so we never checked them with our luggage when flying. We always carried them with us. Of course, we had made backups, but in those predigital days, there was some loss in quality when tapes were duplicated. We didn't want to take any chances.

The great football player Rosey Grier was an inspired choice to sing Carol Hall's "It's All Right to Cry." Carol had written it as a simple poetic statement on the value of expressing emotions. When I played the original arrangement for Rosey, he asked if I could add a stronger beat to it and illustrated by tapping his foot in tempo. I took his foot tapping—some might say stomping—and built the arrangement around that.

For the album, Diana Ross was set to sing my song "When We Grow Up," with lyrics by Shelley Miller. The timing was tight, and I wrote the arrangement on the plane to California. She did the recording in one or two takes, exactly the way I wanted it. For the television version of *Free to Be*, this song was sung by Roberta Flack and Michael Jackson. They were perfect, singing the duet exactly as I had envisioned it without a word from me.

Recordings did not always go so smoothly. Ed Kleban, who also wrote the lyrics for the Broadway show *A Chorus Line*, contributed the song "Let's Hear It for Babies," a new act we created for the television special. Mel Brooks seemed an inspired choice to sing it. Mel immediately strove to make the song his own. I began to feel that the song was getting lost and tried to pull him back to the song Ed had written. After a short time, Mel left the room. Marlo entered and said, "Stephen, what are you doing?" I replied, "I'm protecting the song." She said, "Stephen, you can't do that. That's Mel Brooks. He'll leave." Fortunately, though, he didn't leave. The song was developed into a Busby Berkeley–style puppet production, and it became one of the highlights of the show.

Elaine Laron wrote a beautiful poem called "The Sun and the Moon." I was asked to set it to music, and Dionne Warwick was chosen to sing it. I had always appreciated the rich timbre of her voice and her impeccable phrasing. However, pop phrasing was not what "The Sun and the Moon" called for. As with "Let's Hear It for Babies," this song needed to be sung pretty much as written. In the end, she sang it a little straighter than she was accustomed to and the result, in my opinion, was a perfect recording.

After completing postproduction work on the album, I started to become aware of the cultural force *Free to Be* would soon become. In a country that was politically and socially divided (although not as dramatically as it is today), *Free to Be* had a definite impact. Many young women followed the traditional path of high school, marriage, and family, and for some this was certainly a satisfying choice. But for others, it was not fulfilling. *Free to Be* presented a full range of possibilities.

In some parts of the country, these were radical ideas, and they elicited strong reactions. I remember thinking that this backlash could only help to sell more records. I believe one reason *Free to Be* is passed from generation to generation is that its message continues to be worth repeating.

I am frequently introduced to *Free to Be* fans, and when they learn that I contributed to it, they express gratitude for my role in bringing them this life-changing experience. My daughter, now a twenty-five-year-old Internet writer and editor, enjoyed *Free to Be* a great deal. Of course, her mother and I had tried early on to make her aware of the pleasures of infinite possibility. I have heard from many adults that the record remains a joy in their current lives. And I was delighted when Gwyneth Paltrow appeared on the television program *Inside the Actor's Studio* and told the show's host, James Lipton, that singing along to *Free to Be* as a child had inspired her to become an actress.

When the record was first released in 1972, I phoned record stores to see if they had stocked their shelves with our album. I visited stores to see if it was placed prominently. I didn't need to worry. I think if computers and the Internet were ubiquitous in the 1970s, *Free to Be* would have gone viral. In a sense it has; it's just taken a little longer.

Thinking about *Free to Be*

ALAN ALDA

I remember the day Marlo Thomas called, told me about her idea for a children's record, and asked me to take part. We had worked together on a movie, *Jenny*, and had become good friends. So I knew that this wasn't just an idea—it was something that would actually happen, and in a very classy way. Marlo is one of those extraordinary people who decides to do something, gets on the phone, gets people organized, and makes it happen. She's sort of a benign general.

And this was a great idea. It combined show business with a deeper purpose we both cared about. I learned at an early age how powerful theater can be. My father started in burlesque, was later in vaudeville, and then moved on to movies, television, and the Broadway stage. As a child, I was always standing in the wings, watching his performances. Both Marlo and I had fathers who were in show business; in fact, her father and mine had known each other as young actors. We grew up watching funny people be funny, and in the course of that, we learned to use humor to explore serious issues. I think all that came into play when we worked on *Free to Be*.

After the stories and poems were written, I was given some of the material to act in and direct. (I directed the spoken word pieces, including "Atalanta," "Boy Meets Girl," and the poems by Dan Greenburg, "Don't Dress Your Cat in an Apron" and "My Dog Is a Plumber.") I was looking for ways to make it come alive. I wanted not just to do a reading of the words but to tell the story through the *sounds* of the experience. I used sound montages the way they did on old-fashioned radio shows. I wanted to bring kids into the experience through the power of imagination, the way radio did. So in the poems, we didn't just say there were pots and pans, we added all kinds of clanging sounds to bring the pots to life.

I wanted to get that same vivid quality in the performances. As I remember, the story of "Atalanta" is written in the past tense, but without changing the words, we played it as if it were in the present tense. You hear the footfalls on the track, and our speech is breathless, as if we were running the race in that moment instead of describing it in the past. It was all to bring the listeners into the story for a deeper experience. The power of drama is that it can allow the audience to be the characters for a while, to feel what they feel—the joy and sometimes the pain. I was hoping that the more we were able to involve the kids listening to the sketches, the more they would empathize with the characters.

But aside from the techniques we used, working on *Free to Be* was fun. I remember a happy day directing the "Boy Meets Girl" sketch where Marlo and Mel Brooks played babies. I don't think Mel had ever been directed by anyone before, but he was good-natured and stuck with me. The piece wound up with a nice improvisational feel to it, and Mel had a smile on his face the whole time we recorded it.

We were taking the fun of comedy and music and celebrating the shift in our culture's thinking that was taking place then and that we cared so much about. I was already identifying myself as a feminist and working to get the Equal Rights Amendment ratified. During the 1970s and early 1980s, any time I wasn't in front of a camera, I was traveling around the country, making speeches at rallies and meeting halls and lobbying for the amendment in state legislatures. Marlo was doing the same thing, and at one point we were standing together on courthouse steps in Florida, rallying people before an important vote on the ERA. (Which we lost, but which only made us work harder.)

I think I got involved in the women's rights movement for a number of reasons. People often assume it's because I have three daughters, and I'm sure that's part of it. I know if I saw my daughters (or now my granddaughters) denied equality, I would be angry and fight it. Mostly, though, what I was conscious of at the time was that equality for women just seemed fair—it was simply the right thing to do. My joke then was that I got it genetically because I come from a long line of women. It's more than a joke, of course; we all share a common humanity that can't be ignored.

And on a practical level, I saw I could be helpful because a male voice would be coming from an unaccustomed direction. But I think there was a very personal factor. As a boy, growing up with a strong interest in the arts, I was often the outsider in school. Other guys would be on the football team, while I'd be writing a musical comedy. I was different and a little less than equal. There were times when people would register their interest in me by punching me in the head. So the notion of equality resonated with me. And so did the ideas behind *Free to Be*, which dealt exactly with the feelings I had gone through as a kid.

Looking back, it's clear that *Free to Be* had a big impact. Of course, no one project can take credit for bringing about the kind of social change we've seen—many efforts paved the way, and *Free to Be* was a notable one. All of the struggles in trying to get the ERA passed, all the speeches, all the hundreds of articles that were written, all the television shows and consciousness-raising groups—they all contributed to a huge change in the culture. *Free to Be* helped people to recognize other people's dignity and acknowledge their contributions. It did this in an entertaining way, and it helped bring about real change. There's plenty more that needs to be done, but we shouldn't forget how things have changed for the better.

Concepts like equal pay for women and equal access to athletics for girls are frequently taken for granted now by the same people who years ago objected to those notions. I recently spent some time in Los Angeles, in rehearsal for the play I wrote about the life and work of Marie Curie, a woman who struggled a hundred years ago to be recognized for her groundbreaking work in science. Each day as I walked to the theater, I passed men with their babies—pushing strollers and feeding their children with bottles, with the same kind of concentration that fifty years ago they would have used to take care of their Chevrolets. *Free to Be* helped expand and enrich the roles men can play in their own lives.

And it continues to be enjoyed by new generations. It still circulates in our culture. One of my grandchildren performed in a show based on *Free to Be* at his school—something that's done in schools all over the country. Adults come up to me on the street and tell me they grew up with it and are playing it now for their children and their children's children. *Free to Be* is a cultural object that gets passed down through generations as a way of explaining to ourselves who we are and who we can be. I'm very glad to have been a part of it.

Beyond the Fun and Song

FRANCINE KLAGSBRUN

Click!

It was the sound of our generation. Women had suddenly discovered themselves and the restrictions with which they had lived all their lives without recognizing them.

"Why can't you get the children's stuff put away?," a husband barks at his wife. Click! "You have two hands," she replies, startled at her words yet pleased to have said them.

A woman writer is invited to have lunch in her company's executive dining room. Her husband rocks with laughter. "Ho ho, my little wife in an executive dining room," he says. Click!

Jane O'Reilly introduced the clicks in her article, "The Housewife's Moment of Truth," which appeared in the preview issue of Ms. magazine in 1972. After that, click! became women's shorthand for eyes opening and minds awakening as we reassessed the putdowns ("You think like a man"), diminutives (the "little woman"), and demands ("Honey, what's for dinner?") women and men had simply accepted as the natural order of the universe. Coming one after another and more rapidly with time, the clicks turned into a drumbeat of change that revolutionized society.

For most of us, that change related to our own lives and to the intensity with which we reexamined them. We assumed—if we thought about it at all—that once we made things right, they would be right for our children and grandchildren thereafter. We were, after all, repairing wrongs, revamping the social order, and reconstructing history.

Then came *Free to Be . . . You and Me*, and with it a different kind of click. Suddenly, with music and humor, joy and fun, kids took center stage. And suddenly we realized that that's exactly where they needed to be if we were truly to undo the old tired ways of seeing. The women's movement had begun with our experiences as adults, and we would continue to fight inequality and injustices toward women. But by concentrating on kids now, we could shift the focus away, at least for a while, from the angers and hurts of the past onto our hopes and expectations for the future.

My daughter was three years old when I came to *Free to Be* as its editor, helping Marlo Thomas and the book's creative team pull the project together. It was the second publishing assignment I undertook for *Ms.* The first called for editing an anthology of articles that had appeared in the earliest issues of the magazine. We named that book, published in 1973, *The First Ms. Reader* in optimistic anticipation that there would be others. (They never materialized.) About the same time, I began to immerse myself in the budding Jewish feminist movement, which would eventually lead me to deep involvement in the struggle to have women ordained as rabbis in the Conservative movement, the middle ground between Reform Judaism on the left and Orthodox Judaism on the right. It seemed the perfect moment to be the mother of a daughter. Through her, I could look ahead to sweeping changes in the secular and religious worlds I inhabited.

She was too young at the time to understand all the concepts in *Free to Be.* Much later, I would watch her and her friends perform skits from the book in Hebrew at her Jewish summer camp. And much, much later I would hear her children, my grandchildren, sing its songs at the top of their lungs as my husband and I drove with them to family vacations. But when I began working on the book, she was still too young to appreciate its reach. Nevertheless, I read her the stories and poems our editorial group commissioned, showed her the pictures art director Sam Antupit laid out, and sang the lyrics that graced the record and the printed volume.

As I worked on the project and brought home the delicacies of my labor, I became increasingly aware of the profound meaning behind the lighthearted tales and catchy music that entertained my little daughter. It was as though the serious and provocative essays I had gathered for *The First Ms. Reader* had danced off the pages of that book, rearranged themselves in color and song, and come back to teach children painlessly the achingly difficult lessons many of their mothers had struggled to learn. This children's book, I decided, was downright subversive, in the best sense of the word. It subverted outdated conventions and replaced them in the happiest way possible with a new vision of how things ought to be.

In "The Housewife's Moment of Truth," Jane O'Reilly lamented that "in the end, we are all housewives." Women carried the responsibility for everything that went on in their home, even if they had high-powered jobs outside it. "We would prefer to be persons," she observed drily. Along similar lines, in her classic essay, "I Want a Wife," Judy Syfers spelled out the many family duties that fell exclusively on a wife. "I want a wife who will keep my house clean," she wrote. "I want a wife who will keep my clothes clean, ironed, mended." Finally, she burst out, "My God, who *wouldn't* want a wife?" Sheldon Harnick's "Housework" in *Free to Be* translated the frustration of wives like these into a poem mocking the television saleswoman who smilingly tries to sell women on the virtues of a "detergent or cleanser or cleaner or powder" when the bottom line is what every woman (and man) knows: "Housework is just no fun." The only way for women and men to handle it is "to do it together."

Drawing on their own history, the women writers spoke bitterly about the lot of too many wives who bore all the household burdens alone. Harnick, looking forward, wanted to eliminate the imbalance and prevent the bitterness by letting children know that as men and women, they would need to share the burdens. Some people criticized "Housework" back in the 1970s, arguing that by bashing housework it denigrated paid domestic workers, most of them women. But that missed the point. Harnick echoed O'Reilly, Syfers, and dozens of other women who had come to realize that they had been boxed into roles they had not chosen and wanted to discard.

Roles. Beneath almost all feminist writing in those early days of the women's movement lay rebellion against the stereotypical roles that had been foisted on women. In her dense, brilliant essay, the "Hole/Birth Catalog," included in *The First Ms. Reader*, Cynthia Ozick told of how society defines a woman by "the hole at the bottom of her torso." Through that hole, she gives birth, and even if she doesn't, that chance of anatomy "dictates her tasks, preoccupations, proprieties, tastes, character." But a "hole is not destiny," Ozick cried, lashing into Freud's famous "anatomy is destiny" dictum. A woman cannot be reduced to her anatomy, for therein lies only death—of creativity, of humanity. In some of its most endearing and enduring pieces, *Free to Be* took up Ozick's cudgel and that of so many other women against sexual stereotypes. In the hilarious "Boy Meets Girl," two babies wonder which one is a boy and which a girl. The deep-voiced baby is scared of mice, has "dainty" feet, and wants to grow up to be a cocktail waitress, traits clearly identified with girls. The high-voiced one is bald, unafraid, and hopes to become a "fireman," typical boy signs. When a nurse changes their diapers and reveals their anatomy, the myths fall away as the babies discover that "you can't judge a book by its cover."

Throughout, the answer *Free to Be* offered to society's artificial limitations was the freedom to be—to wear what you want, cry when you hurt, and shine by your own light. In some ways, it carried those ideas even further than many of the feminist writings of the period. The stories and poems in the book celebrate cooperation and comradeship between girls and boys and men and women as they seek their freedom. Although the women's movement did aim to benefit all of society by having men participate more fully in family life while women tested their wings away from it, it placed its greatest emphasis on women's liberation. In *Free to Be*, Christopher John helps Agatha Fry bake a pie, a chorus hails sisterhood and brotherhood together, and Young John feels content to *talk* to Atalanta, not marry her against her will, before she goes off to visit great cities and he to discover new lands. Altogether, a gentle friendship between the sexes supplants sexism, typecasting, and hard feelings.

My favorite piece in the book, "Parents Are People," remains as relevant today as it was back then. I like it because it speaks directly to children themselves, with no intermediary. It reassures them that although parents are away at work or busy with other matters, that doesn't mean they love their children any less. It means that they have room in their hearts and minds for many activities, along with parenting ones. I like the piece because it reassures parents—especially mothers, still—that they can also be "people" pursuing their interests, and the kids will be okay.

On that note I would like to recommend an addendum, maybe for another era: a "Grandparents Are People" ballad. With folks living longer these days, many of us as grandparents find ourselves as busy as ever or more so with "things that we do." Yet some of us who fought the good battle of the women's movement may nonetheless carry in our minds idealized images of our grandmothers in their perennial aprons, chopping gefilte fish for the family or baking cookies for the grandchildren, and wish we could do that. And sometimes we may feel a twinge of guilt when we have to say no to a request to babysit a grandchild because we have an important meeting to attend or a deadline to meet. So we could use a theme song of our own, or maybe a click! or two to remind us that we, too, are free to be.

Free to Be . . . a Child

GLORIA STEINEM

My first glimmer of understanding that a magical classic had been born came on a sunny day in Minneapolis. I was speaking in a downtown park as part of a brown-bag lunchtime lecture series. Most people were from nearby offices, but some women came from home with young children. Since I had a copy of *Free to Be . . . You and Me* with me—it had been published about six months earlier—I decided to give the rows of upturned young faces a treat by reading a story or two.

After a few paragraphs, I looked up and saw children mouthing the words along with me. I read a poem—and the same thing happened. They already knew it by heart.

No one can tell children what to remember. It must be what they love. They might well grow up to repeat these stories and poems to their own children. After all, I remember fairy tales my older sister told me before I could read. I still know the A. A. Milne poems that I first learned to read for myself and to love.

But unlike fairy tales, *Free to Be* stories didn't tell children to be Goldilocks or a prince, Sleeping Beauty or a knight, an object or a subject. On the contrary, they helped little boys to learn that crying "gets the sad out of you" and little girls to rebel against "Ladies First" and the learned helplessness of dresses with buttons in the back. Most of all, *Free to Be* supported a sense of fairness, something that seems to be born into children. Think about it: Why else do little girls and boys around the world say out of nowhere, "It's not fair!" and "You are not the boss of me!"

In my own childhood, I loved even a hint of fairness. For instance, I read the Nancy Drew series about a girl detective. From Hillary Clinton to Supreme Court justices Sonia Sotomayor and Ruth Bader Ginsburg, women confess to loving this female heroine. I also read about the Hardy Boys who solved mysteries together. Both series were created by the same book packager, a man who seemed convinced that a successful female was a loner while successful males were a team—yet the same child was definitely not supposed to read both. Perhaps by putting "feminine" and "masculine" together, I was trying for the fairness of being a whole person.

Otherwise, I turned to stories about animals, as girls especially do—perhaps because we also feel speechless and out of power—and to Wonder Woman, the only female superhero. She was born on Paradise Island, where Amazons found refuge from Mars, god of war, then left to fight for democracy. Actually, she was invented by a male psychologist to counter the violence and sadism of boys' comic books during World War II—so sadistic, there had been a congressional hearing about it.

So three decades later, when *Ms.* magazine needed a cover image for its first monthly issue, Wonder Woman seemed the obvious choice. After all, her message of peace and democracy was needed again in the Vietnam era, and like her, we wanted to convert our adversaries, not kill them. Unfortunately, we discovered she had been transformed by the conservative 1950s and never changed back. Not only had she lost all her magical powers—bracelets that repelled bullets, a golden lasso that forced people to tell the truth, even a girl gang—but she looked a lot like a carhop.

We put the original Wonder Woman on the cover and reprinted her Golden Age comic strips inside. This plus months of fervent lobbying finally ended in a phone call from a harried executive at D.C. Comics. I remember him saying something like, "Okay, Wonder Woman has all her magical powers back. She also has a black Amazon sister named Nubia. Now will you leave me alone?"

Civil rights, feminism, and other social justice movements were at last beginning to sift down into children's worlds. With *Free to Be . . . You and Me*, this went wide and deep. For instance: When Rosey Grier, a powerful African American football star, told little boys, "It's All Right to Cry," it definitely was. When a young Michael Jackson sang "When We Grow Up," kids knew they could dream, too. When Marlo Thomas herself became Atalanta, who ran like the wind, made friends with boys, and adventured in the world, little girls discovered that they didn't have to be rescued. They could rescue themselves.

Nonetheless, just one song, "William Wants a Doll," caused a toothpaste company to refuse to sponsor the television version of *Free to Be*. Homophobia wasn't yet a popular word, but it was a popular reality.

The same was true for Ms. magazine and "Stories for Free Children," a pioneering monthly feature created and carried entirely by Ms. founding editor Letty Cottin Pogrebin. It was probably the subject of more protest—and praise—than the rest of the magazine. Whenever there was a story about a child whose parents were divorced, or who liked the pancakes her mother's boyfriend made on Sunday mornings, or who had two mommies or two daddies, we could count on boycotts by advertisers, fundamentalists who tried to censor us out of school libraries, and even pickets.

Of course, there were many more parents and children who loved seeing real families like their own, and the ACLU supported our legal battles against censorship, so Ms. magazine went right on, albeit with fewer ads. Letty had become an important part of Marlo Thomas's creative team, which included Carole Hart as coproducer. Personally, I count it as my most important contribution to Free to Be that I introduced Marlo to Letty—sort of like introducing Elizabeth Cady Stanton to Susan B. Anthony or the Supremes to Motown.

And here's what you need to know about Marlo: She could run the whole country if she had to. It was Marlo who called and persuaded and organized dozens of creative people—writers, actors, musicians, artists, and more—most of whom had never written or acted or composed for children before. Because they hadn't learned what children could and couldn't understand, they didn't patronize or matronize them. They didn't write or compose or act or illustrate "down." Instead, they created what their own earlier selves would have loved.

Our editors at Ms. magazine, whether or not they had children, also loved Letty's monthly children's stories. I came to understand that each of us is like a nested Russian doll, with all our earlier selves inside. That's why grown-up authors can write great children's stories and why great children's stories appeal to children of all ages.

Now the question is: When so much has changed—when an African American president has brought his two young daughters to live in the White House, female athletes are running faster than Atalanta, and homophobia is giving way to equality in marriage and the military—why is Free to Be still beloved and almost as popular as ever?

I think all we have to do is look around.

Way too many little girls are encouraged to be silly, seek approval only from boys, and be mean to other girls. They are also sexualized younger than ever by media, ads, and popular culture.

Boys are exposed to cruel and dehumanizing war games—not just in movies and TV, but now also on smart phones and home computers where they enter into the conflict. It's not surprising that bullying has become a major danger.

People of color will soon become the majority in this country for the first time, but instead of celebrating the fact that we now look more like the world, some white Americans are so dependent on old hierarchies that they are rebelling against government and saying no to democracy itself.

So yes, there has been a lot of progress, but there has also been a backlash against it. Nowhere is it written that progress will win. It depends on what you and I do every day.

I suggest you read *Free to Be . . . You and Me* again. Like all great classics, it has not only informed the past and present but foretells the future. So, too, does the sequel it spawned, *Free to Be . . . a Family*. Consider just one of its poems, "We and They" by Lucille Clifton:

Boris and Yuki and Sarah and Sue
And Karl and Latanya, Marta too
dreamed of the world
and it was spinning
and all the people
just talked about winning.
The wind was burning.
The water was churning.
The trees were bending.
Something was ending
And all the talk was "we" and "they."
The children all hugged themselves
waiting for the day
when the night of the long bad dream
is done
and all the family of humans
are one
and being and winning are not the same
and "we" and "they" is just a game

and the wind is a friend that
doesn't fuss
and even They is
actually Us.

Remember: If we raised just one generation of children without violence or shaming, we have no idea what might be possible. Thanks to the spirit of *Free to Be . . . You and Me*, we're beginning to find out.

How a Preschool Teacher Became Free to Be

BARBARA SPRUNG

Opportunity on a Three-by-Five Index Card

My *Free to Be . . . You and Me* opportunity arrived at the same time that the record and book were being conceived. In the spring of 1972, while teaching three-year-olds in a small private school in New York City and finishing coursework for a master's degree in child development, I was thinking that my next career step would be to direct a preschool or day care program. My goal was to help parents understand the importance of play and the complexity of learning that happens in the early childhood classroom. With this idea in mind, I went into the personnel office at the Bank Street College of Education and changed my career trajectory forever.

On an index card in the job file was a message: "A job for a feminist. Develop a nonsexist curriculum for early childhood. Call the Women's Action Alliance." This opportunity excited me in ways I didn't fully understand at the time, and I could hardly wait to call first thing the next morning and arrange an interview. Letty Cottin Pogrebin conducted the interview in a unique way. She asked me to comment on three children's picture books. Two, written by child psychologists, were full of sex-role stereotypes. The third book, *Kind Little Joe*, written by Dick Bruna, depicted a little boy who defied the stereotyped vision of what a boy should be. I still remember the opening sentence: "There is a boy whose name is Joe, the kindest boy you'll ever know."

My consciousness was instantly and forever raised by that interview, and I got the job to lead the Nonsexist Child Development Project. Since then, I've never looked back—only forward—to contributing to the movement to let all children become "free to be." What an opportunity and challenge. I received a blank slate to create something unique for the field of early childhood education.

Although it meant working two jobs, I was grateful that the Women's Action Alliance could only offer me a part-time position, which meant that I needed to keep my half-time job teaching three-year-olds. My classroom became a living laboratory of how sex-role stereotypes permeated the learning environment. The picture books typically showed only white, two-parent, two-child (always one girl, one boy) families. The dramatic play area had props that encouraged homemaking roles for girls: aprons, cooking equipment, and fancy dress-up clothes. Props for boys suggested going to work: briefcases, neckties, hard hats, and firefighters' helmets. The children played these roles to the hilt, fully embracing the idea of female homemaker and male breadwinner. These stereotypes persisted despite the fact that they no longer reflected the reality of many children's lives. Nothing in the classroom depicted children living in single-parent families; mothers in the workforce; black or Latino, Asian, or any other ethnic family grouping; or interracial families. Nothing showed a child or adult with a disability.

What I observed was typical of preschools everywhere. In fact, the Women's Action Alliance decided to address sex-role stereotyping in early childhood because Alliance members were hearing from women all over the country who were upset by the messages their children were bringing home. It didn't matter if you were a mother who worked outside the home or a doctor yourself, your child would still say things like, "Mommies can't be doctors, only daddies can."

In addition to books filled with stereotypes, there were traditional block-building accessories—sets of community workers and family people scaled to the size of unit blocks. The community workers set had eight figures—seven men, dressed as a fireman, policeman, repairman, telephone man, postman, businessman, and doctor, and one female, a nurse. The family set included a mother wearing an apron (with a small child clinging to her leg), a father dressed for work, a big brother, and a grandmother and grandfather. These figures now seem almost funny, but in daily use they reinforced powerful messages about social expectations.

Clearly, if children were to grow up "free to be," major changes had to be made, and they needed to begin in preschool. The primary role that early childhood education plays in children's lives is to introduce them to the world around them—a larger world than they experience within their own families. Early childhood educators had to rethink the way they were introducing that world to children. Teacher education institutions had to build awareness of sex-role stereotyping into the curriculum, and books, toys, and learning materials needed to fit the reality of children's lives and the societal changes that were already under way.

The Nonsexist Child Development Project of the Women's Action Alliance was launched to bring about this much-needed change. In addition to what my own classroom was revealing, the project started with observations and interviews with preschool teachers and day care directors throughout New York City. We focused not only on material things in the classroom but also on teachers' often unconscious and well-meaning attitudes and interactions with children that reinforced stereotypes. Greetings in the morning such as, "Hi, Heather, don't you look pretty today" versus "Hi, Jeremy, those sneakers you're wearing will be good for running in the yard." "Billy, you can be proud of that building, it has such a strong base" versus "Daniela, you finished your puzzle, please put it away on the shelf." We also noticed that letting children self-select the areas in which they would play and work reinforced traditional roles and denied them crucial opportunities for skill development.

We learned a lot from these observations and interviews. While many centers perpetuated rigid sex roles, some did not. For example, in one center in East Harlem, I observed that the girls were much more active outdoors. When I mentioned it to the teacher, she said the she *intentionally* ran with the girls to show them that it was okay and fun. In a day care center on the Lower East Side of Manhattan, a skilled teacher regularly turned the dramatic play area into "work" spaces such as a hospital or a store and encouraged girls and boys to try on nontraditional roles.

Another center I visited in the Bronx created a new jolt to my consciousness. It was a Head Start Center, and as mandated by federal regulations, 10 percent of the class consisted of children with disabilities. How did these children see themselves reflected in their environment? Were there any books or puzzles that depicted children who looked liked them or the adults they would grow up to be?

The site visits expanded my view of what needed to be changed. In addition to freeing children from rigid sex roles, learning materials and toys would need to reflect racial and ethnic diversity and to include children and adults with disabilities functioning in the world.

When I was disturbed by the things in my classroom, I did what teachers have always done when they needed something that wasn't available: I made my own materials. Fortunately, I worked in a school with a shop, and the shop teacher helped me make a set of community workers that showed pairs of workers, female and male, doing the same jobs. They were hand-drawn and had rather primitive stands, but they said something very different to children than the commercially available set with the seven men and one woman.

I also cut out pictures from magazines that showed women at work, a boy crying, a girl fixing a bicycle, a man holding a baby, and a person in a wheelchair, and I displayed the pictures at the children's eye level. These pictures were wonderful catalysts for one-on-one discussions with children about what boys and girls and men and women can do. I made nonsexist matching games by mounting pictures on foam core, each with a matching card. I chose pictures that illustrated multiracial and ethnic children and adults, some of them with disabilities, engaged in nonstereotyped activities. It was fun! And one of the most gratifying aspects of being a preschool teacher is that you see the results of your work reflected very quickly in the children. Children were opening up to new ideas, and parents, too, noticed changes.

Spreading the Word

Changing my classroom and sharing my new understanding with my family were valuable but created a very small circle of change. The next step was to take what I had learned from my research and my personal growth and share it with others in my field. This work became the subject of my master's thesis and subsequently a book, *Non-Sexist Education for Young Children: A Practical Guide*.[1]

The book enabled me to conduct informative workshops for preschool teachers and directors. Everywhere I went, the response was electrifying. I usually began by reading Whitney Darrow's book *I'm Glad I'm a Boy, I'm Glad I'm a Girl* (the same book, I've since learned, that provoked Marlo Thomas's ire). Teachers would often run to their bookshelves and give me their copies, so I ended up with quite a collection! Teachers seemed eager for change, and they welcomed the chance to learn hands-on strategies they could implement directly in the classroom.

In the workshops with teachers, I shared the research that professor Selma Greenberg had conducted at Hofstra University, demonstrating how play divided by sex roles deprived both boys and girls of essential skill development. Greenberg's research showed that when children self-selected areas of play based on gender, they became more skilled in those areas and deficient in others—deficiencies that became readily apparent when children entered kindergarten.[2] I also discussed Lisa Serbin's research on the importance of teacher placement in drawing children into new areas of the classroom, which gave teachers practical ideas to allow children to try new things. Block building was of special importance for girls. Serbin found that when the teacher sat in the block area, more girls came to work there, though it was usually dominated by boys.[3] Since block building develops visual-spatial skills, it was important for teachers to have this information. Basing these workshops on solid academic research helped mitigate some teachers' reservations about the need for change. However, by and large, teachers were positive and welcomed the opportunity to improve their practice.

I also conducted workshops with parents, who usually agreed with the idea of letting girls become "free to be." It wasn't as easy to convince parents that boys also needed to be liberated. A girl wearing a hard hat instead of a frilly hat was okay, but a boy with a doll brought out fears of homosexuality that hovered very close to the surface in many parents' minds. Mothers could sometimes make the leap, but fathers had a really hard time. It seemed that a girl moving into a boy's role was perceived as status up, but a boy showing nurturance was perceived as status down. Eventually, though, many parents began to accept the idea of expanding boys' roles as well.

Changing the Toys

Toys and classroom materials had to change along with the teachers, so I took my crude prototypes to the major suppliers of preschool materials. Fortunately, because of the women's movement, Ms. magazine's regular feature "Stories for Free Children," Free to Be, and the pressure exerted by parent and teacher advocates, manufacturers were approachable and willing to retool some of the standard materials. New sets of community workers, flannel boards depicting working people with nonsexist job titles, and puzzles of men in nurturing roles all were produced during this time. The materials that showed children and adults with disabilities functioning in the real world took a while longer to make their way into the mainstream. At first, we

"Our Community Helpers" cardboard play people, ca. 1975. Used with permission of the Sophia Smith Collection, Smith College.

had to self-publish sets of photographs, handmade puzzles, and lotto games. Eventually, however, inclusive materials became commercially available.

Toys and toy packaging also began to change. Now girls weren't always in the background, watching while the boys were in front actively engaged with the toy. Some forward-looking manufacturers made riding toys in primary colors suitable for any child. Publishers also instituted guidelines for using nonsexist terminology.

These welcome changes took place throughout the 1970s and into the early 1980s. Then, as happens in every movement, backsliding occurred. Fortunately, classroom materials and children's trade books continued to depict an increasingly nonsexist, multiracial, and inclusive view of the world. Toy companies, however, soon reverted to producing color-coded toys: pink bicycles that no boy would ever ride, homemaking sets for girls, and violent action toys for boys. Apparently, color-coding sells more toys. Since that time, toys for girls have become more sexist and sexualized, encouraging girls to make a glamorous adult appearance, while toys for boys foster gun use, war games, speed, and danger.

Through the heady years of change, *Free to Be . . . You and Me* was always there to delight and inspire us. Through the backslide years, it helped sustain us and kept us hopeful. Several generations of children have grown up knowing that it's all right for boys to cry, that girls can be leaders, and that both mothers and fathers can take care of babies. That's a lot of change for the better. For me personally, playing a role in helping children grow up free to be has been an exhilarating and energizing experience that continues to this day.

Part Two

Free to Be . . . You and Me

in Historical Context

Where the Children Are Free

Free to Be . . . You and Me, Second-Wave Feminism,
and 1970s American Children's Culture

LESLIE PARIS

On a winter day in the mid-1970s, a group of fifth-grade girls in Tor-
rance, California, south of Los Angeles, spent their "free period" at
school writing to actress and feminist Marlo Thomas. The girls were
enthusiastic fans of the 1972 album, *Free to Be . . . You and Me*, that
Thomas had spearheaded. Wrote Leslie F., "I want to tell you what a
great record you put out, 'Free to be, You and me.' It really goes deep
in to things like womans lib, and its okay, for a boy to play with a doll."
Her classmate, Karen M., concurred: "I'm only in the fifth grade but I
feel I can understand these songs. They are so meaningful and sensitive." Christina F. related that "our class plays it everday and they all
enjoy it! The songs in it are far-out because they all tell a little story
by themselves."[1]

   In the early 1970s, the success of the *Free to Be* series—the 1972
record album and the 1974 book and television special—reflected the
coming of age of second-wave feminism in mainstream American
children's culture.[2] *Free to Be*, aimed primarily at elementary-school-
aged children, was one of the movement's greatest successes, spurred
both by the aspirations of a liberal cohort of adults who wished to
socialize children less traditionally than their own parents had socialized them and by children's delight in the songs, stories, and sketches.
Today, the series has become a foundational text for a specific generational cohort, a kind of shorthand through which adults who grew up
in 1970s liberal (and sometimes radical) families can reflect on the culture of their childhoods. In a recent memoir, for instance, writer Susan
Jane Gilman recalls her youth as the daughter of white hippies living
in a racially and economically diverse New York City neighborhood:
Having been "born just as the women's movement was catching fire,
my classmates and I were being raised by mothers who would be the
first on line to buy copies of *Free to Be . . . You and Me* and multiracial,
anatomically correct baby dolls."[3]

Free to Be also circulated beyond its most obvious market, the daughters and sons of feminists. The album was played in many elementary school classrooms, reaching twenty or thirty children at a time; as one California grade-school teacher wrote to Thomas, "We play it all the time and dance, sing and act it out."[4] Individual children often memorized their favorite songs and taught them to their friends. A number of the songs and skits became "talent night" standards at American summer camps and youth groups. The television special also had a wide audience. In these ways, the series offers a valuable example of the reach of children's culture.

Free to Be attracted this audience through its star-studded cast and its lively style. Some sections of the project were explicitly moralizing; Sheldon Harnick's "Housework," for instance, was an invective against television advertisements suggesting that women find enormous joy in cleaning their homes. But overall, the series' tone was variously inspiring, funny, and joyful, an approach that appealed to parents, teachers, and children alike. In an era when only the minority of girls and even fewer boys self-identified as feminists, *Free to Be* served as a friendly and accessible point of entry for the feminist message of gender equality and self-actualization.

Children figured centrally in second-wave feminism both as young feminists in their own right and as motivating influences for adults. Many feminist women of the period were also mothers eager to consider new ways of raising their children. Feminist writers contributed to conversations about children's culture not only in *Ms.* magazine but also in traditional women's magazines such as *Redbook* and *Ladies' Home Journal*. And many worked to change mainstream child-rearing practices; after Gloria Steinem famously called parenting expert Dr. Benjamin Spock a "symbol of male oppression," he revised his advice to incorporate feminist concerns.[5] *Free to Be* represents an important touchstone of the centrality of young children's socialization to second-wave feminist activism.

For historians of the 1970s, *Free to Be* represents rich terrain. It offers an important example of the continued significance of rights activism and countercultural liberation ideals in 1970s American culture (and beyond).[6] Inasmuch as the series was designed to include a range of contributing artists and to tell stories about a diverse array of children, it speaks eloquently to the impact of the civil rights movement and antipoverty activism in mainstream children's culture. We can read *Free to Be* as emblematic of the new children's rights activism, exemplified by images of bold youth who take risks, defy patriarchal authority, and claim their freedom. We can also contextualize *Free to Be* within 1970s self-help literature, the era's focus on human development, and the middle-class quest for more sincere and authentic "lifestyles."[7] The book's cover art, with its title made of hand-stitched felt letters, speaks to the era's do-it-yourself mandate.

Furthermore, the *Free to Be* series was conceived within one of the most influential spheres of feminist activism—young children's book publishing. In this context, *Free to Be* did not in and of itself radically transform children's culture, but it did expose many adults and children to new gender possibilities. As such, *Free to Be* vividly illustrates the widening parameters of mainstream American children's gender socialization in the 1970s.

"A Social Poison": Feminists and Children's Books

The inspiration for *Free to Be* first came to Marlo Thomas while shopping for a book of bedtime stories to give to her young niece. In the early 1970s, Thomas was a nationally known actress, the star of the ABC comedy *That Girl* (1966–71). Her character, a modern aspiring actress in New York City, was groundbreaking if somewhat daffy: a prime-time single career woman happily living alone, with a steady boyfriend, unmarried (although eventually engaged). During the show's run, Thomas became active in feminist circles. She met journalist Gloria Steinem after the publication of Steinem's first-person exposé of working conditions at Playboy Clubs, and the two women formed a close friendship.[8] By the early 1970s, at Steinem's behest, Thomas was regularly speaking to groups of women on feminist issues. Thus, when she shopped for her niece, she had in mind books that would not repeat old-fashioned gender stereotypes.[9]

Her concern was shared by a wide range of feminists. By the 1970s, both mainstream liberal women's organizations and radical consciousness-raising groups were exploring how representations of "sex roles" in children's culture limited young people's aspirations. Many second-wave feminists focused on cultural factors, arguing that children's gender identities were shaped primarily by their social environment rather than by biological differences between the sexes. If, as feminists contended, gender identities were socially constructed (and thus mutable) to an important degree, early childhood inter-vention offered important political possibilities. Citing new research indicating that children established strong gender identities before they went to kindergarten and that cultural factors were important in the making of gender identity, feminist activists argued that even the youngest children needed better "sex role" models.

By the turn of the decade, concern about sexism in children's litera-ture was a vital part of this broader political intervention. Feminists first achieved visibility on the national children's publishing scene in mid-October 1970, when two New York–area feminist groups pre-sented a talk and slide show to book editors at the annual meeting of the Writers' Guild and the Children's Book Council. The Feminists on Children's Media, a group founded in mid-1970 by a consortium of New York City–area mothers, teachers, and book editors, presented their study, "Sexism in Children's Books." In 1974, they would publish a bibliography of nonsexist readings, Little Miss Muffet Fights Back.[10] The members of Women on Words and Images, an offshoot of the New Jersey Council of the feminist advocacy group National Organization for Women, spent a year analyzing 144 school textbooks for evidence of sex discrimination. In 1972, they published their research as Dick and Jane as Victims.[11]

Reading visibility as an important measure of gendered power, both groups began by tallying the numbers of boys and girls appearing in children's books. The results were striking. The Feminists on Chil-dren's Media focused on recipients of an important prize in children's publishing, the Newbery Award. Books with the Newbery imprimatur tended to sell well and to be purchased by schools and public librar-ies. Among forty-nine Newbery winners, the group reported, stories about boys outnumbered those about girls by a ratio of about three to one. Using a more recent sample, the American Library Associa-tion's list of Notable Books of 1969, the group found that stories about boys were still twice as common as those concerning girls.[12] Women on Words and Images reported similarly: in the 144 schoolbooks they analyzed, 881 stories focused mainly on boys, while only 344 focused mainly on girls.[13] Other studies of the period would come to the same conclusion: Girls were far less visible in children's stories than were boys. Even animals appeared in children's stories far more often in male form.[14]

More to the point, feminist activists contended, the actual content of children's books was often insulting to girls and women. Boys and girls, men and women were portrayed and described quite differently in these stories. Visual images showed boys on adventures or climbing trees, while girls were often homebound, watching admiringly from the porch as the boys played and explored. In written texts, girls also generally demonstrated less independence or required male direction to complete basic tasks.[15] For example, Women on Words and Images cited a story published in a first-grade school reader in which a girl named Sue is allowed to choose a toy duck as a present but remains indecisive. "Oh, my!" she says. "Ducks and ducks and ducks. What will I do?" Her friend Jimmy intervenes, choosing a duck for Sue, which turns out to be just the one she wants.[16]

As feminists further argued, children's books represented men pursuing a wide range of career options but tended to depict women exclusively in domestic terms, even though rising numbers of women, including mothers of young children, were entering the paid workforce. The dearth of professional women in children's books (outside of a few stereotyped fields, such as teachers and dancers) made it difficult for girls to imagine futures for themselves outside of marriage and motherhood.

Feminists on Children's Media noted a particular source of feminist frustration—what they termed the "Cop-Out" genre. In too many books, the group argued, girls who were initially introduced as strong and spunky heroines left their "tomboy" ways behind as a sign of a more mature adolescence. This was the narrative trajectory of such popular older novels as Louisa May Alcott's Little Women (1868) and Carol Ryrie Brink's Caddie Woodlawn (1935); as Feminists on Children's Media reported, the "Cop-Out" scenario motivated recent novels' plots as well. Constance Green's A Girl Called Al (1969), for instance, concerns a girl with a "tomboy" identity who ultimately gives up her pigtails and high energy for a more feminine and restrained style (and ensuing greater popularity). These sudden, last-minute transformations, Feminists on Children's Media contended, reinforced traditional sex-role dictates while stunting the heroines' character development. As the group concluded, "Books that outline a traditional background role for women, praising their domestic accomplishments, their timidity of soul, their gentle appearance and manners, and—at the same time—fail to portray initiative, enterprise, physical prowess, and genuine intellect deliver a powerful message to children of both sexes. Such books are a social poison."[17]

Publishers did listen, and over the course of the decade, greater numbers of images and stories about working mothers and active girls were integrated into mainstream children's books and school readers. Still, the pace of change would remain slow. For one, new editions of textbooks were expensive; older and more traditional books often lingered on library and classroom shelves for many years, remaining part of the officially sanctioned curriculum.[18] For another, from the early 1970s onward, members of the nascent New Right campaigned with success against new textbooks that they felt represented an attack on conservative social values. Textbooks and other children's books would become sources of conflict in the emergent "culture wars."[19]

In the 1970s, a few feminist groups established collective presses to publish the kinds of children's stories they wanted to see in print. The Feminist Press, founded in 1970 by two university professors, published books ranging from the Barbara Danish picture book *The Dragon and the Doctor*, which featured a female doctor and male nurse, to an ABC coloring book to Inez Maury's bilingual *My Mother the Mail Carrier/ Mi Mami la Cartera* (1976).[20] A sister collective press, Lollipop Power, had its origins in a consciousness-raising group founded by feminists in the Chapel Hill, North Carolina, area in the late 1960s.[21] The books published by Lollipop Power, which were aimed at young audiences from two to eight years of age, highlighted racial and class diversity as well as expanded opportunities for girls. In the collective's first book, *Martin's Father* (1971), a nurturing single father cares for his son; in *Exactly Like Me* (1972), a young girl discovers that she can be a girl without wearing frilly dresses; in *Jo, Flo, and Yolanda* (1973), a set of Latina triplets consider their varied career ambitions.[22] By 1975, Lollipop Power had sold more than twenty-five thousand copies of ten books, with its employees working from (and storing books in) their own homes.[23]

Free to Be emerged out of this "do-it-yourself" mandate, albeit on a far grander scale.[24] *Free to Be* was unique among feminist publishing efforts on behalf of children in that it achieved a high degree of mainstream popularity. At the intersection of elite feminist circles and the entertainment industry, Marlo Thomas was well positioned to make a significant impact. She had a knack for publicity and an attractive (and unthreatening) public presence. Deploying these tools to full political advantage, she reached a large and broad audience drawn both to her and her creative collaborators and to the *Free to Be* message of equal opportunity for girls and boys.

Happy Endings for a New Generation

The range of materials and styles in the *Free to Be* album, book, and television special constitutes part of its charm but makes the series difficult to encapsulate. Yet in a host of ways, the *Free to Be* project clearly challenged sexist socialization. A number of the stories and songs, for example, read traditional tropes of children's popular culture against the grain. In "Ladies First," Mary Rodgers's elaboration of a Shel Silverstein poem, a girl who insists on the entitlements of a "lady" turns out to be a little horror. Narrated on the album and the television special by Thomas herself, "Ladies First" playfully considers the advantages and costs of traditional femininity. We first meet the girl (in the book and the television cartoon she is dressed in pink, with fluffy blond hair) staring lovingly at herself in a mirror. She proclaims, "I am a *real* little lady, anybody could tell that: I wear lovely starched cotton dresses with matching ribbons in my lovely curly locks; I wear clean white socks and shiny black patent leather shoes; and I always put just a dab of perfume behind each ear." At school, the other students seem baffled by her but nonetheless acquiesce to her demands for special treatment, whether cutting to the front of the lunch line or eating more than her fair share of mangoes on a class trip to the jungle. Having established the perks available to a "lady," "Ladies First" then offers up the girl as a ritual sacrifice. The girl's vanity compels her to flaunt her softness and sweetness at just the wrong moment; when her school group is captured by tigers, she insists on "Ladies first." So she is first to be eaten, "and mighty tasty too," as Thomas concludes.[25]

"Ladies First" epitomizes the mixture of humor, playfulness, and serious intent that characterizes *Free to Be*. The story asks children to contemplate questions that adult second-wave feminists were themselves considering. What are the attractions and costs of traditional gender roles? From what internal sense of self should girls gain a healthy sense of power and entitlement? What is the role of beauty in girls' and women's culture? "Ladies First" answers these questions primarily through negative reinforcement. A girl whose confidence depends on her performance of traditional femininity, the tale suggests, is blind to the perils and opportunities of the world around her. This "ladylike" girl is thus an object lesson rather than a suitable model for "free" girls.

In contrast, Betty Miles's "Atalanta," which also appeared in all three versions of Free to Be, introduces an exemplar of female talent and determination. In the ancient Greek legend on which "Atalanta" is based, King Schoeneus promises his daughter Atalanta's hand in marriage to any man who can beat her in a footrace. Atalanta outruns many suitors, but a man she admires finally is able to distract her (with the help of the goddess Aphrodite), and he wins both the race and Atalanta herself. In Free to Be, Miles offers a feminist rewriting of this myth. Here, Atalanta is a skilled athlete and astronomer; as Miles explains, "She was so bright, and so clever, and could build things and fix things so wonderfully, that many young men wished to marry her." Atalanta complies on the surface with her father's demand that she submit to marriage with any man who can run faster than she can, but she secretly trains to avoid this fate. "Young John," who also trains alone, is a perfect match for her, both athletically and emotionally. A new kind of man, he seeks companionship rather than possession. After they complete the race "side by side," as equals, John insists that he merely wants to talk to Atalanta, not force her to marry him. The two become friends, and they then set off on their own individual voyages of exploration. "Perhaps someday they'll be married," the fable ends, "and perhaps they will not. In any case, it is certain, they are both living happily ever after."

For many second-wave feminists, traditional myths' and fairy tales' accounts of male adventure and female passivity offered troubling messages to young children.[26] Were women and girls to be judged primarily on their beauty, purity, and desirability in marriage? What right did fathers have to determine the timing of their daughters' sexual awakening? In Free to Be and elsewhere, a new generation of feminist writers challenged these traditions, often using humor to redefine gendered power relations and to reconsider girls' and boys' options.[27] Tales such as "Atalanta" suggested that there were fates more exciting for girls than being selected by princes, just as there were projects of self-discovery more important for boys than the challenge of acquiring royal spouses. In "Atalanta," marriage to an equal remains a possibility, but romance is secondary to the journey of individual achievement and self-discovery that must necessarily precede it.

Free to Be also includes a number of stories designed to encourage more emotionally expressive modes of boyhood. Feminists contended that gender hierarchy hurt men and boys just as it hurt women and girls, forcing males into rigid sex-role stereotypes and refusing them the pleasures of caregiving and tenderness. As the *Free to Be* title song promised, "Every boy in this land/Grows to be his own man." To be a man in this context was to be free to express sadness and vulnerability as well as happiness.

The song "William's Doll," adapted from the award-winning 1972 book by Charlotte Zolotow, delivers a particularly pointed message about boys' emancipation from unfair stereotypes.[28] The story concerns a boy who repeatedly asks for a doll to care for. Despite the taunts of other children and the displeasure of his father (who prefers to buy him sports equipment and other more traditionally "masculine" toys), William persists. Finally, his grandmother supports him on the grounds that he may be practicing for a nurturing fatherhood. William is represented as an able and enthusiastic athlete, but one who would "give my bat and ball and glove/To have a doll that I could love."

In the 1970s, the parameters of American girlhood were rapidly expanding.[29] But the question of boys' right to take on more traditionally nurturing roles remained the site of strenuous cultural contestation. The chorus of voices discouraging boys from so-called feminine activities was real and sometimes insistent. One feminist mother of the period recalled that while walking through her New York City neighborhood with her three-year-old son, who was wheeling his doll carriage, various men criticized the boy directly, including a fireman who said, "Tell your mommy boys should have guns, not dolls!" and a storekeeper who told him, "Your mother should give you a little sister if she wants a girl that badly."[30] Children themselves also participated in policing gender boundaries; in one mid-1970s classroom, a reading of *William's Doll* was interrupted as "giggles and snickers erupted from the class, and then a contingent of boys expressed active hostility by booing and hissing. It was only with frequent reprimands to keep the noise down that the teacher was able to finish."[31] And as Thomas later recalled, when *Free to Be* was first reimagined as a television special, ABC executives asked her to cut "William's Doll," lest it "turn every

American boy into a homosexual." She insisted, and the segment remained, but the conflict suggested the limits of this new version of boyhood.[32] In an era when most mainstream child experts continued to represent heterosexuality as a matter of appropriate socialization, a tender boy who played with dolls could easily be read as sexually subversive or a potentially dangerous model for other boys. As the reception of "William's Doll" suggests, the stakes of heteronormative masculinity remained particularly anxious in 1970s American children's culture.[33]

Free to Be . . . You and Me in Retrospect

Today, part of the market for *Free to Be* consists of parents who first discovered the series as children and for whom this artifact of youth is a happy reminder of their own childhoods. As one father related, he and his wife rediscovered the album as new parents: "Not only did we remember the words but we also came to realize how important of a role the album played in our lives. Thinking about it wistfully almost brings a tear to my eye."[34] Another man wrote that *Free to Be* "truly helped me form the opinions and ideals I enjoy as an adult . . . especially those of gender roles and equality. It is my pleasure to be able to pass those good lessons on to my son."[35]

In the intervening decades, some feminist scholars have criticized the message of individual liberation in *Free to Be* (and elsewhere in liberal feminism), arguing that the series' focus on individual accomplishment and equality of opportunity underplays the ways in which structural categories such as race, class, and gender foreclose some individuals' opportunities. As a consequence, some argue that second-wave critiques of female passivity in literature, for example, place too much pressure on individuals (in this instance, fictional characters) to resolve broader structural issues. Many contemporary feminists also emphasize innate biological differences between the sexes to a greater degree than did their predecessors.[36]

Yet we can acknowledge that young people's lives are indeed constrained by factors outside their personal control while still appreciating the intense appeal of the *Free to Be* vision to young children, most of whom had relatively little control over many aspects of their lives. The series' promise of individual freedom of opportunity might seem utopian, but by no means did *Free to Be* suggest that self-determination would come easily. Rather, *Free to Be* represents freedom as the result of hard work. Atalanta, John, and William all have to strive toward their goals, sometimes in the face of significant opposition. That they all ultimately achieve their desires constitutes their stories' happy endings (while the satisfaction of watching the selfish "little lady" get her just desserts suggests a different form of reading pleasure). Many children found this message of self-actualization deeply satisfying. As one girl of the 1970s later recalled, "I was free to be me, and I took that message seriously."[37]

The work of second-wave feminists to create more varied images of girls and boys in children's culture ultimately was a significant success. *Free to Be* presaged a children's culture that now includes more (if not equal) images of sensitive boys and adventurous girls.[38] Today, the series continues to inspire many children and parents, and what were once bold feminist ideas have to a significant degree been integrated into the American mainstream.

"Little Women's Libbers" and "*Free to Be Kids*"

Children and the Struggle for Gender Equality in the United States

LORI ROTSKOFF

In May 1973, Randi Lewis, a fifth-grade girl from Peoria, Illinois, wrote a letter to the editors of Ms., the first popular, unambiguously feminist magazine published in the United States.[1] While her mother was the household's official subscriber, Randi also looked forward to the magazine's monthly delivery. Although Randi lived far from the Ms. headquarters in New York City, she believed that the magazine's creators would understand some of her deepest concerns. "To the Editor," she wrote,

> I'm writing to you to express my feelings to somebody who understands. At school. When ever we want to play kickball or baceball the boys always say girls can't pitch or girls can't catch. When we play kickball they always have to make some smart remark like look at those terrible outfielders. When ever there is a box or something like that the teacher always picks a boy to take it down to the office. My mom got me into all this equal rights. I believe in it, too. . . . Even though I'm eleven I still believe in equal rights.[2]

In her letter, Randi unburdened her frustration over social injustices she perceived at recess and in the classroom. Her expression of allegiance to liberal feminism—what she called "all this equal rights"—was striking in its simplicity: "I believe in it, too." Perhaps Randi doubted whether most adults would take a child of her age seriously as a thoughtful supporter of sexual equality. But in her act of correspondence, she assumed that the Ms. editors, at least, would value her ideas.

"Equal Rights for Little People." Children demonstrate in July 1976 outside the Democratic National Convention. Photograph by Bettye Lane; used with permission.

Randi Lewis was among thousands of children who expressed a commitment to sexual equality or communicated with national feminist leaders during this time—the same years when *Free to Be . . . You and Me* first hit record stores, bookshelves, and television screens across the country. This was also the moment when *Ms.* became the leading voice of popular feminism, boasting a circulation of nearly five hundred thousand and a readership of three million by mid-decade.[3] Every month, hundreds of readers wrote letters to the magazine, and some of those correspondents, like Randi Lewis, were school-aged children.

I first encountered Randi's letter while working in the archives. My research project had sent me searching for documents revealing how social activists, professional experts, and ordinary mothers created a new mode of nonsexist child rearing during the 1970s. Approaching my subject from the vantage point of women's history, I had simply presumed to find sources composed by adults with vested interests in childhood matters.

Girls protesting about newspaper routes at the *Long Island Press*, October 1971. Photograph by Bettye Lane; used with permission.

What I didn't expect, until I came across a thick file labeled "Kids," was a cache of letters written by children. My first clue was the stationery: pastel pages adorned with rainbows, cards decorated with ladybug stickers, and that perennial staple of the 1970s classroom: newsprint, now yellowed, ruled with blue dotted lines. As I leafed through the kids' letters—some penciled in basic print, some inked in confident cursive, and a few pecked out on the family typewriter—my mind raced as I realized the exciting implications they held for my project: Here were snapshots of children's ideas and actions during the heyday of the women's liberation movement. In this trove of children's voices, young people appeared not as figures of adult imaginations or targets of adult instructions but as historical actors in their own right.[4] Perhaps these letters would reveal whether—and how—kids made a difference in the struggle for gender equality.

In retrospect, perhaps I shouldn't have been surprised by the letters. I knew that the magazine's founders believed that gender equality was for children, too. *Ms.* targeted young readers with its monthly

Girls protesting about newspaper routes at the *Long Island Press*, October 1971. Photograph by Bettye Lane; used with permission.

feature, "Stories for Free Children." *Free to Be . . . You and Me* was by then a staple in many households, including my own. And given the impact of Title IX, which made it illegal for schools and other federally funded programs to discriminate on the basis of sex, it would be surprising if some kids *didn't* report back with stories of their own.

And report back they did. Children found many ways to express their endorsements, confusions—and sometimes their criticisms—of the social changes that affected their lives. Some kids wrote poems, stories, or essays for women's liberation magazines. Others raised their voices in school newspapers, church or synagogue youth groups, or Girl Scout troops. Some even staged public protests, such as a group of girls from Long Island, New York, who demanded the chance to deliver local newspapers on routes long trodden by boys alone.

Across the nation, children responded to and influenced the spread of ideas, policies, and popular culture designed to "level the playing field" between boys and girls, engaging in cultural activism to promote gender equality. By "cultural activism," I mean not just forms of public protest but also individual moments of moral engagement with feminist principles. While some kids penned letters to senators or marched in rallies, others petitioned school administrators, muscled their way onto Little League teams, or belted out the words to "Parents Are People" with ambitious career dreams floating in their heads.

In the file of Ms. children's letters collected between 1972 and 1974, the youngest correspondents were five or six years old, the oldest were in their late teens, and the largest group clustered in the ten- to fourteen-year age range. Geographically, "Ms. kids" were all over the map. Letters arrived from Berkeley, California and Blacksburg, Virginia; from small towns in Massachusetts and Kentucky to the American-occupied Canal Zone in Panama. Most writers were white girls from middle- or upper-middle-class families, but there were a few letters from boys and at least one from a girl who highlighted her Hispanic identity. Although I don't recall seeing any letters whose writers identified themselves as African American, the editors of Ms. occasionally published letters by black children and teenagers that were not preserved in this particular file.

So how did kids like Randi Lewis "get into equal rights" in the first place? How did they incorporate themes from Free to Be . . . You and Me into their play and their future aspirations? How did feminism affect their relationships with friends, peers, teachers, and other authority figures? And in what ways did their actions contribute to the women's movement at large?

These letters captured the voices of children who discovered ways to shape a part of the social landscape they inhabited. These young people engaged with the world as historical actors in their own right, creating and contesting social meanings of gender and power.[5] Throughout history, most children are severely limited in their access to material resources, political influence, and cultural authority. So when kids did act or speak out on their own behalf—and in concert with a major twentieth-century social movement—their stories are all the more remarkable.

Children did make a difference in spreading feminist consciousness both within and beyond the communities that first ignited the women's movement. For adult feminists, children mattered because they would be harbingers of and heirs to a more egalitarian society. The foundations of both liberal and radical feminism were shot through with assumptions about the importance of achieving sexual equality for young citizens. Just as liberal feminists worked to ensure fair employment and equal pay for women, so too did they insist on equal opportunity for girls and boys. For radicals, who sought to eradicate the deeper roots of women's subordination, child rearing was also a crucial matter: What better way to eliminate sexism than to prevent it from germinating in the hearts and minds of the younger generation? This dual influence was reflected in the language of "equality" and "liberation," concepts that coexisted in tension with one another. According to historian Sara Evans, both concepts "challenged the ways women had been differentiated from, and subordinated to, men, but the first drew on the liberal discourse of equal rights and the second proposed a cultural and ideological transformation in which sex roles would be eliminated."[6] Feminist activism regarding children fluctuated between these two perspectives: Activists sometimes sought liberation from gender stereotypes (seen in the promotion of "unisex" toys or clothing), while at other times, they emphasized equality of access to resources and opportunities (as reflected in the passage of Title IX).

As feminism took root in the budding ambitions of young people, it shaped their expectations and values. Some children, in turn, were moved to social action. By campaigning against unfair policies and bonding with like-minded peers, children helped promote gender equality in the United States. Town by town, school by school, gym teacher by gym teacher, kids held adults accountable to the mandate of equal opportunity.

Of course, American schools were hardly teeming with gender revolutionaries. Most young *Free to Be* fans didn't realize that their favorite album was produced by prominent activists. Girls who wore unisex clothing or fought to play football did not necessarily connect their actions to a national women's movement. For the majority of youngsters, feminism simply wasn't a major issue.[7] Children raised by socially conservative parents often hewed to traditional gender norms. And among those who did criticize sex discrimination, few questioned the existence of gender categories or developed a radical critique of sexist society. But many girls spoke out or acted to support a liberal feminist agenda, and their contributions deserve to be recognized.

Taking "Women's Lib" to School

For most American children, feminism filtered into their lives through the mass media. In terms of sheer audience numbers, television topped the list for providing pop-culture takes on sexual equality. In 1971, for example, *The Brady Bunch* aired an episode, "The Liberation of Marcia Brady," in which Marcia, the oldest Brady sister, is interviewed by a local reporter about her opinions on women's rights. When Marcia's three brothers see her later on TV, they taunt and challenge her belief that "anything a man can do, a woman can do better." Typical sitcom shenanigans ensue: after Marcia joins her brother Greg's Frontier Scout troop, another brother, Peter, retaliates by signing up for the Sunflower Girls. Despite her lack of testosterone and rusty camping skills, Marcia blazes a fire with the Frontier boys, while Peter flops in his effort to peddle cookies while dressing in Girl Scout drag. Although the episode ends with both siblings safely returning to their original (and "correctly" gendered) scout troops, the sitcom's mild riff on the "battle of the sexes" clearly scored one for the girls.

The Brady Bunch was a big hit, but the supreme media event of the 1970s gender wars was the nationally televised tennis match between ex-Wimbledon champion Bobby Riggs and the top-ranked female player, Billie Jean King. Filmed live at the Houston Astrodome on September 20, 1973, the Riggs-King face-off attracted more than thirty thousand spectators in person and an estimated fifty million television viewers nationwide. From the moment Riggs challenged King to a match, the event was steeped in the mainstream media's language of women's liberation. King had struggled for years to bring gender equality to professional tennis. Riggs, for his part, was a proud, self-professed "male chauvinist pig." While "making a sexist spectacle of himself at every turn," Riggs branded King a "women's libber," a term he used pejoratively to disparage feminists. To kick off the match, both tennis stars entered the stadium surrounded by harems, playing to the crowd in a frenzied media spectacle.[8]

Despite the hype, it was a serious contest. And when King won the match in three straight sets, female spectators erupted into shouts of joy. Billie Jean King didn't just vindicate female athletes; it seemed she vindicated feminism itself. After the match, the editors of Ms. sent telegrams to both players. To King, they wrote, "From those of us who have grown used to defeat, thank you from the bottom of our hearts for showing us victory. We will never again settle for less." And to Riggs, they cleverly quoted from *Free to Be*, reassuring the defeated tennis player that "it's all right to cry"—a reference to the former football star Rosey Grier's rendition of Carol Hall's song.[9]

The Riggs-King event made a big impact on kids. I was four years old at the time, a bit too young to have sharp memories, but my tennis-obsessed mother was among the ecstatic television viewers, and I must have absorbed her excitement through some kind of osmosis. My friend, Patricia Lewy Horing, remembers watching the match as an eight-year-old in her Chicago suburb. Inspired, perhaps, by suburban Super Bowl parties, her parents invited several families over to watch the tennis match, munching on chips and onion dip and cheering King on to victory. Three decades later, after earning a graduate degree in women's literature and forging a career as an artist, she regards the event as a milestone in her emerging feminist consciousness. "We cheered and hollered for Billie Jean King and her victory over male-chauvinist bravado. I remember feeling really proud to be female at that moment," she recalled.[10]

Written evidence, too, suggests that kids picked up on the positive energy unleashed by King's resounding win. If she was "the women's lib leader," as Riggs had jeered, the joke was now on him. Even before the match, some kids called themselves "women's libbers" as a badge of pride. This was the case for eleven-year-old Donna Roberts of Natick, Massachusetts. In January 1973, Donna wrote to Ms., "I am a very strong women's libber and I don't like it when people always address the girls to set the table or always address the boys to carry the books or machines at school. I used to live in Cleveland Heights Ohio but when I moved, I found it a bit funny. I don't think I could find any woman's libber, but I sure wish I could."[11]

Another girl, who signed her letter a "twelve year old fan," was known as a "junior high school feminist." One day, a teacher "asked for three strong boys to give out books. And if there are any women's libbers, you can help too," the teacher said. "I volunteered," the girl reported. "I think your magazine is great. Keep up the good work." Her matter-of-fact identity as a "women's libber" was a proud sign of allegiance to a worthy cause. Another girl, Grace Kerrigan from Belmont, Massachusetts, reported that her reading teacher was "for women's lib." "She chooses girls to carry books, a relief," she wrote. The twelve-year-old, who had just moved from Berkeley, California, was distressed about the "chauvinistic people" in her new community. Having a feminist-minded teacher was therefore a boon for her. So, too, was a club that she and her friends formed at school: "WIMP: Women In More Power." "We work for equality among everybody," she reported.[12]

The expansion of girls' sports in the wake of Title IX enhanced their pride in their bodily strength. Arthur and Judith Sharenow, who owned the overnight summer camp Kenwood Evergreen in Wilmot, New Hampshire, recalled a shift in the attitudes of counselors when it came to heavy lifting. In the early 1960s, female counselors were upset when asked to help haul the campers' trunks from a central field to individual cabins. "They believed that was a guy's job," the Sharenows recalled. But by the late 1970s, they explained, "the female counselors were offended if we *didn't* ask them to carry the trunks!" Operating a camp staffed in part by teenagers required the directors to take cues from the younger generation, whose expectations were changing rapidly with the times.[13]

African American children who subscribed to *Ebony Jr.* magazine also weighed in on the subject of girls' physical prowess. During its publication from 1973 to 1985, *Ebony Jr.* printed articles about male and female African American dignitaries who excelled in politics, literature, athletics, and the arts. Yet kids didn't always absorb these egalitarian views on women's careers. For the February 1976 issue, editors invited readers to ponder whether "girls are able to grow up and get the same kinds of jobs that boys can get." As one ten-year-old boy opined, "If I was a policeman I wouldn't want a lady to be my partner because a man is stronger and faster. . . . If I was a doctor . . . I'd only ask the lady doctor to hand me what I needed. But if I had a real hard operation I'd ask a man doctor to help me." His younger brother shared similar views: "Girls get hurt playing football," he declared.[14]

Clearly, not all kids went to bat for gender equality during this (or any other) historical moment. Old stereotypes die hard. But youngsters who thought girls the weaker sex didn't get the last word. Two months later, *Ebony Jr.* printed rebuttals from kids who took issue with the previous defenders of masculine bravado. One came from a thirteen-year-old girl who wrote, "I think the boys were wrong. Maybe a girl can't play football but girls don't have to be just nurses, teachers, mothers, models . . . and I think a girl can stand more cold and can wrestle. . . . I just think girls can do anything and be anything they want to." Another girl agreed: "I am not trying to put down your magazine. But the way all the boys were talking about girls . . . upset me. . . . I play football and don't get hurt . . . and I take judo classes every Saturday morning."[15] In a magazine focused on instilling racial pride and literacy skills in middle-class African American youth, some children spoke out about sexual equality as well.

If writing to a national magazine took gumption, standing up against taunting peers took even more courage. In 1973 or 1974, thirteen-year-old Julia Berman of Edison, New Jersey, wrote to Ms. about an older boy who teased her for being a "libber." "My friends know me as Ms.," she wrote. "I think that's great, but once my friend's older brother (age 15) said to me, Here she is . . . the libber. The libber?" she continued. "[They] don't know what the abbreviation Ms. stands for. Not just a word, it's a symbol that means I am participating in the long hard fight . . . that needs every one of our sisters. All of women-kind working together to achieve one goal: equality. Thanks, your sister, Julia Berman."[16] Despite the fact that some kids had teased her for being a feminist, Julia felt emboldened by the spirit of sisterhood and factual knowledge she absorbed from Ms.

Other kids were taunted by teachers who bristled at their burgeoning feminism. For a class assignment, Columbia, Missouri, sixth-grader Stephanie Balsam faulted the publisher of her social studies textbook for using gender-biased language to explain who was eligible to run for Congress or the presidency. But when she advised the publisher to "recall all the textbooks and change the words "men" to read "men and women," her teacher added insult to injury. "Well, we have a little women's libber in the room," the teacher quipped. Writing to Ms. on her daughter's behalf, Stephanie's mother appealed to the editors for a show of solidarity that would take the sting out of the teacher's dismissive comments.[17]

Other kids applied the label "male chauvinist pig" to grown-ups who denied girls equal opportunities. Such epithets shored up their feelings of moral superiority over adults whose authority these young people saw as all but bankrupt. The word "chauvinist" or the abbreviation MCP connoted a clueless adult who was unworthy of kids' respect. Empowered by this confrontational rhetoric, kids pressured school officials to change the rules. When her principal refused to let girls play football at recess, Carolyn Forbes of Northfield, Massachusetts, pushed back. "He became enraged at the prospect," lost his temper, and refused to change his mind. Undeterred, Carolyn fought "discrimination around the school" and petitioned the "male pig principal" to allow girls on the safety patrol. "Many kids along with teachers signed it, and the Northfield Elementary school now has patrol girls!," she reported.[18]

Even young children picked up on the word "chauvinism." Eight-year-old Sara Weston of South Euclid, Ohio, thought it was "very shovenistic" that her school textbook listed certain tasks for boys and certain jobs for girls: Girls could wash dishes, babysit, or amuse younger siblings, while boys could walk a dog or deliver items from the store. "On the top of the page I rote this is shovenistic!," reported Sara. Even better, she added, "Lots of boys in my class think it is very dumb."[19] Apparently, third-grade boys could become "little women's libbers," too.

Other girls underscored the resistance and peer pressure they faced at school, including René Joseph, a ninth-grader from St. Paul, Minnesota. For a class project, René and some of her friends decided to write and put on a play, a comedy about women's liberation. "This by itself is great," René reported, "but unfortunately, the boys (and teacher) are male chauvinists and they want to put the Movement down." The teacher allowed boys to make fun of the women's movement yet complained when René's script depicted chauvinistic characters in a negative light. The boys, too, objected to René's play because they thought "it wouldn't be funny."[20]

René sought validation from Ms. editors but questioned her ability to effect social change. "I have greatly enjoyed your magazine," she wrote, "but just reading doesn't help. There is so much discrimination, especially at my school." In a final anecdote, she mentioned a sign that hung in the school's printing room: "Your mommy isn't enrolled in this class . . . so you will have to clean your mess up yourself." This anecdote exemplified what Ms. readers dubbed a "Click" moment: a situation that was clearly recognizable as sexist, biased, or discriminatory. Indeed, Ms. editors often used this editorial strategy—reprinting offensive remarks unadorned with additional commentary—to expose blatant prejudices.[21]

Many kids regarded Ms. editors as sympathetic mentors. Such was the case for a fourteen-year-old girl from Millburn, New Jersey. "My school is against me," she wrote in 1973. "Any girl who even talks about Women's Liberation is a tomboy. (Ugh! How I hate that word!)"

Even worse, the girl's father disparaged her subscription to Ms. as a "waste of time and money." On a positive note, though, she reported that for the first time in her school's history, a girl carried the American flag during the morning assembly. "This might not be much of an accomplishment to the Average American Female," she conceded, "but to Millburn Junior High girls it's a long-fought for goal."[22]

In issue after issue, Ms. devoted space to children's concerns. In June 1974, the editors published a feature, "What It's Like to Be Me: Young Women Speak for Themselves." According to the editors, many girls "feel that they are not taken seriously by parents, teachers, and friends, who often tell them that being a feminist is 'just a stage they are going through.' The accompanying feelings of isolation and self-doubt contradict their new-found pride and joy in being female." To help counteract this problem, editors created a forum for an "ongoing dialogue of exploration, sharing, and support among young women themselves and with their older—and younger—sisters." The issue featured photographs of fifteen girls, including two African American students who discussed their dual opposition to racism and sexism.

Two contributors to this 1974 feature brought up another sore subject for junior high school students: home economics and industrial arts classes, which became academic pawns in the battle for equality. Wendy Kromash, a Pennsylvania junior high student, was distressed because these subjects were still segregated by sex. Furthermore, she explained, two male teachers requested that "all the girls make cookies for an upcoming dance." When Wendy asked why boys couldn't provide baked goods, the teachers replied, "Yeah, if the boys want to bring in cookies, they can get their mothers to make some." Here was another "Click" moment—a comment that any seasoned Ms. reader could decode as an attempt to relegate girls to the kitchen. Fourteen-year-old Laura Manz of Illinois had a similar view. "When I get older," she wrote, "I will be either an architect or a welder. In our school we have industrial arts for the boys, and that is the class I need. But I couldn't take it because the counselor told me boys aren't mature enough to accept girls in their class." To make matters worse, Laura's boyfriend joked, "No wife of mine will be a welder." In conclusion, she asked, "Why can't males get used to the idea that we are not kitchen utensils?"[23]

Carolyn Forbes, the Massachusetts girl who integrated her elementary school's safety patrol, took on the matter of elective classes when she entered junior high. Required to take home ec in seventh grade, Carolyn fumed, "I really hated the business, making cocoa, baking cookies, and then later sewing cute little skirts." After discussing the matter with her guidance counselor, she was allowed to take industrial arts on a "trial" basis, and her efforts ultimately paved the way to the integration of both classes. "I really approve of the struggle for equality," she wrote, "and I'm glad that at least a few discriminative school traditions have been superseded with some new practices with my help."[24]

Carolyn sent her letter to Ms. in 1974, after which single-sex classes toppled like dominoes in schools across the country. By the time I entered seventh grade in 1981, our local school district in suburban St. Louis, Missouri, rotated all students through quarter-long courses in woodworking, mechanical drawing, sewing, and cooking. The following year, I switched to a private school, and once again, all elective classes were mixed. I don't recall ever thinking about it; we simply took it for granted that boys and girls would take such classes together. Looking back, though, I see what a difference seven years made, and I wonder if some outspoken girls in my own hometown had to fight to enroll in shop class, too.

Some girls, however, defended traditional girls' activities. Thirteen-year-old Suzie Lessing of Greenbelt, Maryland was torn between her social life and women's rights. She liked reading Ms. but set herself apart from "liberated" girls who "won't wear dresses or ever consider keeping house." In contrast, Suzie enjoyed cooking, sewing, and—yes—cheerleading. When she discussed with her fellow cheerleaders a Ms. article "telling how bad cheerleading is," she started "receiving a lot of abuse" from her friends. "I'm a cheerleader," she confessed in her letter. "Big deal. I like cheering but I won't let it interfere with my basketball. . . . To me being liberated is doing what you enjoy."[25] Other girls criticized certain mind-sets they associated with feminism while endorsing personal freedom. As a high school student from Menlo Park, California, remarked, "I know that women's liberation is an important part of today, but sometimes I feel that people are laying it on too strong. I'm getting sick of reading depressing stories and letters written by 'oppressed' women. Maybe I've just never had it bad. . . . As to the oppressed women, hold your head up, keep your back straight, and know what you're saying when you talk. Respect yourself and see the difference. . . . Women's liberation? No. Freedom for the People?

Right on!"[26] Some readers, even those with progressive views on gender issues, interpreted feminist claims as symptoms of a disempowering "victim mentality."

Talking Back to the Television Set

Children's activism for equal rights extended to the mass media. One thirteen-year-old from Spring Valley, New York, reported on her correspondence with the NBC, ABC, and CBS television networks. The problem? Sexism on television game shows. Apparently, when game-show hosts introduced female contestants, they inquired as to their husbands' occupations, but when they chatted with male contestants, they did not ask about their wives' lines of work. "I feel this is one more form of male-chauvinism," the thirteen-year-old complained. "It implies that 1) a woman's position is unimportant. And 2), that her life-style is dependent upon her husband's." Furthermore, the hosts addressed women as "Dear" or "Honey," while they used the honorific "Sir" to address men. "To call a woman by these words is a put-down," she remarked. "This only further proves my point that male chauvinism is being perpetuated in front of . . . thousands of television viewers each day."[27]

The New York teenager wanted the game show hosts to change their ways. While two of the networks replied with dismissive form letters, one offered a supportive response, which the girl quoted with pleasure: "I am going to send copies of your letter to the offices of all our game shows," the television executive replied. "Let's hope it will do some good. The treatment of women will improve in all areas, as long as we have young women like you growing up and going out into the world." Thus she became a cultural critic in her own right, taking action to effect change on the airwaves.[28]

Letty Cottin Pogrebin would have applauded this display of "postage power." In her 1980 book, *Growing Up Free*, Pogrebin advised families on how to critique the media. She counseled parents to watch television with their kids rather than regard it as an electronic babysitter. "Ask your children their opinions of TV programs," she suggested. "People rarely do. Leading questions, critical interventions, and open-ended conversation may be the most underutilized means of getting to know your children's values while raising their media consciousness." By holding "teach-ins" in the den, parents would learn from their children as much as children would learn from adults. "The goal of your teach-in," she explained, "is not a brainwashed TV-resistor but a skeptic with a firm finger on the 'OFF' switch."[29]

In *Growing Up Free*, Pogrebin documented girls who "talked back" to the media. One of them, in fact, was Pogrebin's daughter, Abigail. In a July 1973 letter, the Manhattan eight-year-old took issue with the General Mills Corporation for the masculine bias of its Wheaties television commercials. The ads featured action shots of boys jumping, climbing, and riding motorcycles while a man's deep voice intoned, "He's ready for Wheaties; he knows he's a man." To protest the cereal makers' exclusion of her sex, Abigail boycotted the breakfast flakes, vowing not to touch even "one tasty bit of those Wheaties" until advertisers allowed girls into their breakfast club. The boycott soon became a family affair, with Abigail's twin sister, Robin, and their younger brother, David, also sealing their lips against Wheaties. The next month, Abigail received a reply from General Mills in which the cereal maker defended its branding of Wheaties as a "male oriented product."

This rebuff fueled the Pogrebin children to continue their boycott, which reportedly lasted for several years (and during which time they joined in the filming of the *Free to Be* television special). It took a while, but in 1975, General Mills began to include girls in its primetime Wheaties commercials. When Letty called the company to find out why they had finally changed the ads, they told her it was due to "the emerging woman concept and the fact that everyday folks of both sexes were becoming more concerned with sports and fitness." Yet whatever the corporate rationale, "Abigail believed that her letter played a part in the company's change of heart."[30]

Other girls, too, protested the exclusion of girls in toy marketing campaigns. Caroline Ranald, who also grew up in New York City, loved to assemble and play with her father's electric train set. But Caroline was bothered by the fact that the Lionel train company featured only photographs of boys in its promotions. So in 1972, the seven-year-old wrote a letter to the model train maker: "Dear Sir: I don't like your new ads. Girls like trains too. I am a girl. I like trains. . . . Your catalog only has boys. Don't you like girls? I love the metroliner."[31]

Lionel's executives were persuaded by Caroline's plea. Just one year later, the company launched a new promotional campaign depicting girls and touted its commitment to overturning gender barriers in children's play. Lionel's press release even quoted Dr. Florence Denmark, president of the New York State Psychological Association, who endorsed the new commercials as "a real breakthrough." According to Denmark, Lionel was "helping to provide more exciting and adventuresome roles for girls through a change in behavior. . . . Girls will become more active in their play and exhibit more creativity and curiosity. . . . Lionel will help girls aspire to be something other than simply pretty and compliant."[32]

By enlisting a psychologist to endorse the new ads, Lionel joined the ranks of toy makers who characterized their products as part of an educationally enriching hobby. Upscale toy manufacturers had been making similar claims for decades, but Lionel's adoption of nonsexist child-rearing expertise was novel for a commercial toy firm. Not surprisingly, a copy of Lionel's press release made its way to Letty Pogrebin's desk at Ms. What impressed Pogrebin most, though, was the fact that a second-grade girl had made the change happen.[33]

Given her cameo role in American toy history, I contacted Caroline and asked her how she came to challenge gender stereotypes at such a young age. Both of her parents were English professors, and they fostered in her a love of books. While her mother discouraged her from playing with Barbies or tea sets, Caroline recalled being "pretty girly" in most of her toy choices. But the trains were her favorite because they allowed her to share a special activity with her father. After her mother spurred her to write to Lionel, both parents accompanied Caroline to the media event where Lionel launched their new "coed" ad campaign. At the press conference, she displayed her finesse with the trains, but she was dismayed when she was asked to share the spotlight with a "little blonde girl who had no idea how to put the trains on the tracks properly."[34] Rounding up a girl simply to pose and look adorable—and who showed none of the manual dexterity train play fostered—only reinforced stereotypes of female inferiority.

A final letter from the Ms. children's file is relevant here. Nidian Ruiz, the sixteen-year-old daughter of Puerto Rican immigrants living in New York City, wrote to complain about a Spanish-language radio program that her mother enjoyed. In contrast to the daughters of well-educated feminists, Nidian struggled to enlighten her ethnic, working-class mother about feminism. "Most Spanish speaking women don't know anything about women's liberation," Nidian lamented. And the Spanish program syndicated by a local radio station—a talk show "supposedly for women . . . but more beneficial for the men"—wasn't helping her cause:

> It's all about cooking, taking care of the home, and how to raise your children. I've never liked the idea of someone telling you how to run your life, so I was immediately turned off by it. Then came the day when I could no longer listen to that horrible voice . . . that of a man. Why is that man telling women what to do? The least they can do is give us tips on how to progress. Instead he says ways of how to make our husbands happy. He also said you should be pretty and perfumed when he comes home from work. Why can't he . . . leave women to do what they think is best? . . . It's a pity there isn't a club or organization to open up their eyes. (If black women have done it, what's keeping us back?)[35]

Nidian's analysis of her mother's radio program, along with her discussion of black women's activism, showed a perceptive awareness of the diversity of feminist thought and action that swirled outside her home.

CHILDREN DON'T INFLUENCE historical change in a vacuum. Rather, they respond to specific, sometimes conflicting, educational and parenting strategies used by teachers, parents, advisers, and other adults they encounter. Young people's participation in second-wave feminism thus emerged in the context of dynamic relationships they forged with adults. Many leaders of the women's movement, including *Free to Be*'s creators, welcomed youngsters into the feminist fold from the start. The editors of *Ms.* encouraged children to write letters about issues that mattered to them. Not only did the editors print many of these missives, but during the magazine's early years, they also responded personally to every writer.[36] This archive provides just one set of documents that reveal why, when we look back on the history of second-wave feminism, we need to take both adults and children into account.

For children of activists, marching for the ERA or answering the doorbell when it was mom's turn to host the consciousness-raising group were common experiences. For them, *Free to Be . . . You and Me* dovetailed with the political commitments and values that infused their everyday lives. Other kids were exposed to feminist ideas in smaller yet potent doses. Maybe they had a sixth-grade teacher who insisted on being called "Ms." rather than "Miss." (Full disclosure: that was me.) Perhaps they listened closely when overhearing their mother rant about a "chauvinistic" acquaintance who condescendingly called his wife a "little woman." (Yes, that was me, too.) Or maybe, when it was their turn to have a bat mitzvah—after years of singing songs about equality—the synagogue wouldn't let them read from the actual Torah scroll because, in 1982, that privilege was still restricted to boys. (Ditto. For the record, they changed the rule a few years later, which helped quell the resentment still smoldering inside me.)

Paradoxically, nonsexist child rearing advocates were both more and less successful than they set out to be. Within limits, they empowered children to claim greater measures of gender equality for themselves: at home, on the playground, and especially at school. They shifted the landscape of common sense so much that by the mid-1980s, most middle-class American families would deem it utterly unacceptable for girls categorically to be denied a Little League baseball bat or a turn at the woodworking lathe. Conversely, their efforts at collective parenting—like those of all adult generations—did not come with a guarantee that kids would march in lockstep to the progressive beat of their elders' drums. Feminist parents were optimistic that their strategies would yield certain results, but we've learned that just because a girl plays with a toy chemistry set doesn't mean she'll grow up to be a scientist. Furthermore, adults have continued to this day to create toys and other products that perpetuate gender stereotypes.

Although self-identified feminist kids were a small minority, they were far from silent on the subject. Children were not powerless to help define new gender parameters that shaped their lives. That's what thirteen-year-old Randi Lewis did in 1973 when she wrote her letter about equal rights. By encouraging children to stake a claim for equality, adults paved the way for kids to create their own caravans of social progress. To be sure, those caravans haven't traveled as far or as wide as second-wave activists hoped. We still haven't arrived at a magical "land" where boys and girls—not to mention grown men and women—can conduct their lives unconstrained by powerful gender assumptions.[37] No single magazine, no one children's record, no toy can transform the world. Nor should we ever expect it to.

But irrefutable social progress has been made since Marlo Thomas and her colleagues created their entertaining primer on self-empowerment. Despite their limitations, feminists educated a new generation of children to be mindful about sexism and gender equity. And some of the biggest achievements occurred in arenas where kids themselves talked back, acted up, and sang aloud. The "*Free to Be* kids" and "little women's libbers" of the 1970s are now the parents and teachers of children confronting new challenges on the road to full equality and personal freedom. They are heirs to a women's movement whose complex legacy is still being sorted out—and sung about—today.

Child's Play

Boys' Toys, Women's Work, and "Free Children"

LAURA L. LOVETT

When my first daughter was born in the early 1990s, I was determined to be a feminist mother: She would wear only primary colors; read books about smart, strong girls; and never play with a Barbie doll. That lasted until she went to preschool and demanded to wear a frilly dress like her friends and until her grandmother created a Barbie World refuge at her house. What's worse is that they were once my Barbies, which my mother had kept tucked away waiting for her future grand-daughters. It seemed obvious to me that these disproportionate plastic dolls were a legitimate focus of feminist ire.[1] But why did I think that these bits of leggy, lumpy plastic were so significant? Could they really influence my daughter's thoughts and opinions? After all, they hadn't stopped me from becoming a feminist or a women's history professor.

Like many parents, I am convinced that toys matter. They foster creativity, exploration, and imaginative play. They also carry messages about acceptable behavior, gender roles, and social norms. As a historian trained to read all sorts of materials as cultural texts, it's not surprising that I now interpret toys as reflections of broader social trends. But children's toys were not the "texts" examined in any of my classrooms when I was in college. Rather, I learned to think critically about toys by reading Ms. magazine.

CHILDREN WERE AN important part of Ms. from its first issue in 1972. Letty Cottin Pogrebin, a founding editor, created a special section of the magazine for "free children" that featured stories without sexist stereotyping. One of Pogrebin's other important contributions, "Toys for Free Children," was an article that explained why parents needed to take toys seriously. In her view, toys were not "magic talismans" capable of dispelling the "spirit of sexism in a society that is obsessed with notions of 'manliness' and 'femininity.' A nonsexist toy cannot transform a child growing up in a home, a school, and a society where

"What Shall I Be? The Exciting Game of Career Girls," game by Selchow and Righter, 1966. Photograph by Laura L. Lovett; used with permission.

gender roles are inflexibly cast as stereotypes." Nevertheless, Pogrebin argued that toys are powerful influences on children's "character, personality, and temperament." Because toys can "inspire occupational choice, unleash artistic talent, and leave an emotional imprint for life," toys mattered.[2]

Consider the board game produced by Selchow and Righter in 1966 called "What Shall I Be?" This "exciting" career game came in two versions, one for boys and one for girls. Each version required players to assume various career identities and then make their way around the board while facing certain challenges.

So what careers were available to girls? The possibilities included teacher, airline hostess, actress, nurse, model, and ballet dancer. The game allowed career women who were models or actresses to get ahead if they drew cards declaring them to be pretty. Sloppy makeup, however, would hold them back. In the boys' version of the same game, players could be statesmen, scientists, athletes, doctors, engineers, or astronauts. The contrast is starkly stereotypical. (Of course, all of the images are of white men and women.) The same company followed up in 1969 with "What Shall I Wear? A Fashion Game for Girls." As far as I can tell, boys did not get a fashion-oriented version of their own.[3]

For feminists focused on childhood, toys could reinforce sexist stereotypes as easily as they could inspire creative potential. Pogrebin challenged parents not to buy toys that insulted, offended, or excluded one sex. In her words, "We're refusing to buy toys 'for girls' that teach hypocrisy, narcissism, and limited aspirations. We're avoiding toys 'for boys' that promote militaristic values and a must-win attitude."[4] Instead, she urged parents to apply feminist values when considering toys for their kids. This faith in the power of socialization and the impact of parenting placed children at the center of the women's movement.

Stemming from the journalistic hub of Ms. magazine, the Women's Action Alliance, a national feminist organizing group, questioned women across the country about the social changes they believed were necessary to raise children free from stereotypes. Beginning in 1972, the WAA received nearly five thousand letters from parents across the United States asking for advice: "How do we keep young children from developing the rigidities of sex-role stereotyping? How do we help little boys realize that love, affection, and nurturing are indeed part of the proper role of a man? How do we help little girls realize that the world is theirs to have and to hold? How do we help them in their earliest years make choices that will not one day limit their choices?"[5]

In response, the WAA created the Nonsexist Child Development Project (NSCD) and hired Barbara Sprung, a New York teacher, to direct its growing grassroots efforts at nonsexist parenting. Sprung drew from Pogrebin's research in the child development literature, which suggested that three-year-olds had already internalized gender stereotypes. As a result, Sprung focused her pioneering efforts on preschoolers. As she assessed the books and toys that were available, Sprung realized that "the art work was outmoded and totally unreflective of human variation"; moreover, these books and toys "did not reflect the ethnic and racial population of the country."[6] Indeed, when Sprung and her coworkers later developed programs for parents and teachers, they began with examples of commonly available sexist or racist toys as a way of raising the conscience of these caregivers before presenting new, progressive alternatives.

Inspired by similar concerns, the creators of Free to Be . . . You and Me made children's toys a crucial feature of several songs, poems, and skits. In "William's Doll," Alan Alda sings the lament of a boy who wants a doll but instead receives a basketball, a badminton set, marbles, a baseball glove, and "all the things a boy would love." William's wish is granted when his grandmother recognizes that he wants a doll to practice nurturing so he can be a caring father some day. Other Free to Be selections also depicted children or personified animals playing with toys or other objects in less conventional ways. Dan Greenburg's poem, "My Dog Is a Plumber," depicts a dog who is both handy with "manly" tools and fond of playing with pots and pans on a pretend stove. In Carol Hall's song, "Glad to Have a Friend Like You," Greg admits that he "still hugged teddy bears," while Peg likes to "make things out of chairs." Together, they construct rocket ships out of pillows and pretend to be astronauts. In these vignettes, Free to Be . . . You and Me intentionally represented less rigid gender roles through the kinds of toys its male and female characters embraced.

Many middle-class white feminists did not question the significance of children's toys, probably because these activists themselves grew up in homes stocked with educational and creative playthings. The marketing of "educational toys" began in earnest after World War I when the toy manufacturing firm Holgate, later acquired by Milton Bradley, hired Norman Rockwell's brother, Julius, as the company's main designer. Nursery schools, where children played to learn, were still a relatively elite phenomenon. They began in the 1920s and through the 1930s and 1940s moved into middle-class culture. Objects such as Carolyn Pratt's unit blocks, designed to foster "creative pedagogy," moved from schools to middle-class playrooms in the 1950s.[7] Moreover, in the 1950s, parents began to place more value on creativity and toys that would foster it in their children. During the postwar era, as historian Amy Ogata puts it, "creativity becomes desirable, consumable and redemptive."[8] This emphasis on creativity was mirrored in the adult world, as reflected in popular television programs of the early 1960s that were populated with creative professional jobs, including the Dick Van Dyke Show (a writer), Bewitched (an advertising executive), and even Marlo Thomas's long-standing fiancée, Donald, on That Girl—a magazine writer. At least for many middle- and upper-class white parents, then, child's play was understood to be very influential for later career success.

The Science of Sex Roles

When Letty Cottin Pogrebin began at Ms. in 1971, she was assigned the task of writing her first article on the subject of nonsexist child rearing, since she was the only founding editor with children at the time. This led to an eight-year "obsession" as Pogrebin dove into contemporary research on child development, education, and sociology.[9]

Psychologists and sociologists had been studying sex roles since the nineteenth century. Freud, for example, famously rooted adult behavior, especially gender roles, in a child's relationship to his or her parents.[10] In the early twentieth century, Edward A. Ross and the other founders of social psychology argued for the profound impact of socialization on gender roles and behavior more generally.[11] James Watson took this socialization approach to its extreme in the 1920s with his behaviorist proclamation, "Give me a dozen healthy infants, well-formed, and my own specified world to bring them up in and I'll guarantee to take any one at random and train him to become any type of specialist I might select—doctor, lawyer, artist, merchant-chief and, yes, even beggar-man and thief, regardless of his talents, penchants, tendencies, abilities, vocations, and race of his ancestors."[12] Watson acknowledged that his claim was largely speculative, but his confidence in the power of socialization and rejection of biological instincts marked one end of the continuum associated with debates contesting the relative influence of nature and nurture.[13]

Children's toys were brought into the fray over the influence of instinct versus the environment in 1933, when Mildred Parten, a researcher at the Institute for Child Welfare at the University of Minnesota, emphasized the social value of toys.[14] Describing herself as a "genetic sociologist," Parten believed that the key to distinguishing between what we are born with and what we acquire lay in our earliest social influences.[15] As Parten watched groups of children under five play, she noted differences between what she called solitary play, parallel play, and cooperative play. Different toys were associated with different forms of play: house and doll play was the most cooperative, while playing with trains was often a solitary pursuit. Girls tended to choose doll play, while boys strongly preferred the trains.[16] From Parten's perspective, toys fostered cooperation but did so more often among girls than boys.

When psychologists and sociologists resumed studies of children's toy preferences after World War II, they reframed their work more explicitly in terms of the social origins of sex roles. Leading experts included R. R. Sears, who initially worked at the Iowa Child Research Station and later moved to Harvard.[17] In the early 1950s, psychologist

Eleanor Maccoby joined Sears's research group at Harvard and began using doll play to study how parents influenced children's ideas about gender roles and "appropriate" toy selection. [18]

Although Maccoby noted that her career did not really suffer as a result of sexism, she always considered herself a feminist, and her research on gender roles and sex differences became a foundation for other feminists. Maccoby and Carol Jacklin's 1970 book, *The Psychology of Sex Differences*, had a profound effect on the women's movement as it rekindled the dispute about the relative impact of biology and society on gender roles.[19] In fact, *The Psychology of Sex Differences* is in the first footnote of Letty Pogrebin's *Growing Up Free*. When the WAA launched the NSCD, Barbara Sprung started by poring over Pogrebin's research on sex-difference literature, which greatly informed her work.[20]

Maccoby and Jacklin's research on sex roles centered on toys. From thirty-eight different studies, they concluded that boys and girls do differ in some of their toy preferences and tend to prefer playing with children of the same sex. Many toy studies are about more than preference, though. Beginning in the 1950s, Daniel Brown began using a cutout doll called "It," to observe whether boys had the doll perform more masculine activities and whether girls had the doll perform more feminine activities. These tests supposedly demonstrated that boys have a stronger and earlier sense of gender identity or sex typing than do girls.[21] In other words, how kids play with toys can be an indicator of how much they have accepted their sex roles, and boys seemed to conform more to their sex roles and did so at an earlier age.

The "It" tests were somewhat controversial, and the disagreements centered on how sex roles are learned. Imitation of same-sex parents and same-sex role models was the most common explanation. Maccoby and Jacklin concluded that the ability to learn through imitation does not depend on biological sex. According to their theory, children play an active role in their socialization by selecting and imitating what they think are appropriate behaviors. They learn what is appropriate—and what is not—through socialization.[22] So sex role differences are based not in biological or cognitive differences but in social factors that influence how children decide what behavior is appropriate for a boy or a girl.

For the feminists who created the NSCD, the psychological literature of the time furnished two foundational claims: first, that sex role constancy (the idea that your sex will not change) develops early; and second, that early socialization has a profound influence on how children perceive and create their own gender expectations. Moreover, of all the social influences on a child, stereotypes were seen as the most damaging because they acted like a "cultural sledgehammer" that flattens human complexity.[23] Fighting stereotypes was intended not to eliminate sex roles but to open up a full range of possibilities for all children—to help create "free children."

Child's Play and Women's Work

Stories and songs encouraged children and parents to free their minds of cultural biases, but feminist criticism also led to direct action that changed the substance of toys and children's books. One of feminists' primary goals was to create toys and games that would expand girls' aspirations for future careers. In her 1973 Ms. article, for example, Letty Pogrebin took issue with Playskool's "educational" game, "When I Grow Up." This matching game featured cards depicting twenty-one males and three females poised to be paired with a range of occupations. The only occupations that matched with the female cards were teacher, violinist, and dancer. The remaining occupations, from milkman to scientist, matched only with men. This game clearly minimized the range of "appropriate" careers for girls and women. Ironically, though job bias was illegal and gender discrimination was increasingly under fire in the adult world, the supposedly educational "When I Grow Up" game evoked a workplace where women were subject to bias and discrimination.[24]

Under pressure from feminists, Playskool began to change its tune. Patience Merriman Fahey, the coordinator of the Delaware County Feminists in Pennsylvania, wrote to Playskool about an ad for a toy toolbox that read, "In every little boy who picks up his first tool, there are 100 thousand years of history at work." Fahey questioned Playskool's erasure of women from history, from tool use, and from the benefits of learning from construction toys. Playskool found her objections "completely justified," and the second ad in its "Playtools to Shape a Child's World" campaign read, "Putting something together all by yourself is a big thrill when you are three. . . . [H]ave you ever seen the look on a little girl's face the first time she finishes a puzzle? . . . And every time she does a puzzle, she learns a little more about how to get that feeling of achievement in other situations."[25] While the toolbox itself was not objectionable, feminists criticized the fact that it was packaged as a toy appropriate for boys only.[26] At the vexed intersection of toys and women's work, playthings became part of the national agenda for the women's movement.

In 1975, toys officially became a major feminist issue. To set their national agenda, the WAA sent letters to more than one hundred national women's groups asking them to identify their "priority issues." The results were summarized in a revealing memo, "WAA: Agenda, Advice and Toys."[27] The agenda included issues such as "physical safety," "adequate housing," "equal access to economic power," and "fair representation and participation in the political process."[28] These are all familiar feminist concerns.[29] Yet this memo is also about toys. It describes the WAA's founding focus on nonsexist education and child care, two of the eleven priority issues on the National Women's Agenda. Some of the women who supported this platform were themselves mothers intimately acquainted with the challenges of parenthood and child care. But it wasn't just the everyday experiences of mothering that put toys at the center of a national feminist agenda in the mid-1970s. Nonsexist education and child care also spoke to broader social concerns about the ambitions and abilities of all women to forge and maintain careers in a male-dominated workplace.

According to economists, during the 1980s, more than 80 percent of teenage girls expected to be working when they were thirty-five. When I was growing up in the 1970s and early 1980s, I had similar views, and I took it for granted that I would have a career of some sort. In 1968, though, only a third of teenage girls expected to be working when they reached thirty-five. When you consider that about 30 percent of their mothers were working at that time, this expectation makes some sense.[30] The difference between then and now also becomes that much more striking. Women entered the workforce in unprecedented numbers throughout the 1970s, when even mothers with children under six were working full time. Career options and child care were becoming significant issues to more women than ever before in American history.

These broader societal changes in women's work and sex roles motivated Sprung and her colleagues at the NSCD. The traditional stereotypes embodied in the nuclear family sitcoms of the 1950s, which enshrined mothers as domestic icons and fathers as breadwinners, were rooted in "sex role socialization patterns developed for an agricultural, under populated, frontier society." Echoing Betty Friedan's rejection of domesticity in *The Feminine Mystique*, Sprung declared that these sex roles would "no longer work for urban, industrial modern America."[31] Her reasons were not grounded solely in feminist ire. "Economic necessity," in Sprung's words, demanded that "both parents work." With both the cost of living and the divorce rate rising rapidly, women had no choice but to enter the workforce as never before. Fighting gender stereotypes, then, was not just a matter of feminist ideology but a way to keep up with changing social and economic realities for women in the 1970s.

The first set of materials that the NSCD developed and evaluated were "occupational" puzzles and flannel board sets as well as a new lotto-style game. These items were intended to "show both men and women in counterpart roles in community work and in the nurturing role; to show both boys and girls in active and quiet play (instead of showing boys always in action and girls always passive); to show the cultural diversity of our society; and to show a more open view of the family." In the late 1970s, Sprung worked with major manufacturers of children's toys, including Milton Bradley and Instructo, to produce nonsexist and multiracial materials, but only after she had tested the materials in four preschool centers.[32]

To develop these new materials, Sprung and her coworkers observed twenty-five different preschool programs in the New York metropolitan area. Based on detailed interviews with school directors and teachers, they developed new materials to reflect the social, occupational, and racial diversity already present in their students' lives.[33] Teachers in the New York preschools developed five study units that year: one on families, another on jobs people do, and others on homemaking, sports, and the human body. These units were then incorporated into a curriculum guide, *Non-Sexist Education for Young Children*, a filmstrip, and a cassette tape for classroom use. The filmstrip emphasized tasks related to nurturing, such as cooking and caregiving, as well as more subtle things about what paid work means—emotionally and financially—to parents.[34] Sprung's influential guidebook informed new preschool study units adopted everywhere from California to Kentucky in the late 1970s.[35]

Jobs and careers were also on the minds of *Free to Be . . . You and Me*'s producers when they dramatized the song "Parents Are People" for the television special. Marlo Thomas and Harry Belafonte sing about the range of jobs open to mothers and fathers, presenting a "we can do it all" vision.[36] Mommies are people with children who can also be "ranchers"

Or poetry makers
Or doctors or teachers
Or cleaners or bakers
Some mommies drive taxis
Or sing on TV

Conversely, we are reassured that daddies are also people with children:

Some daddies are writers
Or grocery sellers
Or painters or welders
Or funny joke tellers
Some daddies play cello
Or sail on the sea.

But both mommies and daddies "can be almost anything they want to be." "Parents Are People" conveys an expanded sense of possibility in terms of career choice. More important, it instills an expectation that women will work while reassuring listeners that working women will still be loving mommies at the end of the day.

In the TV version, Thomas and Belafonte happily sing the upbeat song while switching roles. In this sense, the TV show echoes the presentation of the song in the book, where the poem is surrounded by pictures of men and women at work. The images are multiracial and highlight men and women in nontraditional roles; for example, women are depicted as construction workers, while a man is caring for a child.

Efforts to combat sexist toys extended to other realms of activism as well. The New York chapter of the National Organization for Women, for instance, formed an education committee that joined together with Parents for Responsibility in the Toy Industry to monitor, lobby, and pressure toy manufacturers to stop producing sexist toys.[37] Since 1964, Parents for Responsibility in the Toy Industry had been protesting violent toys, like the GI Joe action figure, at the American

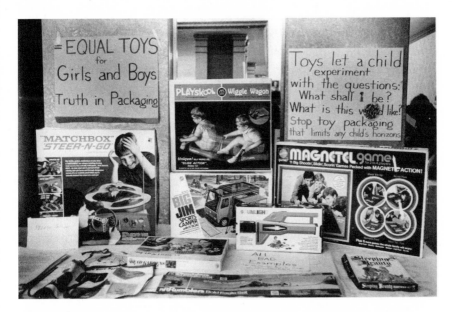

Toy and game packaging display organized by the National Organization for Women, Washington, D.C., in February 1973. Photograph by Bettye Lane; used with permission.

Toy Fair.[38] In 1970, Edward M. Swartz wrote a powerful exposé on dangerous toys, *Toys That Don't Care*.[39] The same year, the federal government began monitoring toy safety.[40]

In November 1971, Jacqueline Ceballos, head of the New York NOW chapter, picketed Nabisco headquarters with eleven other women. At issue was a set of monster toys, including "The Girl Victim," "Vampirella," and "Pain Parlor," made by a Nabisco subsidiary, Aurora Products Corporation. The *New York Times* reported that the protesters carried signs reading "Sick Toys for Children Make a Sick Society!" and "A Toy Should Be a Toy! A Toy Is to Grow!" while chanting, "Sadistic Toys Make Violent Boys."[41] Nabisco was in the process of halting production of some of the most violent and sexist of these toys, but they remained available on many store shelves.

NOW chapters continued their efforts with local protests against toys and their packaging. Photojournalist Bettye Lane visually captured one such protest at the NOW conference in Washington, D.C., on February 17, 1973: Members set up a display table of toy and game packaging with hand-lettered signs saying "Equal Toys for Girls and Boys/Truth in Packaging." Featuring "bad examples" ranging from Matchbox cars to Magnetel games, the display highlighted packaging that only showed boys engaged in active play. Equally offensive were a beading kit and a "Sleeping Beauty" game marketed exclusively for girls. While NOW activists promoted nonsexist toys at conferences, rallies, and grassroots meetings, Pogrebin did so in the pages of *Ms.*, where she made the same case against toy packaging and called for a boycott.[42]

In 1976, two New York–area teachers, Ellen Goodman and Fran Gustavson, created *Toys That Care*, a mail-order catalog of toys and educational materials.[43] This unprecedented catalog sold knitting patterns for kids, wall posters depicting women in sports, and an original line of "dramatic career play props" encouraging kids of both sexes to dress up as doctors, chefs, and riverboat captains. Not surprisingly, *Toys That Care* also sold *Free to Be* records and books. "Bridge the generation gap with this award winning record that pokes fun at our outdated ideas about masculinity and femininity," the caption read. The back page bore a checklist for evaluating children's books, inviting readers to compare male and female characters according to how inventive, helpless, active, or passive they were. For years, Goodman and Gustavson helped stock homes, schools, and libraries with such items, many of which had never before been marketed.

Yet despite the success of this catalog, a 1983 survey of ten thousand women found that 75 percent of those surveyed believed that the marketplace still offered too few toys that conveyed positive attitudes toward women in the workplace. Significantly, this survey was conducted by the National Association for Female Executives. So what kinds of toys did they want to see? "Doctor's bags and lawyer's briefcases, a business wardrobe for dolls such as Barbie, and indications ("perhaps a tag stating 'For the executive woman'") that such items as attaché cases and file cards are used by women as well as men."[44]

Boys and Their Toys

Free to Be . . . You and Me and the Women's Action Alliance were not formally related, but the producers and organizers overlapped and they shared a common agenda. Sprung used *Free to Be* in her preschool programs, and the WAA funded the creation of a poster with a verse from "William's Doll." With the slogan "He May Be a Father Some Day," the poster speaks to the impact of toys on sex role socialization, espe-

"William wants a doll
So when he has a baby some day,
He'll know how to dress it,
  put diapers on double
And gently caress it
  to bring up a bubble
And care for his baby
As every good father
  should learn to do...'"

He may be a father some day.

"William's Doll," lyrics by Sheldon Harnick,
based on the book *William's Doll* by Charlotte Zolotow;
reprinted from *Free To Be...You and Me*, published by McGraw-Hill Co.
©1974 Free To Be Foundation, Inc., in cooperation with the
Ms. Foundation for Women, Inc.

Photo: ©1983 Michael Weisbrot & Family
Design: Nina Reimer

TABS Copyright © 1983 TABS: Aids for Ending Sexism in School. Posters are featured in every issue of TABS, a quarterly journal— 744 Carroll St., #1D, Brooklyn, NY 11215.

"He May Be a Father Some Day" poster, 1983. Photograph by Laura L. Lovett; from *TABS: Aids for Ending Sexism in School*, 1983.

cially for boys. Playthings and careers were major issues for girls and women, but toys and boys brought their own set of concerns.

From the beginning of Sprung's efforts in preschools, some parents and teachers were concerned that nonsexist roles would feminize boys and make them homosexual. The perception of the feminizing effects of boys playing with dolls drove Sprung to focus on psychological literature that paradoxically claimed that rigid sex roles might cause homosexuality. According to this notion, sons were more likely to identify with fathers who were "warm and nurturant," not "stern" and "authoritarian," and those sons were more likely to develop heterosexual identities.[45] In Sprung's words, "When the question of homosexuality arose, one project director always made the point that although we live in a society rigidly divided along sex lines, homosexuality is rife and perhaps we should be open to looking for new ways to rear children."[46] Sprung concluded that this information would help alleviate parental anxiety about boys' doll play. Her theory countered the argument that doll play would emasculate boys or make them "sissies" and even turned the proverbial "William's doll" into a kind of vaccine against homosexual sons. Of course, it did so by reinforcing heterosexuality as the ideal norm for both children and adults.[47]

Letty Cottin Pogrebin also weighed in on this topic. In her 1980 book, *Growing Up Free*, she named three common fears: the fear that "sex roles determine sexuality," that "specific ingredients make a child homosexual," and that "homosexuality is one of the worst things that can happen." Pogrebin accepted no direct relationship between sex roles and sexuality and emphatically claimed that "no one knows what causes homosexuality." Her strongest reaction, though, was reserved for homophobia, which she called the "malevolent enforcer of sex-role behavior" and an "enemy of children." Homophobia, Pogrebin reasoned, "cannot prevent homosexuality;" instead it destroys female assertiveness and male sensitivity. Of course, if there were no sex-role stereotypes, there would be no homophobia. So what was Pogrebin's advice? "Don't worry about how to raise a heterosexual child; worry about how not to be a homophobic parent."[48]

Moreover, Pogrebin argued that the right wing played on fears of homosexuality to prevent social change—in this case, to halt the progress of nonsexist education. Chief among these right-wing traditionalists was a new child care expert, James Dobson.[49] Dobson spoke often to local church groups about child rearing, and in 1970, a friend at a Christian publishing house persuaded him to write his first book, *Dare to Discipline*. The volume's introduction was penned by Paul Popenoe, a eugenicist turned marriage advice expert, who saw in Dobson's book a way for parents to "get the results that they want."[50] Set as a conservative answer to a permissive society, Dobson styled himself as a replacement for Dr. Spock, whom Dobson viewed as corrupted by socialism and the counterculture.

Like the feminist educators in the NSCD, Dobson was a strong advocate of the power of socialization. However, he advocated strict parental discipline and corporal punishment to reinforce "correct" behavior. Unlike feminists, who sought to encourage nurturing behavior in boys, Dobson directly advocated violent toys for boys. To prevent effeminacy and presumably homosexuality, Dobson believed that boys *should* play with guns: "Young boys live in a feminine world. . . . In this sugar and spice world, I think it is healthy for boys to identify with masculine models, even if the setting involves combat."[51] In retrospect, Dobson told his biographer, Dale Buss, that *Free to Be . . . You and Me* was written to "shame parents into raising androgynous children." Moreover, according to Dobson, the "people behind this movement weren't married, or mothers; hadn't raised kids; didn't like men; had no academic training in this field [yet] influenced a whole generation of parents and just about everything else in the culture, including schools, and the entertainment industry."[52] Although Dobson did not mention *Free to Be* in any of his writings during the 1970s, he clearly sought to counter nonsexist child rearing and did so by advocating violent toys for boys.

THROUGH FLANNEL BOARD DOLLS, stories for free children, and the music of *Free to Be*, feminists became educators who created new resources based on the idea that socialization influences the formation of gender roles in early childhood. They sought to convince parents that sex stereotypes embodied in toys, books, and games unfairly limited their children and hindered them from understanding the diversity and complexity of the people they encountered every day.

In 1975, the *Free to Be . . . You and Me* book and record both won awards as two of the top ten Toys of the Year from the Public Action Coalition on Toys (PACT). Created two years earlier by consumer advocate Ralph Nader's staff, PACT emphasized toy safety and promoted playthings that were "life enhancing," nonsexist, and nonracist. Ironically, the bestselling commercial toy that year was a plastic Evel Knievel action figure manufactured by the Ideal Toy Corporation.[53] Apparently, lots of real-world Williams favored masculine action figures in 1975, and there was no concurrent outcry that such toys would make boys gay. These plastic figures enacted stereotypical manly ideals of courage, action, and risk taking the year after Knievel tried to jump the Snake River Canyon on his motorcycle. But feminists did not campaign to have mothers buy their daughters Evel Knievel action figures. Indeed, Pogrebin campaigned for different kinds of male play figures that were not "the 'Action Jackson' type."[54] Her vision was not for children to bounce between the extremes of stereotypical masculinity and femininity but to "learn to cope with all the surprising shadings of diverse human behavior" that lie in between.[55]

From this perspective, when Marlo Thomas and Harry Belafonte sang the words to "Parents Are People," they embodied the gray area between traditional male and female careers. Gender itself was neither threatened nor eliminated when Thomas sang that mommies can be ranchers and Belafonte crooned that daddies can be painters. Critics who fixated on the dangers of crossing gender barriers feared the imagined ramifications of gender diversity for heterosexuality and its codified sex roles. Homophobic scare tactics drew attention to the powerful influence of toys, guns, and dolls but obscured the real aim of *Free to Be . . . You and Me* and the nonsexist child-rearing movement, which was to counter gender stereotypes and create play opportunities that reflected the true range and diversity of children's interests and experiences. Embracing diversity was intended not to create androgynous people but to break down stereotypes that placed restrictive limits on girls, boys, men, and women. But with toy stores just as segregated by gender as they were before the *Free to Be* era, the time has come again to seek out the "surprising shadings" of gender diversity for a new generation.

Getting the Message

Audiences Respond to *Free to Be . . . You and Me*

LORI ROTSKOFF

No analysis of *Free to Be . . . You and Me* would be complete without an overview of how original audiences responded to it. As the three versions of *Free to Be* were absorbed into homes, classrooms, and libraries between 1972 and 1976, listeners and viewers registered their reactions in detailed reviews, celebratory raves, and occasional rants. Sales figures reveal its popularity: Selling more than five hundred thousand copies in the first few years after its release, the album achieved Gold Record status, a fact that delighted the album's creators and early supporters. And because many children who did not own a copy of the record at home heard it replayed in schools and other social settings, its influence was greater than those numbers alone suggest. Collectively, the album, book, and television show amassed prestigious Emmy and Peabody Awards, a Grammy nomination, and honors from specialized organizations such as the New York City High School Arts Festival, the National Conference of Christians and Jews, the National Education Association, and the Chicago International Film Festival. In 1974, the American Library Association bestowed special recognition on the book, attracting a swell of media attention and resulting in a big jump in purchases by librarians, teachers, and parents nationwide.[1]

That *Free to Be* garnered so many awards reflects the extent to which it impressed, influenced, and surprised listeners and viewers with its bold message and entertaining style. Written evidence reveals an even more nuanced and complete picture. From *New York Times* critics to part-time journalists for local newspapers, reviewers offered evaluations that ranged from tangential judgments about the tone or implications of particular songs to commentaries grounded in ideological viewpoints antithetical to *Free to Be*'s liberal feminist politics. Moreover, critics who disagreed with the underlying premise that childhood socialization can be harnessed to shape more egalitarian attitudes about gender were reacting not only against *Free to*

Be specifically but also against the broader nonsexist child-rearing movement and indeed second-wave feminism itself.

The *New York Times* ran two pieces on December 24, 1972, just in time to give readers an idea for last-minute Christmas shopping. In "A Women's Lib Message for Children," reporter Nadine Brozan summarized the record as "18 consciousness-raising songs of individuality, equality, and the joys and problems of growing up" and used media shorthand to refer to the feminist movement and call attention to the gendered messages within. Less a critical review than a reported story based on an interview with Marlo Thomas, Brozan's piece explained how Thomas's traditional family upbringing, combined with social pressures to marry young, spurred her to create an album that would chip away at assumptions of masculine privilege and encourage kids to celebrate their own autonomy.[2]

Deborah Jowitt, a choreographer and author who was beginning her career as a dance critic, offered a more analytical assessment in the *Times*. On balance, Jowitt praised the record, noting that it was "obviously put together with thought, integrity, and skill" and endorsing its "happy message that biological sex need not determine careers, tastes, skills or personalities." Furthermore, she remarked, "there are enough catchy tunes and hearty rhymes to . . . to appeal to small children's love of predictable rhythms and patterns." The creators and performers, Jowitt concluded, "deserve the gratitude of liberated parents. The children will be too busy enjoying themselves to say thank you to anyone."[3]

In Jowitt's view, the story of Atalanta was "told in sure-winner fairy tale style." She also described the song "Girl Land's" eerie sound (in which Jack Cassidy "cries out like a nightmarish carnival barker") as an interesting contrast to the "sunniness" of the other numbers, appreciating the song's discordant tone rather than dismissing it as too scary for kids. But Jowitt took issue with two pieces she thought could cause "slight confusion" for listeners. Given how deeply curious people were to discover the sex of a newborn baby—a fact that the "Boy Meets Girl" skit implicitly recognized by staging the dialogue between the puppets as a relentless quest to know their own and each other's sex—Jowitt wondered why *Free to Be* seemed so insistent on teaching children that "a person's sex should make absolutely no difference as to how he/she conducts his/her life." In other words, Jowitt pondered whether *Free to Be* went too far in suggesting that biological sex doesn't matter. At the same time, though, she suggested that Carol Hall's song "Parents Are People" might be too constraining in terms of gender. When Harry Belafonte sang in his "husky, knowing voice" that women "can't be grandfathers . . . or daddies," Jowitt provocatively asked "Why the hell not?" Perhaps in light of individuals including Christine Jorgensen, who publicly spoke about undergoing sex reassignment surgery during the 1950s and 1960s (and prefiguring tennis player Renee Richards, who famously transitioned from male to female in 1975), Jowitt's question progressively poked holes in prevailing assumptions regarding two stable gender categories.[4]

Jowitt also raised questions about Sheldon Harnick's "Housework" sketch, a satirical monologue enacting the second wave's edgy politics of domesticity, performed on the album by gravelly voiced actress Carol Channing. While Jowitt agreed that men and women should share housework, she noted that the skit "unintentionally demeans those who accept the clean-up chores without fuss, and makes those who take pleasure in such chores sound like real suckers." By denigrating all housework as drudgery at the same time that it challenged assumptions that women should be the only ones to perform it, the "Housework" skit, in Jowitt's view, overstated its case. Part of raising children, she suggested, means teaching them that "cleaning up and hosing down are necessary processes." A primer joking about how "everyone hates housework," therefore, was problematic.[5]

Several people wrote letters to Ms. magazine with a similar take on the "Housework" sketch. Given the overlap between the magazine and the Free to Be project, some readers wrote to Ms. to air their opinions about the new album. One devoted Ms. reader wrote from her home in the suburb of Port Washington, New York, to "express doubts about" Channing's voice-over. After heralding most of Free to Be's music as "great . . . entertaining . . . and sometimes inspiring," the author reported that she became upset when playing the album for her three-year-old daughter one day when her paid housekeeper was working in her home. "I heard it from the point of view of a woman whose 'career' is housework," she explained, and "it seemed too demeaning and insensitive to this woman, who does derive a sense of satisfaction and accomplishment from her work." Concerned that the piece unnecessarily "hurt and alienated some women," she asked Ms. editors if they could "avoid this" in the future. A writer from Nicholasville, Kentucky, made a similar point. Children, she argued, should be taught that housework, "like brushing their teeth, needn't be glorified or expanded to fill the whole space of their lives," but "neither should it be negatively charged." Domestic chores "were best accomplished as efficiently as possible in order to make time and energy for . . . a larger endeavor." She also defended her housekeeper against the skit's implicit denigration of her work. "Doesn't her job, dignified by a salary, have dignity itself?," she asked. "While the rest of the record sounds terrific," she told Ms. editors, she didn't want her children listening to it "in its present form."[6]

Free to Be's creators took these criticisms to heart when planning the televised sequel and, demonstrating a willingness to grow and learn from experience, decided to cut the "Housework" sketch from the show. While they still upheld the vignette's clever critique of advertising and media sponsorship, they did not want to air a segment that inadvertently insulted workers who perform socially valuable domestic labor.[7]

When the Free to Be book was published in 1974, a flurry of reviews appeared in local and regional papers across the country. The syndicated columnist and humorist Erma Bombeck, hardly known for her radical views, praised the volume in the New York Times as a "positive, refreshing read" for the "the crayon crowd." In Bombeck's view, the book "tells you not who you should be or ought to be, but who you can be." Similarly, a journalist for California's Oxnard Press-Courier called the book "a new form of entertainment and . . . adventure which opens new possibilities for growth and change. It is a happy potpourri . . . and delightful exercise in didacticism."[8] Many other local news outlets published reviews filled with similar positive remarks.

In an astute review for the Washington Post in 1974, writer Gabrielle Burton called the Free to Be volume "a utopian book." Dismissing critics who would dismiss or attack a work of children's literature simply on the grounds that it endorsed a specific "political" standpoint, Burton argued that it was not possible, in the social climate of the 1970s, to separate artistic or cultural narratives from the realm of politics and ideology. "Time was when a distinction was made between the political writer who writes solely to effect change and the creative writer whose primary obligation is to tell a story," she remarked. Her assumption here was that all works of literature necessarily (even if implicitly) take some kind of political stand. To those who would shrug off or denigrate Free to Be as feminist propaganda, Burton countered, "Propaganda is a dirty word when someone you don't like does it." In her view, the *Free to Be* book *was* inherently political—but it deserved praise not for its politics (which Burton admitted to sharing) but for its merits as a crafted, creative work. Between the book's covers, she wrote, "people of all ages, shapes, sizes, colors, and sexes appear, and everybody is happy they came. Although politically conceived, much of the content can be measured by other standards—literary, musical, design, pure entertainment—and emerge with flying colors." Conversely, she also suggested that the book would have been more useful if it was packaged and sold with the album as a set. Because so many of the book's pages featured sheet music, they were of little use to people who couldn't competently play an instrument, and the separate $7.95 price would unfortunately "preclude many children from making this book their own."[9]

As part of a long *New Yorker* review of "children's books for Christmas," writer Jean Stafford offered one of the harshest evaluations of the *Free to Be* volume. Well versed in children's literature, Stafford was irritated by Marlo Thomas's claim that she couldn't find any decent books to read to her niece. "It seems not to have occurred to her to go to a public library, where she would have found shelves and shelves of books which would have made her young kinswoman sit up and take notice and not get a wink of sleep for excitement and . . . laughter." While Stafford offered mild praise for Linda Sitea's story "Zachary's Divorce" as an "up-to-date no-nonsense treatment" of the topic, she objected to most of the book's content, which she described as "nonsectarian, interracial, genderless, utopian, boneless, humorless bunkum." Worse, she argued, *Free to Be* reflected the "propaganda" and "the inflexible piety of the *Ms.* manifesto." "Poor children!" Stafford wrote. "They are being brainwashed in the nursery, in kindergarten. Their enemies are their parents, their teachers and librarians, and the author and publishers of condescending and misleading trash." Stafford's critique went beyond a dismissal of nonsexist child rearing as overly prescriptive or controlling. Her caustic comments, her obvious disdain for *Ms.* magazine's feminist politics, and her refusal to notice *Free to Be*'s obvious humor suggest that she was unable to put aside her biases and offer a measured assessment. "Poor Jean Stafford," scrawled one unnamed *Ms.* editor on a copy of Stafford's review that was later saved in an archive.[10]

When it premiered in March 1974, the ABC television special attracted even more press coverage. The *Seattle Daily Times* commended the show for providing a "delightful, witty, and thoroughly joyous" alternative to the "dry diatribes" and "heavy, radical discussion programs" that too often "made women's liberation seem a subject devoid of such human qualities as humor or joy." Each segment of the special, the writer noted, "has something different to say about the rights and responsibilities of parents, children and just-plain people. Each is done in a clever, entertaining fashion and the dedication and talent of the myriad guest stars shine through." The *Hollywood Reporter* was also fulsome in its praise, describing the show as "innovative, clever, and completely different from anything ever done before. The kids will love it, and it is a must for adults to see so they can become enlightened, too. . . . No longer should little boys be afraid to play with dolls or cry. Little girls should be able to dream of being firemen or doctors and not be thought of as weirdos." As a young woman writing for Virginia's *Richlands New Press*, Anne Gordon Greever was "quite sure that [she] enjoyed it more than all the five and six year olds for whom it was intended." Moreover, she claimed, the show was "the best introduction" she had "ever seen to what the Women's Movement is all about."[11]

This is not to suggest that all reviewers praised *Free to Be* wholeheartedly. In 1975, one Michigan father writing for the *Petoskey News Review* admitted that he was gradually warming up to feminist ideals. Thus, he harbored mixed feelings about his eight-year-old daughter's favorite album. What would happen to his daughter's generation, he wondered, after spending years listening to Carol Channing gripe about housework, Rosey Grier extol the virtues of crying, and Alan Alda plug dolls over trucks? "I can just see it," he wryly predicted. "I'll go to see my daughter and her [future] husband some day and it'll be a bad experience. The house will be dirty as heck. And her husband will be sitting in the corner crying. He will be holding a doll. I love my daughter, and I believe in steady social change. But I think I'm going to break that record."[12] His tongue-in-cheek bit of gender forecasting combined acceptance of some feminist goals (such as equal opportunity) with lingering fears about effeminacy among boys (who might not grow up to become "real men").

His remarks, though, were a far cry from the harsher critiques of nonsexist child rearing offered by unwavering social conservatives. As Laura L. Lovett also explains in her essay "Child's Play," in this volume, traditionalist family experts affiliated with the Christian Right held views antithetical to the creators of *Free to Be*. The most influential spokesperson for this evangelical perspective was James Dobson, whose 1972 parenting book, *Dare to Discipline*, and whose multifaceted political initiative, Focus on the Family, advocates rigorous parental discipline and corporal punishment to enforce traditionally divided gender roles and hierarchical family structures. Unlike the Michigan father quoted above, who used humor to express his discomfort with a more open, nurturing style of masculinity, Dobson and other evangelical conservatives were adamant in their conviction that sexually egalitarian family arrangements and homosexual "lifestyles" would corrupt the nation's moral fabric.

Most parents, of course, didn't have a local newspaper column where they could pontificate on children's culture, but some wrote letters to *Ms.* endorsing the project. In March 1973, for example, a mother from Pasadena, California, wrote, "I ordered the album for my four children for Christmas and they listen to it constantly. They have taken it to school to share with their friends. They dance, sing, and have the spoken parts memorized. They may not understand the implications but the seeds of thought will stay with them. Already, I see some attitudes changing about 'girls' games' and 'boys' games,' just to name a few." Similarly, a first-grade teacher from Versailles, Ohio, told *Ms.* that the children in her class were "very impressed with each song and story and have no trouble agreeing with the ideas. They play the album on their own—singing along with the songs they are beginning to learn."[13]

One mother had especially high hopes for the album's potential influence. Denise Kanes congratulated Marlo Thomas for creating "a truly enlightening album . . . unlike any other created for the listening ears of children." One-year-old Sally Kanes was "too young yet to understand the meanings of these delightful poems and songs," but one day, her mother predicted, she would "be able to overcome the hampering patterns of sociology" that had stultified Denise's 1950s girlhood with "narrow-mindedness, suppressed creativity, and a lack of mind-expanding freedom." Thrilled to offer her daughter "the benefits of such an album," Denise expressed the strong wish that "talented artists . . . will continue to 'stick their necks out' for children forevermore so that the little people will realize that they DO have a choice and the right to decide what or who they will be."[14]

Children also left a paper trail of opinions—mostly praise. Marlo Thomas received many letters from elementary school students who chimed in a chorus of enthusiasm. As Leslie Paris also notes in her contribution to this book, a group of California schoolchildren wrote to express their joy in the music and their budding awareness of "womans lib." One girl from this group offered Thomas a bit of sage advice about her singing career: "You have a great voice, so watchout for that Ludicrous monster, Larengites!" This way, Thomas could keep spreading the message that "divergency is the key to the world!" Another young writer requested that the television special be aired again: "Would you please put it on TV [again] and put it on early"— presumably, before her bedtime.[15]

Free to Be clearly made a huge impression on kids during the 1970s. To be sure, its popularity was hardly universal. Some youngsters encountered it in much the same way they watched *Speed Racer* episodes or played with hula hoops: It was a fleeting part of their childhood, nothing special. Yet for many children, *Free to Be* was a dynamic form of popular culture that saturated their recreational lives. Today, many adults recall *Free to Be* in reverent, even ecstatic tones. Currently, Facebook features a *Free to Be . . . You and Me* fan page that has attracted over twenty thousand enthusiastic devotees. Most fans are adult "children of the 1970s" who adored the album in their youth and whose public comments about the project today reveal the profound influence it had on their lives in the past.

THE CONTRIBUTORS featured in the rest of this book continue to ponder the ideas, impact, and implications of the original *Free to Be* material. Yet unlike the voices of the adults and children whose impressions remain artifacts in the cultural amber of the 1970s, these authors write from multiple vantage points today, circling from past to present and weaving a kaleidoscope of experiences, memories, interpretations, questions, and opinions.

Part Three

Parents Are Still People

Gender and Child Rearing across Generations

Genderfication Starts Here

Dispatches from My Twins' First Year

DEBORAH SIEGEL

"He looks like a boy and she looks like a girl," say my parents over and over again at the hospital as the four of us peer over two bassinettes at my newborn twins on their first day of life. "Her features are just so fine!," my mother explains. My husband, Marco, and I sit there, beaming and dumb. Our boy and our girl have arrived.

The hospital has furnished each of our babies with a pink-and-blue-striped hat and blanket. And how quickly we replace that headwear with hats of our own, carefully selected from a bag of hand-me-downs tucked into the hospital suitcase along with my toothbrush and socks. Right up to the last week, I felt too sick to feign interest in baby clothes. Choosing these hats and now placing them on two tiny skulls is my first step toward understanding these kids, now on the outside, as real.

The hat for Baby Boy is yellow and too big and sits perched on his head, giving him the semblance of a miniature rapper. He looks, dare I say it, macho. Baby Girl's hat is girly—white with pink and green flowers. Uh oh.

As I stare down at these new life forms, my postpartum brain goes wild: *Did I choose these hats to adhere to gender norms? Maybe. Who cares? The stuff was free. Dear friends gave us those hats. Should I have put the flowery one on Baby Boy to make a point? Oh, stop worrying about color and pattern as long as it's clean and warm. We're talking a hierarchy of needs. It's clothing. Did I mention that it was free? To hell with color. Color obsession is an affluent woman's craziness. The feminists don't know I'm here. It's a maternity ward. No one's noticing these hats. Except . . . me.*

I go in and out of ideological awareness the way I go in and out of alertness, thanks to the heavy dose of Percocet I'm on. Part of me cares only that my babies are healthy and safe. And part of me cares—very much—about what they're wearing. Because *that* part of me knows that this same morning, babies at hospitals across the land are undergoing the same process: induction into a highly gender-differentiated world. Raised to believe that boys and girls are created by the expectations of their culture and not just born that way, I, for one, know better than to stereotype by rote. What, dear goddess, is going on?

And that's when it hits me: Forty years after the gender-equitable child-rearing anthem *Free to Be . . . You and Me* unleashed its utopian vision, well-intentioned new parents like me are reproducing gender stereotypes as instinctively as our newborns wail.

Over the next weeks and months and ultimately my twins' first year, I'll become obsessed by this conundrum. I'll move through phases in my thinking as my babies graduate from breast milk to formula to milk. At times I'll think that the pendulum has swung in the opposite direction. "The more we parents hear about hard-wiring and biological programming, the less we bother tempering our pink or blue fantasies, and start attributing every skill or deficit to innate sex differences," writes neuroscientist Lise Eliot in *Pink Brain, Blue Brain*, a book that argues that social expectations—not biological differences—have the upper hand in shaping who our children become.[1]

Yes, at certain moments during this surreal first year of parenthood, I'll come to believe that we sons and daughters of feminism have grown convinced of children's innate gender sensibilities, even as we take pains to surround our boys with dolls and our girls with trucks. Three decades of media stories hawking the latest in neuroscience have emphasized the nature side of the nature-nurture debate, the side that our mothers' women's movement famously upstaged. All that noise about biological determinism has to have some effect on our psyches. No?

Sometimes I'll start to think, during early dawn feedings when I haven't had enough sleep, maybe we're just lazy. Maybe my generation just isn't interested in fighting our mothers' battles once we become parents—older ones, many of us—ourselves. Or maybe it's just those of us coming to parenthood in hip, liberal enclaves like Seattle, San Francisco, and my particular corner of Brooklyn, where "gender" has joined the ranks of food allergies and chemical toxins as a focal point for parental concern. Maybe those of us living in these epicenters of correctness are tired of all the pressure. You can rid your pantry of peanut butter and find replacements for paraben-laden shampoos. But short of creating a gender-neutral environment, as if such a thing were possible, experts rarely agree about what you can do to ensure that your boys grow up sensitive and your girls grow up, as the national nonprofit Girls Inc. urges, "strong, smart, and bold." If you fervently believe in nurture, then a lot depends on you as a parent. If social expectations, not biology, are destiny, doesn't that put an unfair burden on us to create the self-confident, truck-loving girls and sensitive, doll-hugging boys we ourselves were raised to become?

As the sleepless nights pile up, I'll sometimes even start to think—heretically—that maybe second-wave feminism got it wrong. Maybe nature is feminism's dirty little secret.

Or maybe . . . maybe I just need more sleep.

But I'm getting ahead of my story here. Allow me to back up. On this particular day when I become a mother, the last thing I want to do is check my feminism at motherhood's door. So I decide to start a journal, a gender diary of sorts, in which to observe the gendering of childhood as it plays out in my own private petri dish. The scholar in me figures she'll record some of the contradictions at play in the larger culture in which these new lives begin to grow. The third-wave feminist in me reasons she'll try to monitor some of her internal contradictions in an effort to document the space between ideology and diaper changes where modern parenthood is lived, and where today's parenting philosophies are born.

Day 1

The boy comes first, as predicted. In twin parlance, he's Baby A—the one nearest the exit. The girl, known officially as Baby B, arrives two minutes later. I can't distinguish their wails, though Marco says he thinks he can make out two cries, one high, one low. To me, they both sound like mice.

But human they are, the doctor assures us, holding them up one at a time over the blue barrier that separates the rest of me from my head. Miraculously, they are safe. As Marco fumbles with his camera, I turn my head in his direction, arms splayed crucifix-style, tubes running every which way, and tell him I feel better already. This C-section is a breeze compared to the pregnancy, which was rough. In spite of how very much I wanted this pregnancy—coming to it as I did later in life after a divorce, a second marriage, and rounds of fertility interventions we really couldn't afford—I did not enjoy it. Yet I loved those dots on the ultrasound. Marco said they looked like stars.

We learned their sex as soon as we could. I was ecstatic to learn one was a boy, happy to offset my own fraught mother-daughter relation-ship by mothering a son, and I let out a war whoop when we learned the second one was a girl. One of each. An instant family. A foursome, just like that. The sheer bounty of what I carried got me through nau-sea, hormonal depression, premature contractions, bed rest, and the disappointment of not enjoying my pregnancy so much.

Given my mood and energy level, we didn't do much to prepare. But we did what we could and what felt important. Marco, a graphic de-signer and corporate brander by trade, had taken pains to brand these babies before my water broke. With a craftsman's care, he created an electronic birth announcement, marking the babies' names in type with a thick slab font like the letters on children's building blocks. For a palette, he used muted blue and mauve and polka dots and stripes, careful to mix both colors throughout both names. How I marveled at seeing those names writ large.

Here we all are, new mom, new dad, and two new people. For a few timeless hours inside that hospital cocoon, like babies in the *Free to Be* skit "Boy Meets Girl," they are genderless.

Or are they? Just when will gender begin?

Day 5

Today we'll bring them home. Dressed in outfits given to us by others, their gender seemed already assigned. And I'm far too exhausted—also elated—to care.

As I fold the tiny white onesies issued by the hospital and place them into my suitcase next to the outfits we brought ourselves, I think of my friends' generosity. When someone showed up with a bag of hand-me-downs, sparing us the expense of purchasing baby clothes during a recession and with Marco out of work, who were we to re-fuse? I rejected the items that raised my hackles: The onesie with "MVP" emblazoned across the chest (neither Marco nor I are athletic) went straight to Goodwill. The footies for "Daddy's Little Princess" got passed along too. But the rest we tucked in drawers—one overridingly pink, the other overridingly blue. I'm cheap. I'm practical. Resistance felt futile, I swear.

For their homecoming, Baby Boy sports blue and green dinosaur pajamas. Baby Girl wears a white top and pants trimmed with pink ribbon. We snap pictures of them lying on my hospital bed while we wait for the cab to pull up. What lovable, sleeping mice. My own.

Pulling up to our apartment, I see my mother outside, attaching two balloons to our railing—one pink, one blue. Stepping gingerly out of the car, I find the sidewalk while she and Marco each carry a baby over the threshold. I follow them in. They place the babies, still in their car seats, on the dining room table. And then we all just stop and stare.

What tiny munchkins I have borne. I marvel at twenty wriggling fingers and four squinting eyes. My midsection throbs in agony. But my heart floats buoyant, like a thousand pink and blue balloons.

Day 8

In Jewish culture, the eighth day of life is a milestone. My babies have arrived during a swine flu outbreak. So far, every day has been a miracle, it seems.

Today is Baby Boy's *brit milah* and Baby Girl's *brit bat*, parallel ceremonies designed to welcome babies into the Jewish community and connect them to ancient roots. I've explained to Marco, who is in the process of converting to Judaism, that before the late 1960s, there had been no comparable ceremony among the Ashkenazi (Jews from Eastern Europe) to celebrate the arrival of a girl but that Sephardic Jews (from Spain and the Middle East) had been greeting the birth of daughters with traditions for centuries. Marco is Puerto Rican. We joke about his ancient Sephardic blood.

The ceremony begins as each of our mothers carries a baby into the room. Wrapped in a colorful prayer shawl, the female *mohel* (more properly, *mohelet*) says something about the chair of Elijah, an honored "guest" at every *bris*. She lays out her metal tools on the white cloth covering our dining room table. Marco and I light candles for Baby Girl. The *mohelet* performs fast work on Baby Boy while our fathers feed him sugar water and stroke his bald head. We all drink wine. Each baby gets a drop. The covenant is renewed.

The *mohelet* asks Marco and me to make silent wishes for our children. *May you be healthy, happy, and whole.* They're given Hebrew names, along with two official certificates peppered with Stars of David, children's blocks, teddy bears, and cupcakes. Maybe it's the cupcakes, but

I find it hard to take the certificates too seriously. At the bottom of each, the artist has drawn a pair of booties—one pair pink, the other blue.

Pink and blue. It's only Day 8 and already there seems to be a conspiracy designed to color code my mice. The color coding of humans who have yet to express themselves strikes me as canned. But I'm so happy to have made it to this season that I can do little more than merely note it down here in my journal, to absorb later. We sing the Shehechiyanu, a Hebrew prayer of gratitude.

I'm soaking up the melodies. I look around the room at our family and friends and revel in the archaic vocabularies that provide language for our most sacred occasions. And then, as if on cue, a dear friend, trapped at home in Philadelphia with the flu, joins us via phone to offer some words in closing. We put her on speaker and she leads us all in a rousing rendition of "Free to Be"—the modern progressive corrective to decades of predetermined rules.

Month 3

At three months in, I'm waking up, slowly, from my postpartum haze. The feisty feminist returns, somewhat rested, back in touch with her principles after listening, a few thousand times now, to the *Free to Be* album downloaded onto the iPod plugged into the babies' room. No longer merely the backdrop of my youth, it is becoming the early soundtrack of theirs.

The monkey dress arrives from a beloved family friend who I'll call Susie. The dress takes the form of a pink tutu sewn onto a onesie, adorned with a Paul Frank monkey and sequins. I put the dress on Baby Girl, snap a picture, and text it straight to Marco and my mom with the caption "OMG!"

"Um, she just looks wrong," my snarky husband texts back.

"You know, Susie *made* that dress for you," my mother scolds me gently when I tell her about it later that day on the phone. Oy, the guilt when etiquette and ideology collide.

A few days later, my mother flies in from Chicago bearing a suitcase full of gifts. We sit together on the floor in the babies' room, the zippy music blaring, as she pulls out the treasures. "A dolly for Baby Girl," she says proudly, bestowing a pink stuffed baby doll, "and a gorilla for Baby Boy."

"Mom, *really?*" Something about the way I say it that makes me feel like a teenager. But honestly, did the woman learn nothing from "William's Doll"?

When we put the babies down for a nap that afternoon, I make sure that they have the "right" objects tucked beside them. In front of my mother, I make a big stink out of reversing the recipients and gifts. Doll: Baby Boy. Gorilla: Baby Girl. My mother leaves the room. I come out a few moments later to find her in the living room reading the newspaper, looking a little miffed.

When I come back two hours later, I find the babies laying placidly head to toe, Gorilla and Doll tangled in an anxious heap.

Month 6

By six months out, my personal library has grown at the same rate as that of my twins. I'm secretly spending the Barnes and Noble gift card a friend gave us for the babies on books about "packaging" girlhood and boyhood, with subtitles like *Rescuing Our Daughters from Marketers' Schemes* and its corollary, *Saving Our Sons from Superheroes, Slackers, and Other Media Stereotypes.* While other moms I know are midway through *What to Expect the First Year*, debating the consistency of poop and the best time to introduce solids, I'm searching for clues about nourishment and excrement of another sort.

Surely, I think while combing through the pages of *Marketing to Girls*, Marco and I will be on board with a healthy media diet when the time comes. Surely we will rescue our daughter and son from the cultural myths and media stereotypes and marketers' schemes destined to box them into rigid gender categories, Marco's geek love for superheroes notwithstanding. And surely that moment is now.

I know what I need to do.

The first two pages of the *My First Words* book we read them at night contain photos of children, labeled "boy" and "girl." Are these really the very first "first words" my babies should know? I remember from my feminist theory classes in graduate school how gender is defined in opposition. A "girl," in particular, is defined in opposition to that which she is not. So I skip those first two pages and start the reading with "cat" and "banana" instead. Soon, I'm altering pronouns in the book about firemen. I'm reversing the genders of snuggling bunnies and pouncing rats. My babies' library becomes populated with a rotating cast of gender-bending creatures. I'm remastering the narrative! I'm remixing the tale! This feels good and right and true.

And then one night around this time, I stop mid-reading and look down at my babies and wonder what they're thinking. For all my efforts to rewrite the tale, part of me imagines they're really just thinking something mundane like *I wonder how that book tastes.*

I revisit the chapter in *What to Expect* about starting solids. And I start wondering what, exactly, I'm so hungrily searching for.

Coda

At the one-year mark, I'm still searching, still reading, and still trying to resist the stereotypes within.

I don't have answers. I have only questions. My babies have a few years to go before their gendered identities and their characters take form. The goal back in the days when *Free to Be . . . You and Me* first appeared, similar to the goal now, was never to eradicate gender but to create open spaces in which our children can choose for themselves. But what will my babies choose to become, and what will choose them? Will Marco and I "naturally" encourage freedom of expression and gender equality, or will we continue to fall into gendered ways of being without thought, the way we did with those hats? And is there really such a thing as free choice? Or is gender always already prescribed?

My reading takes me back to the lessons of an earlier generation. Back in the 1970s, I learn, there were families who attempted to create environments of gender neutrality. It didn't work. The most famous case was Sandra and Daryl Bem, two psychologists who decided to raise their young children, a boy and a girl, in a gender-neutral way, much like the fictional parents had done in "The Story of X," a science fiction fable written by Lois Gould for *Ms.* magazine and published as a book in 1978. The Bems' goal was to restrict their children's knowledge of the signs of gender until they were old enough to be critical of stereotypes and sexism themselves. They went beyond merely offering both children dolls and trucks. They dressed both kids in pink and blue and made sure that as parents, they divided labor and parenting equally. And then the Bems one-upped themselves: They took White-Out and markers to their children's books, changing the sex of main characters and deleting sections that described males or females in sex-stereotyped ways. In their conversations with their children, they took pains to instill the idea that the only difference between males and females was anatomy.[2]

One day their little boy, Jeremy, wore his favorite barrettes to school. Another little boy teased Jeremy that he must be a girl, because only girls wear barrettes. Jeremy tried to explain that wearing barrettes doesn't matter. Being a boy means having a penis, he explained. But the boy wasn't convinced. So Jeremy pulled down his pants as a way to make his point more persuasively and prove that indeed he was a boy. His little friend was not impressed. "Everyone has a penis; only girls wear barrettes," he said. The fictional story in Ms. ends more optimistically, with the experiment succeeding. Influenced by X, X's classmates throw off the mantle of gender tyranny, and no one cares about categories like "boy" and "girl" anymore. But that was fantasy.[3]

As much as the creators of Free to Be may have wanted Girl Land and Boy Land to be things of the past, childhood today remains far more sex segregated than one might have hoped it would be by now. Maybe it's because even the most well intentioned among us slip. "Babies are born to parents who have a host of assumptions and expectations about gender, whether or not they consciously endorse those expectations," says Cordelia Fine, author of Delusions of Gender.[4] According to Fine, studies show that parents have a tendency to see boys as more boyish and girls as more girlish than they actually are.

Until my babies reach age two, they apparently won't know which side of the gender divide they're on. And here, on their first birthday, I sense that their gender is still largely something we impose.

At the same time that my twins turn one, Marco officially becomes a Jew. We decide, together, to add a blessing for our children to our weekly Friday night ritual of candles, challah, and wine. We search for words that speak to us across cultures, ideologies, and time and settle on a modern interpretation of an ancient prayer:

May you be who you are.
And may you be blessed in all that you are.[5]

To that I say, Amen. I'm not always sure how we'll get there, but I know somehow we will. Come with me, take my hand, and we'll run.

Free to Be Conflicted

ROBIN POGREBIN

As the daughter of one of the contributors to *Free to Be . . . You and Me*, I absorbed every one of its catchy lyrics as wisdom to live by:

> When I grow up, I'm gonna be happy and do what I like
> to do . . .

> In this land, every girl grows to be her own woman . . .

> Mommies can be almost anything they want to be . . .

Most of it proved true. I weathered the social rejection of my physically awkward adolescence by believing that it was my brains that mattered, not my flat-chested body or metal mouth (braces). I pursued my love of journalism and became a professional newspaper reporter. I married a man who appreciated my independence. I grew up confident that I could be and do anything.

But then I became a mother. And that blissfully smiling *Free to Be* picture of kids riding around on a carousel proved far more complicated.

It was the one thing feminism didn't prepare me for—how wrenching it would be at times to leave my kids at home and go to the office, or how I'd beat myself up about not doing either thing fully: parenting or work.

Motherhood was also something my mother, Letty Cottin Pogrebin, never talked about—how she balanced work and home, whether she found it a struggle, how to move between those two worlds. She made "having it all" look easy.

And from my childhood perspective, my mother did have it all. A leader of the feminist movement, she had a stellar career and the freedom to work from home as a writer after her office years as a founder of *Ms.* magazine. She and my father, Bert, had a strong marriage and an active social life. And despite a packed schedule that always included public appearances and political activism, my mother still managed to edit our school essays, make crispy potatoes, and help my sister, brother, and me conjure homemade Halloween costumes.

Strong, busy, accomplished, content—my mother has been a powerful role model for me throughout my life. One that I assumed I would be able to emulate.

But when I became a parent, I slammed into the reality that I could not have it all—at least not all at the same time. Yes, I managed to have kids and continue working at a fulfilling job, but along the way, I kept coming to crossroads, crucial junctures where I felt compelled to make a choice. Did I want to raise my hand for a reporting position that would involve constant travel around the country covering a presidential campaign, or did I want to get home to have dinner with my kids and be able to attend parent-teacher conferences in the middle of the day? Did I want to try for a demanding beat like covering City Hall, or did I want the flexibility of being able to occasionally work from home? How ambitious should I be? How successful could I get and still be able to tuck my kids in every night?

The way I came to see it, because I wanted to be both an accomplished professional and an involved parent, certain routes were just closed off to me, untenable. I can't be the Seattle bureau chief if I'm not prepared to fly off to cover an Alaskan oil spill at a moment's notice. I can't chase late-breaking news if I don't want to file stories after hours. So I have grown to accept certain—sometimes painful—limitations. I won't get on the front page as much as other reporters. I'll probably never win the Pulitzer. I may never be a bureau chief or a name everybody knows.

And I've seen my female peers make similar compromises. So many of my friends have left the workforce entirely or opted for part-time jobs. My college roommate said she couldn't justify leaving her four sons to write advertising copy. I couldn't blame her. I now get why so few women are CEOs, members of Congress, chief surgeons, managing law partners. It's hard to reach the pinnacle of your profession if you don't want to miss the school play.

Nobody talked about motherhood in college, and I understand why. Those halcyon days were all about aiming high, pursuing our goals without any consideration of someday raising children. That's probably how it should have been. I'm glad no one factored in which jobs were family-friendly; even if they had, I imagine my younger, driven self wouldn't have paid much attention. I'd want my daughter to have the same sense of boundless opportunity. But I've also begun to think she and her peers could use a little dose of reality about what's ahead so they can make their career decisions with open eyes.

We should continue to fight for social change that would make all of this easier—for the corporate world to become more flexible for women wanting to work from home or to work fewer days a week. We should keep encouraging men to play a larger role in child rearing and housework. But that's still an uphill climb, and it's only part of the equation.

Just look at the recent decision by a federal judge to dismiss claims that Bloomberg, the financial and media services giant, engaged in a pattern of discrimination against pregnant women and new mothers returning from maternity leave. "The law does not mandate 'work-life balance,'" wrote the judge (a female one, incidentally) in the August 2011 decision. "In a company like Bloomberg, which explicitly makes all-out dedication its expectation, making a decision that preferences family over work comes with consequences."

And a recent study by the nonprofit group Catalyst shows that last year, women held about 14 percent of senior executive positions at Fortune 500 companies, a number that has barely changed since 2005, in part because of "entrenched sexism."

To be sure, I attempt my version of balance covertly, trying to play down the parenting side of me in the workplace for fear of being pigeonholed as someone on the "Mommy Track." I'm not proud of it. Whereas my mother made change by marching in the streets and making very public demands, I am quietly—decorously—trying to chart a new path without helping redefine conventional ideas of professional commitment, without paving the way for similarly conflicted women coming up behind me.

How much better it would be if I could do things out in the open: "Look at me! I can leave work early to pick my daughter up from school but then go back to my computer after she's asleep and file a story at night! Face time shouldn't be the test of a good work ethic! We should be judged on our quality and productivity!"

But an enlightened workplace is only part of the solution. Being in a 50-50 marriage in which my husband is fiercely committed to being a fully involved father has forced me to realize that it's not just about freeing women up to be able to work more. We don't want to miss out on anything. Even if my husband can take my kids to their doctors' checkups, I want to be there too to hear how much they've grown. Even if my husband is happy to handle the home front if I travel for work, I don't *want* to be away more than I am.

Even liberated women like me, therefore, impose some of our own career limits. We don't reach the professional top in part because we don't want to make the parenting sacrifices required to get there. That's the complicated, conflicted reality.

I want to have it all—to be a present, available, in-touch mother. And I want to be a present, committed, successful professional. So all I can really hope for is to try to strike a balance on a day-to-day basis. On rare occasions, it feels like I do. I interview an interesting public figure, write a lead I feel proud of, or wake up to my byline in the paper. And then I hear my kids share the details of their day at the dinner table, listen to my son play a song he wrote on the guitar, or help my daughter prepare for a test on ancient Rome.

Having seen so many of my friends feel fried at the end of a full day at home with the kids—dealing with the often-thankless logistics of child care—I feel fortunate to be able to go to an office where I feel valued, to interact with colleagues, and to come home feeling refreshed and ready to give my kids energy and attention.

And I like that my children see me doing a job that I love and inhabiting a separate world of my own, with important rewards and responsibilities—even as they know they matter most of all.

My achievements may not be as groundbreaking as those of my mother and her compatriots, but it is progress nonetheless.

Sometimes, my husband and I talk about how we don't necessarily have to do everything at once. Life can happen in stages; we can opt for less high-powered jobs and fewer nights on the town now so that we can consistently be around for our kids. And then someday—after they've gone off to college—we can ramp up our careers and our extracurricular pursuits.

For the time being, I've come to accept that this is simply how it's going to be: my particular version of the proverbial—imperfect, sometimes maddening, but ultimately satisfying—juggling act between work and kids. I constantly question whether I'm managing either thing well. But I never doubt that it's worth trying to master both.

Ringside Seat at the Revolution

ABIGAIL POGREBIN

It's strange—and perhaps somewhat pathetic—to be so proud, at age forty-six, of something I did when I was seven. But *Free to Be . . . You and Me* is that badge that allows me to say, "I was there."

I WAS THERE WHEN Mom brought home the prospective songs for the show, and I remember listening to them for the first time in our living room. I remember when she read "Atalanta" aloud, and then hearing Marlo Thomas and Alan Alda bring it to life on the album.

I was there on that crisp morning when we shot the opening sequence of the TV show in Central Park; I was lucky enough to be holding Marlo's right hand as she sparkled in her fabulous red cape and we ran south on the park's west drive. We had to do take after camera take, smiling till our cheeks hurt.

Afterward, we all posed on the jungle gym in my childhood playground at 67th Street for what became the black-and-white photo on the back of the record album. I remember holding onto the cold metal bars and feeling again the honor of being so near the star.

I was assigned a painted horse on that cheerful carousel that the set designers plunked down in the Sheep Meadow, and I'm one of the kids who morphs into animation when the horses bolt.

Most memorable of all, I sat in that odd geodesic dome under TV lights, facing Marlo and answering—very self-seriously—her questions about siblings:

MARLO: Is it really great having a twin?
ABBY: Oh, YES. Like when I have a secret or I did something at school and my brother wouldn't understand it, but my sister, she would. It's good to have someone to bring it out to . . . who's my age.

To this day—no joke—people recognize me: "Wasn't that you . . . ?" Or, more accurately, since they often know I'm an identical twin: "Was that you or Robin talking to Marlo in that dome contraption?"

They're asking because they're still watching it. And they're still watching it because they now have kids of their own and want them to watch it. *Free to Be* lives on—for all the right reasons. It managed to distill—in accessible, tuneful, endearing vignettes—one acid-clear message: You can do everything the world offers. Period. Don't let any person or prejudice stop you.

In some ways, I believe that *Free to Be* had as seismic a cultural impact as any speech, protest, or legislation during the women's movement. Because it was entirely entertaining and nonthreatening, everyone could embrace it without appearing overtly "political." Also because it was unimpeachably logical: Girls and boys possess nothing inherently different that should prevent them from choosing the same pursuits and following the same passions. And it didn't hurt that the message was coming from beloved, telegenic celebrities.

The only hitch in this fairy tale, as far as I'm concerned, is the standard it set. I grew up believing everything was possible and kind of painless. So it was disillusioning to learn as an adult that being "free" didn't mean being free of ambivalence, free of pressure, free of self-reproach. *Free to Be* painted a sunny, uncomplicated picture, underscored by my mother's seemingly effortless juggling act at home. So later, when I became a mother myself, I was unprepared for the moments when I felt I wasn't balancing everything as breezily as advertised. I felt guilty when I traveled for work, and then I missed being at work when I was at the playground with my kids. I judged women who stayed on the fast track and those who got off.

When I left my job as a producer for *60 Minutes*—because I no longer wanted to leave my sleeping infant before dawn to catch planes—I was embarrassed to tell my mother I was switching from TV journalism to print reporting just so I could stay closer to home. I didn't think she'd disapprove, but I did worry I'd deflated or dented the New Role Model.

I realize it's unrealistic to have expected *Free to Be* to prepare us for the pull between parenting and profession, between feeling accomplished one minute and middling the next. I don't see how they could have added the message that it's fine to feel inadequate or average and that the key takeaway in life is to savor where you are, not to focus constantly on what you should have done or should still do.

I don't blame feminism; I see how the battles at the birth of *Free to Be* had to be fought forcefully and often without nuance. And in my girlhood, I think its lessons were decisive in seeding my confidence and a sense of aiming high. But as an adult, I was caught off guard by the persistent anxiety that I wasn't quite as successful or unambivalent as I was supposed to be.

Which brings me to my contribution to this anthology: a rewritten lyric to the tune of our enduring anthem, "Free to Be . . . You and Me." My version is for adults, not kids, and it's meant to be tongue-in-cheek, of course—because sometimes it's easier to sing our neuroses than to write about them.

"Free to Be"—New Lyrics for a New Moment

There's a land that I see
Where the moms are guilt-free
And they know it's okay
To fall short day after day.
Take my hand, come with me
Where moms talk honestly
Come with me take my hand
And we'll run . . .
From a land where we need to be thin
From a land where we should be vegan
From a land where we speak flawless Russian.
And you and me are free to be: strong but imperfect.

I see a land bright and clear
Where we don't have to fear
That we're not as top drawer
As our mothers were before.
Take my hand, grab your Spanx
Lend your voice to my angst
We are not CEOs, we're not famous . . .
I have not—been profiled in the *Times*!
I have not—volunteered in Mumbai!
Yes I bought
Halloween costumes online!
And you and me are free to be: smart but imperfect.

Every mom in this land
Has more guilt than a man

'Cause she knows that she can
Be a better superwoman.
She should have three degrees,
Corner office,
Do good deeds.
She should coach Little League
Read the classics . . .

But we're torn—should we work or stay home?
We feel bad—when we're glued to our phones.
We're deprived—of some time on our own.
And you and me should make our peace
Juggling work and family . . .
You and me are free to be: you and me.

Free to Be the Dads We Want to Be

JEREMY ADAM SMITH

When I was a kid in Saginaw, Michigan, I made a horrible mistake: I chose to play the flute in my school band. I was the only boy to do so. And at first, I was just awful. There were twelve chairs, and for the first half of the first year, I was dead last. The girl flutists ignored me. The all-male drum section made it their habit to inflict on me the full range of junior high school torments, from tripping me up in gym class to writing "faggot" on my locker in magic marker to straight-up beat downs. But like William with his doll, I wouldn't give up my flute.

William was the protagonist of a cartoon segment featured on the 1974 television special *Free to Be . . . You and Me*—a little boy who was far ahead of his time. "A doll, a doll, William wants a doll," chant the children, their faces taunting. In response, William's father knows just what to do: He buys a basketball, marbles, a baseball glove, "and all the things a boy would love," sings Alan Alda, just before he would become a fixture in America's living rooms as star of the hit TV series M*A*S*H. Then Grandma comes to William's rescue:

> So William's grandma, as I've been told
> Bought William a doll, to hug and hold
> And William's father began to frown
> But Grandma smiled, and calmed him down
> Explaining, "William wants a doll
> So when he has a baby someday
> He'll know how to dress it, put diapers on double
> And gently caress it to bring up a bubble
> And care for his baby as every good father
> Should learn to do"

> William has a doll, William has a doll
> 'Cause someday he is gonna be a father, too.

I was only five years old when this cartoon appeared, but I remember it. I may have seen it in reruns when I was older, although I have no specific memory of that now. Watching it today as a middle-aged father, it is familiar to me in the same way that *Happy Days*, *The Brady Bunch*, and *Gilligan's Island* are familiar, a pop comfort food that reminds me of running home after school and switching on the TV.

Today, I don't even own a TV, and my seven-year-old son doesn't spend more than a few hours in front of a screen every week. It horrifies me that I spent so much of my childhood absorbing countless, commercialized messages about who we are and how we should live, from the shows as well as the advertising. Most of those messages said there was one way to be a man and one way to be a woman. Although *Free to Be . . . You and Me* was just a pebble of dissent in an ocean of gender conformity, it meant something to me as I grew up. It meant something because I felt like William did, and I never, ever saw anyone like me on TV, which was probably the only form of culture I consumed in the deracinated suburbs where I grew up.

After I made my ill-fated choice to play the flute, "William's Doll" consoled me, but it didn't stop the other kids from tormenting me. Still, I played on. Do I sound like a rebel? A gender nonconformist? Don't be too impressed. I was just clueless. Eric would call my friend Jim a "fag," and Jim would say, "I'm not a fag! You're a fag!" Then Eric would give Jim a push into the locker, and that would be that. But when Eric called me a fag, I would just shrug. *What's a fag?*, I wondered. I had no idea. I was just a kid, and so was Eric; I don't think he really knew what a fag was either. I still got pushed into the locker, but unlike Jim, I just didn't see the problem with the whole "fag" thing.

And yet an undeniable menace lurked inside the word. Being called a "fag" meant that you were weak, an easy target—in short, a girl. But the word's true menace, I now realize, arose from its inchoate intimation of sex. Real sex. It was more than an insult. "Jerk" was an insult. "Fag" was a cage that boys built around other boys, one that was intended to stand between the alleged fag and true manhood. A boy in the cage would never be permitted to experience the glories of fucking. Instead, he would be fucked. Like a girl. This is how children learn to enforce a social order that sees men as dominating and women as submissive. My mistake, my fatal blind spot, was that I didn't see the cage being built. I just wanted to play the flute; I liked the way it sounded and looked. In my sixth-grade naïveté, I didn't realize that it was a girl's instrument and that boys of my age should not play with girly things.

When I finally started to see the bars that divided me from everyone else, I fought back in two ways. First, I started to furiously practice the flute, two to three hours a day. And so one fateful Monday I zoomed past all the girls from last chair to first, and I held that first chair for the rest of my time in the band.

At roughly the same time, I challenged one of the asshole drummers to a fight. I went down in a hail of fists, of course. The next time someone called me a faggot, I threw myself into him as well, arms flailing. I lost that fight, too. In fact, I lost every single battle I was in that year—perhaps twelve in all. Of course I lost: I was a skinny kid who weighed in at a lower class than my opponents.

But ultimately, I won the war. Eric called me over to his kettledrum one day, like Fonzie on the TV show *Happy Days* calling Potsie and Richie into the bathroom that served as his "office."

"Jeremy," he said. "Why are you always trying to fight me?"

"Because you hassle me all the time," I said, perhaps a bit sullenly.

"So you're just trying to stand up for yourself?," he said, surprised, as though the idea had just come to him that I might try to do this.

"Yeah," I said, dumbfounded. "Of course."

"Okay," he said. "Let's not fight." There was no handshake, and we certainly never became friends; this was not an after-school special. There was never a Grandma to save me, like she saved William. But after that terse little interaction, the bullying evaporated.

It wasn't just the boys who seemed to gain new respect for me; my fellow flutists finally noticed me and started talking to me. Michelle Gase, on whom I had a huge crush, even invited me over to her house. I didn't know what to do once I got there, but the journey of one thousand miles begins, my friends, with a single step.

Perhaps it goes without saying that I didn't stop being a geek: The following year, when my friend, Colleen, communicated my romantic interest directly to Michelle, Michelle reportedly laughed out loud, an event from which I am still recovering. But I had found a comfortable niche in the junior high school (and later high school) social ecology, and it was a niche in which I could thrive on my own terms.

Do you see the lesson I learned, the one that every American boy must learn? The formula is simple: (1) dominate the girls and (2) fight other boys. It's never good for a boy to do a girly thing, but if you must, you'd better be better at it than any girl, and you'd better be willing to punch any boy in the face who says that doing it makes you a girl.

There is a third item on that list: Pick on boys who are even more different and thus more defenseless than you are. This formula worked for me, I am sorry to report. It's worked for millions of American men of my generation.

That is why "William's Doll" seems so simultaneously tame and revolutionary today.

The tone is gentle throughout. William is teased, but he is sure of himself in a way that real-life children seldom are, and you don't get the sense of terrible aloneness that picked-on children come to know so well. By the end of the song, all is well with the world, and William seems to discover a peace that I, for one, never did.

But these qualities can cause us to miss the uncompromising radicalism behind the quaint, tender images, a radicalism that provided some degree of solace to this lonely, nonconformist child of the 1970s. The loneliness didn't end with childhood, of course, because we still live with gender boundaries. When I became a father in 2004, I worked part time and took care of my infant son, Liko, for most of the day while my wife, Olli, was at her job. In sunny, desperate playgrounds I taught Liko to walk, his little fists clenched around my aching forefingers. Pushing a swing, I'd eye the mothers and they eyed me, or so I imagined. I was typically the only father. The moms seldom spoke to me, and I was frankly afraid of them. I feared—it sounds ridiculous to admit—that if I initiated a real conversation, they'd think I was hitting on them. Deep in my bones, I felt that I didn't belong on weekday playgrounds. Not just because I was a dad; I didn't even feel like a parent, not then. I felt like a spy, an interloper, an anthropologist studying a lost tribe of stroller-pushing urban nomads.

In truth, I wasn't alone. I did find other fathers on the playgrounds, and I became friends with many I met. But there were also mothers who didn't fit that easy mother-father binary.

At the time we lived on the border between San Francisco's Noe Valley and the Castro, a mad scientist's laboratory of new family forms whose representative on the city's board of supervisors was a gay man who coparents a biological child with his lesbian best friend. But at first I didn't realize how many of the other parents on the playground were gay and lesbian; despite the fact I had had many queer friends, at this time I still assumed breeding was what straight people did. And I remember the first time I met Jackie and her smiley toddler Ezra; beckoned by her friendly smile, she was one of the first stay-at-home moms I decided to talk to. Later I saw Ezra with a woman named Jessica, and I thought she was his babysitter.

Wrong. Jessica was one mommy and Jackie was the other. Fortunately, I figured this out before my new friends discovered my ignorance. In time, I met many other families, both gay and straight, and we formed a new kind of child-centered community, one I never expected to have. After we became close, Jessica (the nonbiological mother) told me that it drove her crazy when people assumed she was the nanny, which constantly put her in the position of having to explain her relationship to her own family. Embarrassed, I didn't tell her about my early assumption, and she didn't find out until I published an essay in the *San Francisco Chronicle* about my experience being a straight parent among queer ones. She forgave me, and then she made fun of me.

Such encounters reveal the degree to which our lives have changed since 1974, when the *Free to Be . . . You and Me* television special first aired. Partnerships between men and women have changed dramatically, mainly because many women have gained the ability to support families. This has created more options for men as well. When I was born, my parents debated only whether my mom would work or stay at home. "We opted for her to stay home," says my father, Dan. "That was the question of the day. The idea that a mother could have a career and be a mom was the radical thought of the time. The idea that Dad would stay home was not considered. If it was, nobody told me, and the thought never entered my head." That wasn't true for my wife and me. We always assumed that we would share parenting and breadwinning responsibilities, as indeed we have.

The same is true for many families in our community. True, fathers as a group still make more money than mothers, and mothers as a group are still most responsible for children. But dads take care of kids, too, and moms do have careers. As a result, it's a community where stay-at-home dads forge friendships with stay-at-home moms, and female breadwinners discover they have a lot in common with male counterparts. In embracing more flexible gender roles, we broaden our conceptions of friendship and community. Here, playgrounds are not just for mothers and their children. In child-centered spaces, there's a place for fathers as well. It's a smaller place, to be sure, but it seems to grow a little bit every day.

The changes go even deeper than that. As Exhibit A, I submit myself: I had assumed that Jessica was the nanny. Despite being as gay-friendly as straight people come, I still had a picture in my mind of a mother and a father. That picture is gone, friends, and it's not coming back. This isn't just happening in San Francisco. It's happening all over the country, in Iowa, Massachusetts, Vermont, Maine, New Hampshire, Connecticut, and many other places. There is little doubt (at least in my mind) that marriage will ultimately open up to include people of the same sex and that this evolutionary advance will affect family law and every nook and cranny of community life. If gay men can now get married in Iowa, nothing can stop it. It's like a strapping, corn-fed freight train, roaring wholesomely past the amber waves of grain and purple mountain majesties on its way to the coastal American Sodoms.

I agree with conservatives who say that childhood is what is at stake in debates about same-sex marriage. But while they see gay and lesbian couples as the threat, to me the threat comes from the bullies I faced in school, the kind of children who taunted William for wanting a doll. My greatest fear as a father is that my son will face the same ferocious teasing and fighting I did. Worse than that, I fear that he will embrace the same solutions I did, and that he will stand back and watch other boys be teased and beaten up.

That's not the world I want him to live in; that's not the person I want him to be. I want the world to be entirely different by the time my son turns twelve, though I know that's impossible. I want him to be freer than I was; I want us all to be free. The solution is not as simple as just giving dolls to our sons, though that's part of it. Women still face discrimination on the job, something that needs to end. Fathers still lack support for their caregiving roles—at work, only 7 percent of American men have access to paid parental leave, and fathers face other structural limitations to full participation at home. The next step, I believe, is an education campaign to help men of all social classes advocate for workplace and public policies that can help them be the fathers they want to be, plus legal campaigns that will defend their jobs against backward attitudes at work. We also need to shift the language we use to discuss work-family issues in a more inclusive direction, to include fathers as well as mothers. That language may end up stressing resilience and meaning to men instead of the language of equality that has mobilized women, but I believe the outcome will be more freedom for both sexes. We've come a long way since "William's Doll," but our journey is not yet over.

Little Bug Wants a Doll

LAURA BRIGGS

Normally, my eleven-month-old son loved swim class, but that day he refused to budge from the side of the pool.

He had found the waterproof doll the instructor kept around to demonstrate what we were trying to teach our kids to do, and nothing was going to pry it from him.

"Hey, Little Bug, why don't you give that to Mama Laura, and we can do 1, 2, 3 under!" I suggested brightly, unpeeling his hands. His outraged shrieks of protests brought the swim teacher over to see what was wrong.

"Let him hang on to it if he wants to," our Montessori-esque, kid-centered swim instructor gently suggested. "If he doesn't want to swim today, that's okay."

A smile lit up Little Bug's face as she handed the doll back to him. "Doesn't he have a doll at home?," she asked.

I think my partner and I actually blushed when we had to explain, shamefaced, that good lesbian feminist parents that we tried to be, we had never gotten our son a doll.

You would think I would have known better. Until I was thirteen or fourteen, long past when other people had given it up, *Free to Be . . . You and Me* was still in heavy rotation on the turntable in my bedroom. Little Bug had a copy, too—albeit on his iPod—and I danced him around to "William's Doll."

It just didn't occur to me that he actually wanted one until he called me out in swim class as a bad feminist.

What I want to teach my son about gender has been more confusing to me than it was with my daughter, older and now grown. When she came to live with us from foster care at the age of eleven, she had a pretty highly developed sense of herself as a "girly girl"—her phrase. There, I understood my job: just to offer her a diversity of gender possibilities, so she felt like she could put on boots and go hiking sometimes, too, and get a break from the relentless heterosexualization the United States imposes on tween and teen girls.

I failed; she never once went hiking unless I made her, and now, in her early twenties, she wouldn't dream of going out without makeup. We wryly acknowledge that she and I are different genders.

But I have to confess that there was comfort in all that girliness, too; I never had the thought that she was anything but heterosexual.

If there is a lot of homophobia swirling around parental anxieties about gender nonconformity in their offspring, it doesn't always go away when the parents in question are lesbians. The public discourse about gay parents centers on the question of whether our children will turn out to be gay. In the right-wing model, gay is like a disease that you can catch or a set of dance moves that you almost unconsciously start mirroring: Gay influences cause children to become homosexual. The progressive answer, though, is almost as bad: Have no fear, the children of gay people are no more likely than heterosexuals' children to turn out gay. And that would be a . . . bad thing?

The sheer amount of homophobia I had imbibed in trying to be a model lesbian mother came crashing down on my head the day my daughter nervously and tentatively came out to me. I managed to say supportive words, but in my head, I think I was as horrified as any conservative evangelical Christian.

I tried to explain my feelings about my daughter to a straight friend who was a model of coolness as her two-year-old son started to wear a tutu every day to day care. She looked at me like I was from Mars.

My daughter actually didn't last long as a lesbian. The feeling she was struggling to put words to then was that she felt *culturally* gay, the same way you can be culturally Jewish but not practicing. As the daughter of lesbian parents, her struggles were our struggles, and our people were her people. When I couldn't register her for school or get her health care, that was her problem, too, and she was angrier about it than even I was.

I'll never forget the day when I took my daughter to the emergency room, throwing up blood, and I was in a dead panic. My then-partner and I were spelling each other in the waiting room—she had gone to find a sandwich—when my daughter finally got called.

"You're not her mother," insisted the nurse, looking around for the more plausibly maternal woman with whom she had seen my daughter before.

Her other mother came up behind us, and she just tried to solve the problem with as little discussion as possible so our kid could get seen: "I'm her mother," she said.

The nurse wouldn't let it go. She turned to me and said, "Well, then who is *she?*"

My daughter, then thirteen, answered her fiercely and actually did put an end to it: "She's my father!"

Then Little Bug came along and forced me to try to think it all through again.

WHEN JENNIFER went in for the twenty-week ultrasound of Bug, the technician asked if we wanted to know the sex of the fetus. We said yes. "There it is," she said. "That's the gender. He's a boy!"

"Well that's his sex," Jennifer gently corrected her. "We'll have to wait and see what his gender will be."

This, I think, is the positive thing that gay families have to contribute to raising free children and contribute to social change—not just a defensive insistence that our children will *not* be gay. At least some of us are steeped in a queer conversation about butch and femme, transmen and transwomen, tomboys and drag queens that begins to imagine a whole complex world of gender possibilities that children, youth, and adults can take up, permanently or temporarily.

I'm not sure I really believe any more, as some of us did in the *Free to Be* moment, that gender is something that you can lightly take up or refuse, that it comes in some straightforward way from parents and schools and toys, games, and friends. But when I was a boy, as singer-songwriter Dar Williams says, *Free to Be . . . You and Me* was a huge resource and comfort to me because those are many of the ways that gender rules are enforced. As a gender nonconforming child, even in the relatively freer world of the 1970s, I was acutely conscious of the intensely, anxiously gendered world of childhood. Even in first grade, *Free to Be* gave me a way of understanding that all those people who thought I shouldn't climb trees, play with boys, and wear jeans were wrong and narrow and antifeminist. I was against that. That was the year I got in trouble for hitting a boy who said he didn't believe in equal pay for equal work. As the teacher tried to discipline me, I knew she was at a loss. I guess that didn't happen a lot.

When Little Bug was born, my partner and I tried to find some middle ground about not playing out our gender politics on his head—not wanting to dress him in a way that made him conspicuous or odd—but trying to expose him to plenty of gentle men who could show him a lot of models for masculinity.

I didn't really get my feminist back up about the gendered implications of raising a boy child until he was about two months old. We were looking for something for him to wear to our friends' wedding. We started at the last minute, of course, being sleep-deprived parents of a little baby with no time and even less ability to plan. My partner, Jennifer, went out to the store in the morning and didn't return for hours. When she did, it was with a tuxedo onesie that was at least a size too large. "I've been to every store in the city of Tucson," she said. "There is nothing out there for boys. There are all kinds of cute party dresses for girls, but for boys, only camouflage."

"Apparently little girls go to parties, and boys go to war."

No, I thought. The world of commercialized childhood does not get to turn this beautiful, precious two-month-old baby into a soldier. They will have to go through me first.

As my colleague, Kari McBride, once said, it's not even clear why we think children have the same gender as adults. With little hair anywhere, no secondary sex characteristics, and not even that much difference in their genitals to speak of, it would make at least as much sense to say children all have one gender and adults have two others. We have to work at it to look at a baby and see masculinity, much less a soldier.

But that's when I started to really hear it. As he learned to sit up and crawl and take pleasure in moving his body and grabbing things, people said, "He's all boy." When he would sit quietly and listen to a book, people said, "That's unusual for a boy. And he's normally so active." When he wrested a toy from another child, a parent tried to stop me from frowning at Little Bug, saying, "That's boys for you!"

All I could think of was babies in camo—and his eventual entrée into elementary school as just another hyperactive boy with learning problems who had never learned to curb his aggression or experience empathy for other kids. I don't really know what we get out of teaching boys such dysfunctional models for masculinity, except young men who will decide to go into the military because they lack the grades or the skills to go to college. But I know that I feel at least as angry about the masculinity that too many people want my Little Bug to learn as his only choice as I ever was about the frilly femininity that landed on my daughter's head.

Within a day of that swimming lesson, Little Bug had gone to the toy store and picked out a doll. For his big first birthday, he got another one from my ex and her partner. Now that he is fourteen months, it really is his favorite toy. He holds it and cuddles it and pushes it around in his wagon.

When he does pirouettes in his gender-neutral red and orange overalls and long blonde curls while I sing along with the album I once loved so much, about a land where the children are free, I'm not really sure how I ever got persuaded to be afraid that I could make him gay.

We still are waiting to see what his gender will be. But my fierce hope for this baby boy is that the answer will be a long time coming, that he will be full of the grace to try on different ones to see what fits—gay or straight, jock or scholar, girly or boyish.

Growing a Free to Be Family

NANCY GRUVER & JOE KELLY

Talking in bed the night before our first child was born, we broached a subject that hadn't come up before. "Maybe one is enough." We'd always agreed about having two children. But with the due date only three weeks away, we were suddenly worried about whether we'd be up to the challenge of juggling two careers and two children. We felt overwhelmed by the mountain of unknowns that lay ahead.

As it turned out, we didn't have to decide about one or two in the end. In those days before ultrasounds were performed during pregnancy, Mavis and Nia surprised us by being twins! Ever since, we've joked that they heard us talking that night and told each other, "We better get out of here before they decide they just want one!" The surprise of twins showed us right away that things wouldn't go as we expected. Our family started with an earthquake, unsettling and rearranging our pre-birth assumptions and naïveté about what coparenting really is.

One thing we certainly didn't predict is that it was easier to share parenting when one of us was out of town. Before Nia and Mavis were born in 1980, we mutually committed to feminist parenting: raising them equally, sharing the daily responsibilities, drudgery, joys, and delights. That sounded wonderful to us. When they were infants and toddlers, it was key to our survival as parents. But as the girls got older and added their special ingredients to the stew of family plans and decision making, it dawned on us that there were also benefits to being the solo pilot of the family plane when one of us was away.

This became crystal clear when Nancy went to graduate school and lived fourteen hundred miles from our home in Duluth, Minnesota. When she came back for a long weekend once a month, we were all delighted to be together, whether snuggling on the couch to watch *Pride and Prejudice* or just running errands. But when normal family conflicts over schedules, food preferences, and chores arose, Joe noticed that they seemed harder to resolve than when he was the only parent at home.

The same thing happened when Joe got back from a monthlong research trip. Nancy and the girls were glad to have him—and his weekly chocolate chip cookie baking—back home. But we also experienced a longer than usual "reentry period." That's what we dubbed the family readjustments that happened every time one of us was away for more than a couple days.

It was a striking realization that the daily grind felt calmer in the absence of parental negotiation and compromise. If Joe was home alone, the kids knew that they'd have their fill of homemade mac and cheese for dinner. And if it was Nancy, the girls knew that they'd be picked up late from ballet and expected to tag along on a few errands on the way home. Fewer questions needed to be asked. Fewer negotiations needed to be made.

Fittingly, our memory of this revelation serves as a perfect metaphor for our experience as we sit down to write twenty years later—as we reflect back on our lives and our decision to create a feminist, "free to be" family. Just like coparenting, writing this collaborative personal account together is difficult and inconvenient, even clunky and awkward at times. The narrative voice doesn't flow quite as smoothly as it would if one of us wrote alone in the first person. Our dual authorship reflects collaboration and compromise—it's a joint production—and like coparenting itself, sometimes it seems like it would be easier if just one of us took over the job.

We were eager to be parents, partners, and spouses together—and equally eager to remain two individual people who draw meaning from things (like career and community) outside our family. Maintaining that individuality while sharing the child rearing, income earning, and householding is not as simple as making a task list and dividing it down the middle. It's a journey on seldom-charted seas, tacking back and forth between work, parenting, partnership, and other realms of life.

But we wouldn't have it any other way. When we were asked to contribute our reflections on the impact and legacy of *Free to Be . . . You and Me*, we knew we wanted to share the intertwined story of how we've grown our own "free to be family." From the moment our daughters were born, only eight years after the original *Free to Be* album was released, we've incorporated feminist family values into our lives. Beyond singing or reading about *Free to Be*'s principles, we've done our best to live by them on a daily basis. In our family, we all have the right to be who we are, knowing the others will back us up when the going gets tough.

The biggest test of our commitment to partnership parenting came in the unpredictable seas that delivered unexpected twins. Some waves were filled with mystery and warmth, while others seemed to overwhelm us with their brilliant heights and dark, dark depths. Even at their smallest, our little women were amazing people. Like all children, they were miracles in their own lives as well as ours.

When Nia and Mavis were little, they loved listening to the original *Free to Be* LP. To indulge their toddlerish love of repetition, we played the record over and over again—just as often as we played *Sesame Street* and Raffi albums. Inevitably, we came to know the lyrics word for word. (When reducing our vinyl collection to a few best-loved LPs, *Free to Be* made the cut easily. It still occupies a place of honor on our shelf of classic albums.)

Stories from the book were frequent bedtime requests. Some of *Free to Be*'s impact was inspired by its straight-out silliness and the laughter it provoked. Dan Greenburg's "Don't Dress Your Cat in an Apron" tickled Joe and the girls to create our own family's nonsense rules, including:

Don't put the dog in the dryer.
Don't put your bed on the ceiling.
Don't sit on the cheese.

Decades later, our daughters still use these rules to entertain toddlers.

Betty Miles's story, "Atalanta," made us more conscious of a disturbing fact: Young children's books provided precious few girls and women of action and heroism. Even most animal and fantasy characters were male! *Free to Be* inspired dedicated searching for other rare treasures, like Jay Williams's *The Practical Princess and Other Liberating Fairy Tales*, now sadly out of print. His and other stories of brave, practical girls (often with equality-minded male friends) were a joy for us to read aloud.

Free to Be . . . You and Me lent inspiration, affirmation, and support for our journey of feminist family-ing, which many of our peers didn't quite understand. It reminded us why we wanted to stick to the unconventional path we'd chosen. We took Carol Hall's song "Parents Are People" especially to heart, remaining determined to share child rearing and income earning. We wanted to have emotional space to pursue our individual dreams and to nurture Mavis and Nia, all at the same time.

Our commitment to equally shared parenting has entailed sacrifices, especially in regard to our respective careers. Soon after the girls were born, we decided that we would both work part time so we could coparent equally. For the first five years, this choice meant we lived in poverty and restricted many other freedoms in our personal life. But our often stubborn commitment to being free to be ourselves as parents, to learning and taking risks, brought us opportunities and experiences we never imagined when we first fell in love in 1978.

With such high expectations for our family journey, we've faced plenty of bumps and detours along the way. The first bump was more like shock therapy when the babies were born prematurely. We both kept our jobs but worked on opposite schedules to reduce child care costs. Sometimes it felt like we were handing the babies off to one another like batons in a relay—attending to their feedings, colic, dirty diapers, food allergies, and too-short naps—when we really wished we could both stay home and care for them together. Like one stressful evening when Nancy worked days at a craft gallery and Joe worked nights and weekends at Catholic Charities' Shelter for victims of family violence:

"Joe, the colic is acting up again. I can't get them to stop crying!" Nancy was on the phone, frantic: "I need you to come home."

Working an evening shift alone at the shelter, Joe said, "I'm the only one here; I have to answer the phone and we're full tonight. I can't leave; it's my job."

In tears, Nancy replied, "But we were going to share this. I need help now!"

Talk about feminist dilemmas! We were proud that Joe's job provided support for victims of domestic violence and women in the broader community, but we simultaneously butted up against the ways that work sometimes clashed with his parenting responsibilities.

Caring for an infant with colic is an awful experience, and being one parent trying to soothe two babies meant carrying the girls in two Snugglies at the same time. Fortunately, Joe turned out to be a "baby talker," with a nonverbal second sense, and he still has a soothing effect on infants. But he felt frustrated that he hadn't gotten the information girls get with lifelong baby-folklore training. Like most men raised during the 1950s and 1960s, he wasn't socialized to be a primary nurturing caregiver for his babies. He felt unprepared and incompetent despite his years of experience babysitting and caring for younger kids.

Conversely, all of Nancy's babysitting experience didn't prevent her incredible frustration at the fact that these helpless infants couldn't articulate what was bothering them. She felt more confident as the girls started speaking and communicated beyond crying, eating, or sleeping.

But at times, even Joe had trouble getting our infants to settle down. Sometimes, Joe would call Nancy at the gallery.

"What am I supposed to do? They only eat two ounces, and then fall asleep. Then the colic kicks in, they wake up and seem hungry. But I can't tell whether to feed them again or not. Help!"

Nancy replied, "A customer just walked in, Honey. I'll be home by six. Try calling my mom for some advice in the meantime."

Nancy knew she wanted to be a person first and then a mother, with an outside work life and income. Even with the babies' exhausting demands, she needed her independence. But she felt guilty about it, wondering, "Am I heartless to even think about my wants when they're so tiny and needy?"

Meanwhile, Joe's guilt was rooted in the conflict between his deep need to spend time caring for the babies and what he calls "the provider demon." He battled thoughts like "Fathers are supposed take care of their families financially. I work part time at lousy pay. We're on WIC in a crummy apartment. How can I be such an inadequate provider for my daughters?"

We often worried that we were letting our kids down by choosing to meet our individual needs. Our desires flouted the roles defined for mothers and fathers by our culture, but ignoring them was wasted effort. In retrospect, though, we see that our "selfishness" had a positive effect on Nia and Mavis. It gave them the gift of two totally involved parents with whom they built different relationships and from whom they learned different things. And it gave them the example of parents who were open to learning, making mistakes, and adapting to changing circumstances.

One of those changing circumstances was the fact that our daughters inevitably outgrew their favorite music and stories from *Free to Be*. As they entered what are now described as the tween years, we searched vigorously and in vain for books, records, or other materials that would appeal to them—literature that would nurture their imaginations and ambitions the way *Free to Be* did when they were smaller. While the world of feminist children's literature was blossoming, there was a cultural void when it came to high-quality nonfiction for girls on the cusp of adolescence.

When Mavis and Nia were eleven, we responded to the paucity of empowering media for tween girls and expanded our commitment to a "free to be" world beyond our own family. In 1992, Nancy was inspired to launch *New Moon Girls*, a girl-edited magazine that supports girls during the often treacherous transition from preadolescence to adolescence. This inspiration caught all of us by surprise: At the time, Nancy worked in the field of health care planning, and Joe was a reporter for Minnesota Public Radio. The only thing we had ever done with magazines was read them. But when Nancy read *Meeting at the Crossroads* by Carol Gilligan and Lyn Mikel Brown, it planted the seed that in less than a year grew into *New Moon Girls*.

In the attic of our Duluth, Minnesota, home, we gave ourselves a crash course in periodical publishing. We began to meet with our daughters, their friends, and friends of friends—about twenty-five girls in all—functioning as the Girls Editorial Board while scattered around the living room and kitchen. Together, we created the *New Moon Girls* model of an international, multicultural magazine without advertising and with girls' opinions, stories, artwork, poetry, women's history, science, cartoons, girl-to-girl advice, and "How Aggravating," a section where girls identify sexism in their daily lives. No other children's magazine or media (in that pre-Internet era) provided such content or enabled girls themselves to select and edit the media.

We're glad to report that *New Moon Girls* continues to help girls resist social pressures, including the hypersexualization of girls and the prevailing belief that how women look is more important than who they are. Before she hits adolescence, a girl is likely to stand strong in her body and not hesitate to speak her mind. But then, as she begins to emerge sexually, she is increasingly perceived and treated as a sexual object whose voice is irrelevant and whose body exists as the object of others' desire. The second-wave feminism of the 1970s produced resources for adults to resist these pressures. Work like *Free to Be . . . You and Me* gave young children resources, too. But the tween and early teen girl of 1992 had few resources to help her claim and express her own public voice.

Shortly before we published the first issue, our local newspaper ran a story about the enterprise, and it was picked up by dozens of other papers around the country. As a result, five hundred unsolicited subscription requests arrived. Two months later, our sample issue came off the press and garnered a flurry of national media attention.

We included girls in the creation of a magazine because our family gave us firsthand experience with Mavis and Nia speaking up for themselves, acting as agents in their own lives, and handling the responsibilities that accompany this way of living. We believed that other girls could do the same as editors of *New Moon Girls*, even if they had little experience with agency in other parts of their lives.

New Moon Girls gathered a paid circulation of ten thousand by 1995, and its girl editors (including Nia and Mavis) and Nancy won numerous awards over the years. But adults still struggled to understand what we were doing. During our second year, our young editors hosted a Take Your Parents to Work Day so their folks could see what the girls did. A reporter for a large newspaper tagged along for a story about this interesting twist on Take Our Daughters to Work Day.

Afterward, standing in the kitchen, the reporter told Joe, "I expected this to be a 'cute' story about a pro-girls project. I thought that the 'girl-edited' thing was hyperbole, and that the girls would be—at best—a focus group for you two. But they really are editors, like the ones at my paper. With one major difference."

"What's that?," Joe asked.

He replied, "The girls are far more efficient. At my paper, editorial meetings include lots of jockeying for position and authority. Today, I saw girls saying 'This sucks, this sucks, this is good, this sucks'—in other words, just doing their work."

Through the years, we've learned how capably girls deal with the workload, criticism, disagreement, creativity, authority, success, risk, and other real-life experiences of working in media. And, together, we've continued to confront (and prove wrong) the ageist assumptions that children can't handle responsibility or conflict and can't share power as peers with adults and one another.

Meanwhile, *New Moon Girls* has lived through its own adolescence. Adapting with the times, it still supports the original *Free to Be* message with new ways of creating community through technology and the Internet. With our interactive online social network, girls now share their opinions, writing, videos, photos, art, poetry, activism, problem-solving creativity, and sisterhood every day.

We're still inspired by *Free to Be . . . You and Me*. As Marlo Thomas noted on the original album cover, she conceived *Free to Be* because of her disappointment at finding "shelf after shelf of books and records, for boys and girls, which charmingly dictated who and what they *must* be, colorfully directing new minds away from their own uniqueness."

After four decades, we're grateful to *Free to Be* and other feminist efforts that supported our ambition to forge the kind of family we needed and wanted to be: a family where we all find support to dream our personal dreams, share them with others, and then try to live them, wacky or inconvenient or imperfect as they seem. That's our definition of a "free to be" family.

Can William Have a Doll Now?

The Legacy of *Free to Be* in Parenting Advice Books

KARIN A. MARTIN

Growing up in a working-class town in Massachusetts in the 1970s, I didn't know that a feminist movement was afoot across the country. And despite the fact that my mother was part of the same generation as many second-wave feminists, I don't think she knew about it, either. When I ask her now if she saw a movie or heard a song from the 1970s, she often replies, "I was too busy raising you kids; I missed a whole decade of politics and culture." Fortunately, though, she didn't miss *Free to Be . . . You and Me*. A fan of *That Girl*, she bought my brother and me the record album after hearing Marlo Thomas interviewed in the media. Between the ages of seven and ten, I spent countless hours on the living room floor listening to the record. I knew every song by heart and fought with my brother over which songs to play first and most. I memorized every word of Carol Channing's quick-rhyming "Housework," a feat that so impressed my parents that I was asked to recite it when visiting cousins and grandparents. Suffice it to say, *Free to Be* was an integral part of my childhood and my first introduction to feminism. As a teenager I stumbled across and became enthralled with Gloria Steinem's *Outrageous Acts and Other Everyday Rebellions*, and then, as a college student in the mid-1980s, I quickly became a fully committed feminist.

Years later, on the eve of the new millennium, my partner and I had a son, and I began to look for tools for feminist parenting. In an era when Nickelodeon was considering separate television channels for boys and girls and toy stores were (and today remain) color-coded for gender, I began to wonder whatever happened to gender-neutral child rearing. What happened to the ethos that produced *Free to Be*?

Unlike my mother, who had relied religiously on Dr. Spock, when I became a mother, I was inundated with parenting advice and was part of a generation of middle-class mothers who relied more than ever on experts' advice for rearing children.[1] As I read the advice books suggested to me by family and friends, I found them to be infused with traditional notions of gender for families, mothers, and children, and they were particularly unhelpful with respect to gender-neutral child rearing. Any discussion of how to raise a feminist boy (or girl) was nearly invisible in my little pile of books. So even though I had years of feminist theory in my back pocket, I had little in the way of everyday tools or strategies for parenting. I decided I was going to have to make it up as I went along, so I returned to the only tool I knew, *Free to Be . . . You and Me.*

I bought the CD of *Free to Be* for my son, but I had just as much fun listening to it twenty-five years later as I did as a child. However, I was now also in awe at the radicalness of it. In the context of the new millennium and post-second-wave feminism, it remained visionary and unique. There was nothing in contemporary kids' culture that even came close to delivering the messages (and with such fun and wit) that boys could play with dolls, or that girls might not want to marry ("Atalanta," my son's favorite at age four), or that everyone should share the housework. In fact, I felt that most of kids' culture was delivering the opposite messages: Girls were princesses; boys were fighters, warriors, superheroes. Girls dreamed of princes and getting married and played with toy vacuums while boys—well, were fighters, warriors, superheroes. This stark contrast between the content of *Free to Be* and the content of the contemporary kids' culture in which my son was already immersed led me back to the advice books. Why hadn't I seen much advocacy for gender-neutral parenting there? Sociologists have long recognized that advice books can provide a window into how social issues are culturally understood, so I began to consider what these advisers had to say about gender-neutral child rearing.[2] Had feminist ideas become part and parcel of what doctors and psychologists advocated? Were these ideas culturally normative? As a sociologist, I set out to investigate this question through an analysis of popular parenting advice.

Advice to Parents about Gender-Neutral Child Rearing

Beginning in 2003, I decided to take a close look at contemporary parenting advice about gender. I examined thirty-four comprehensive parenting manuals and fifteen websites that were most recommended by a variety of parenting, medical, and educational organizations. I wanted to know if these experts advocated gender-neutral parenting and how they recommended coping with a child's gender nonconformity.[3]

Nearly a third of the experts that I read advocated at least minimally for gender-neutral child rearing. Advocating for gender-neutral parenting is different from simply saying that it is okay for a boy to play with a doll if he wants to. By "advocating," I mean that these advisers believed that parents should not only permit but encourage children to move beyond gender stereotypes for their own good and possibly for the good of society. These advocates encouraged parents to disregard stereotyped toys as well as to raise self-confident daughters and emotional sons. Two parenting books, Shelley Butler and Deb Kratz's *Field Guide to Parenting* and Laura Davis and Janis Keyser's *Becoming the Parent You Want to Be*, most fully advocated gender-neutral parenting by providing parents with specific advice on how to counter gender stereotypes in children. These books referred parents to earlier resources, many written or produced during the 1970s, including Letty Cottin Pogrebin's *Growing Up Free*, Charlotte Zolotow's *William's Doll*, and, not surprisingly, *Free to Be . . . You and Me*.[4]

In contrast, nearly one-fourth of the parenting advice books I read were explicitly critical of gender-neutral parenting. Experts who thought gender was rooted in biology were most likely to hold negative views, and they provided a range of negative comments from "it won't work" to "it could be harmful." Three of these critical experts also mentioned some positive aspects of gender-neutral child rearing, but they were often undermined by suggestions that the effort was futile or potentially harmful to a child's development. For instance, *What to Expect: The Toddler Years* (a sequel to the enormously influential pregnancy manual *What to Expect When You're Expecting*) portrays gender-neutral parenting as hardly worth the trouble because most children "fit comfortably into their respective gender molds" and parents who are careful to raise children in a nonsexist environment often end up with gender-normative children.[5] The American Academy of Pediatrics advice book offers similar cautions, and both books warn parents that "forcing" a child to play with an opposite gendered toy or "ignoring" biological differences could harm their child's development.[6]

While such comments hardly celebrated gender-neutral child rearing, only a quarter of the advice was this negative. Overall there was more support for the practice than not. The picture became more complicated, however, when I turned to what experts advise when confronted with gender-nonconforming behavior in a child.

Advice about managing gender usually emerged in answer to the question, "Is it a problem that my child is doing something gender deviant? And what should I do about it?" At first glance, it appears that all of the child-rearing experts I examined answered "No, this is not a problem." Gender nonconformity was considered "unhealthy" only in its "extreme" or "exclusive" form. However, only two experts gave feminist answers to this question, where they explicitly stated that boys' playing with dolls and girls' playing with trucks or some other version of gender nonconformity is good for children and society. In the seventh edition of their legendary parenting tome, *Dr. Spock's Baby and Child Care*, Benjamin Spock and Steven Parker wrote, "When individuals feel obliged to conform to a conventional male or female sex stereotype, they are all cramped to a degree, depending on how much each has to deny and suppress their natural inclinations. Thus, valuable traits are lost to the society. And they are all made to feel inadequate to the degree that they fail to conform to the supposed ideal."[7]

Similarly, Penelope Leach wrote, "If you try to make a boy stick to the 'right' gender, however good your reasons, you deprive him of exploring the potential of half the world, and if you are happy to let a girl switch over but not a boy, you inevitably contribute to the basic gender inequalities that still bedevil us all."[8] Another small handful of sources, while not interested in social change, said, "There's no harm in that" without elaborating on its benefits.[9]

Most experts, however, offered some acceptance of gender nonconformity in children and advised parents not to worry. However, their advice also implied that gender nonconformity is troublesome. They gave qualified and tenuous answers to parents seeking advice about their gender-nonconforming kids. These answers fell into three categories.

First, some experts told parents not to worry about their child's gender-deviant behavior, as it was only a phase and worrying about it would create problems. These authors suggested that "we may inadvertently cause the very thing we fear if we react [to a boy wanting a dress] with anxiety, however understandable that may be."[10] Experts suggested that parents' discomfort with a child's gender nonconformity created or worsened "the problem." For instance, in *Parent Power,*

John Rosemond advised, "Your son's preference for dolls and 'girl' toys is unusual, but not necessarily abnormal. . . . The problem is that you have made his choice of toys into a major issue. . . . As long as you fight with him over whether he has a right to like dolls, he has no choice but to fight back. . . . *He won't have the freedom to expand his range of interests until you put an end to the battle*."[11] Rosemond also suggested more father involvement and recommended that the family seek counseling.

Similarly, Jan Faull, an adviser for family.go.com, in two different columns of advice to mothers of "hypersensitive" sons (three and five years old, respectively), wrote, "By trying to make him less sensitive, you'll accentuate a personality trait he was born with. . . . Instead of talking him out of it, accept it, validate it and then move on about your day, focusing on other aspects of his personality and behavior," and "If you try talking or forcing him into being less sensitive, you'll only magnify this delicate personality trait."[12] This admonishment that a parent's attention to a child's gender "deviance" will ultimately *create* gender deviance implies that (despite frequent assurances of normality), parents should not encourage gender nonconformity in their children. These experts ultimately provided advice about how to prevent such nonconformity.

Second, some experts reassured parents about children's gender nonconformity by claiming that the behavior was not about gender. They offered parents new ways to interpret or recode their children's behavior so that it would not look like a problem of gender deviance. Perhaps the best example of this can be seen in an advice column from naturalchild.com. A mother wrote that her "soon to be 4" son "is obsessed with wearing dresses" and that she does not "want to hurt, or interfere with [her] son's true identity. Please help." After a brief discussion of "sexual aberrations," the adviser offers a long recitation of reasons for why a three-year-old boy would want to wear a dress. This exhausting list included dresses being more comfortable, dresses being easier for managing toilet training, an expression of "resistance in general," family stress, the need for more time with a father or male, difference from his sister, being "ahead of his time" since men in other cultures wear dresses, and a need to wear costumes to experiment with being a different person. Having consulted with a colleague, the adviser then offers several solutions including "a compromise, such as a kilt or other ethnic dress," or acting classes.[13] In a short piece of advice, this "expert" gave the mother many options for transforming her boy's dress wearing from a sexual aberration into a normal, sensible desire and behavior. All of these are implicitly more acceptable than his simply being a four-year-old boy who likes to wear dresses. By offering all these interpretations, the expert signaled that this behavior required both explanation and transformation into gender-normative behavior.

Naturalchild.com was not the only site that offered this kind of recoding. Spock and Parker said that boys' doll play was "parental rather than effeminate."[14] Advice from parents.com asserted that a four-year-old boy's Barbie play was merely a sign that "chances are when he grows up, he will want to date girls who look like Barbie." Similarly, parentsplace.com advised a parent whose three-year-old son loved to dress up as Cinderella that "the Cinderella fairy tale also includes themes of rescue and protection against evil so common at this stage of development."[15] By offering interpretation, these advisers attempted to make gender nonnormative behavior understandable and acceptable. Yet in so doing, they reinforced parental notions that such behavior needed explanation.

Finally, despite the fact that gender nonconformity is rarely posed as a question about a child's sexual identity, more than half of the experts commented on supposed connections between gender non-conformity and gay identity. They frequently suggested that gender nonconformity was not a sign of homosexuality but implied that homosexuality was a problem. Drspock.com, for instance, advised, "Relax. There isn't one shred of evidence that play that crosses typical sex-role boundaries is bad in any way unless it's the *only* sort of play your child engages in. It doesn't make boys sissies or girls tomboys. It doesn't lead to homosexuality. All it does is give children a wider range of fun things to do, and parents more options for presents to buy."[16]

Experts almost uniformly viewed homosexuality as a problem. They often sympathized with parents, describing the prospect of homosexuality as understandably "alarming." For example, "Any parent in this situation would be alarmed. You are probably worrying that your child is a transvestite-in-training or gay."[17] Only Spock connected this "alarm" that parents felt to social prejudice: "When parents think that their little boy is effeminate or their little girl is too masculine, they may wonder whether the child will grow up to be gay or lesbian. Because of prevailing prejudices against homosexuality this can create worry and anxiety in parents."[18]

Other experts described homosexuality as an abnormal, problematic sexual orientation. They described homosexuality as "skewed" and a less "appropriate sexual orientation" that comes with "warning signs," implied that it was an "unhealthy" sexual identity and a "sexual aberration," and suggested that such "eccentric" behavior would "alienate or draw fire from others" and thus warranted parental intervention.[19] Many advisers then told parents to seek professional help. For example, in a footnote to a sentence about what is not "a predictor of sexual orientation," Arlene Eisenberg, Heidi Murkoff, and Sandra Hathaway wrote, if "a three-year-old plays only with dolls, shuns male playmates, and/or regularly wants to dress in girls' clothing, a discussion with his doctor may be helpful."[20] Many advisers medicalized and stigmatized boys who wanted to play with or dress in girls' things.

While in many ways, the call of second-wave feminists, especially as it concerns girls, has been heard, my survey of advice literature suggests that the feminist transformation of gender has not been fully translated into a shift in attitudes about sexuality. Many experts do not fully advocate gender-neutral parenting, because in doing so, they confront the prospect of "advocating" homosexuality. While there continues to be debate about the relationship between gender nonconformity and homosexuality, in much popular consciousness, gay identity is linked with gender inversion. Furthermore, homosexuality remains stigmatized in the United States. While many people and institutions "have a strong interest in the dignified treatment of any gay people who may happen already to exist," there are few, if any, institutions—including feminist or lesbian, gay, bisexual, transgender organizations—that offer suggestions on how to raise people to be gay. As Eve Kosofsky Sedgwick proposed in her provocative essay, "How to Bring Your Kids Up Gay: The War on Effeminate boys," "The presiding asymmetry of value assignment between hetero and homo goes unchallenged everywhere. . . . On the other hand, the scope of institutions whose programmatic undertaking is to prevent the development of gay people is unimaginably large."[21] Child care experts continue to advise parents from within such normative institutions, including medicine, organized religion, and education.

Epilogue

I originally surveyed parenting advice in 2003 when my son was three years old. Nearly ten years later, has anything changed? As a mother, it is easier to find tools to challenge gender stereotypes with a near-teen than with a three-year-old. My partner and I and *Free to Be* laid a foundation that makes everyday conversations the best tool of all. But has the current parenting advice changed? A quick review of the most current advice suggests that it remains largely the same in content (although there is greater quantity), providing both some acceptance of gender-neural child rearing and a suggestion that boys playing with girls' toys is problematic and potentially linked to gay identity. In the last several years, numerous media stories have suggested that gender-neutral child rearing still has not been fully embraced. For example, several boys have been asked to leave preschool for hair that is "too long" and in violation of gendered dress codes, and last year the retail store J. Crew received much criticism for an ad that pictured a mother painting her young son's toenails his favorite color: pink.

Recently, however, there has been a proliferation of accounts about, media coverage of, and especially blogs by parents of young children, nearly all boys, who like girls' things (such as "Raising My Rainbow," "Accepting Dad," "Mother of Pink Boy"). These parents tell stories—agonizing, funny, and ultimately accepting—of boys who like pink, want to be princesses, wear their hair long, love glitter, or want to play with Barbies. My hunch is this proliferation has been made possible by the strides in lesbian and gay rights over the past decade and especially by the burgeoning transgender movement and its critiques of gender identity disorder in children.

While second-wave feminism, including the *Free to Be . . . You and Me* project, made much of this rethinking of gender possible, these contemporary parents and advocates of gender-nonconforming boys differ in several ways from second-wave feminists in their pursuit of transforming gender. First, they encourage and endorse the use of hypernormative feminine attire and toys intended for girls. Barbies, toy kitchens, pink tutus, and glittery heels are the material resources for parenting "gender creative" boys. Second-wave feminists eschewed such toys and clothing for the ways in which they objectified women and symbolized passivity, deference to men, docility, and consumerism. Second, parents of gender-creative children build their advocacy for children's gender freedom on an understanding that their children were, in the words of Lady Gaga, "born this way." This discourse is a defense of the personal attributes of their children and suggests that while gender may not align with one's body, it is not as socially constructed as second-wave feminists' argued it was. But these narratives of individual acceptance of particular children who were born gender creative do little to transform larger systems of gender inequality. In this new model, William can have a doll first and foremost because he was born wanting one, not because it will lead to him to be an involved coparent and to transform gender roles in the family and society. The latter is still the unfinished business of feminism.

Part Four

How Free Are We to Be?

Cultural Legacies and Critiques

Free to Be or Free to Buy?

PEGGY ORENSTEIN

The girl in the photograph looks at me with mock surprise, her mouth and eyes as round as the cotton-ball shaped "Jew-fro" she sports on her head. She's wearing a T-shirt with wide, bright-colored stripes tucked into cutoff denim shorts. Rainbow suspenders, à la Robin Williams in *Mork and Mindy*; toe socks complete the ensemble. God help me, that girl is me, circa 1978, at age seventeen, living in St. Louis Park, Minnesota, a suburb of Minneapolis. And that is my cast photo from a year spent touring with my high school's production of *Free to Be . . . You and Me*. We traveled to elementary schools, church basements, community events. I met my first "real" boyfriend when, during "It's All Right to Cry," everyone leaped off the stage to serenade the audience members (I sat on his lap and stroked his hair—he asked for my phone number). Two of our troupe married (years later, of course). Another (with whom I performed "Agatha Fry") became a songwriter known for penning powerful anthems for female artists: He cowrote Adele's hit song, "Someone Like You," and won a Grammy for the Dixie Chicks' "Not Ready to Make Nice."

And one of us—okay, I—became a somewhat prominent feminist writer.

That said, we were a little old for *Free to Be* to act as a crucible. I'm sure I saw the TV special when it came out, if only because I was a big Rosey Grier fan (a pro football player who wrote a book on *needlepoint?* What could be cooler?). But I was twelve at the time, more enamored with *That Girl*'s glamorous diamonds and rainbows than the pre-Raffi light strains of "Parents Are People."

I am, however, a product of the progressive, optimistic zeitgeist that created that show and made it a hit. Feminism nipped at the heels of my childhood. Title IX, the Equal Opportunity in Education Act, passed the summer I was ten, though it would take years to reach us. My junior high still had girls' and boys' gym. My male classmates were still assigned to wood and metal shop courses. We ladies were schooled in cooking (101 meals based on Campbell's tomato soup!), sewing

185

(I stitched a boss khaki jumpsuit) and—*oh yes, they did!*—the proper way to decorate our homes and give ourselves manicures.

In our other, more academic, classrooms, though, the times they were a-changin'. Our eighth-grade English teacher assigned us a biography of Lenny Bruce and the poetry of Joni Mitchell and Bob Dylan. In social studies, we read John Hersey's *Hiroshima* and debated the ethics of dropping the Bomb. Hard to imagine those things happening today, when learning is measured in percentiles and evolution is taught as a "theory."

By the time I entered high school, those classic feminine rites of passage had vanished, become instantly archaic. Still, the messages to girls about who we were and who we should be remained as weirdly mixed as a lime Jell-o parfait. The yearbook from my senior year features those *Free to Be* cast shots, for which we were told to strike silly poses. One boy pulled the strings of his hoodie tight across his face so that only a rather prominent nose protrudes; another stuck out his tongue, his fingers stretching his mouth wide; a third grins while hanging himself from a noose. The girls, however, are all doing a version of "cute": smiling with a teddy bear; twirling an index finger in a dimple; peeping coyly from behind a long braid. Maybe we could aspire to Joni Mitchell (and believe me, I tried), but Lenny Bruce? Forget about it. All those decades before the movie *Bridesmaids*, humor—broad humor, blue humor, noisy humor, exhibitionist humor, *angry* humor—remained the realm of guys, at least if you hoped to get a prom date.

IN MY TWENTIES AND THIRTIES, I put *Free to Be*—along with the toe socks, rainbow suspenders and bad hair—far, far behind me, though occasionally the jingling strains of the title song would bounce through my head. (How could they not? I had probably sung it a thousand times that year.) Then, at forty-one, I had a daughter. Naturally, I wanted—expected—her to feel totally "free to be." I didn't want her to believe either that some behavior or toy or profession was *not* for her sex or that it was mandatory for her sex. I wanted Daisy to be free to pick and choose the pieces of her identity; that was supposed to be the prerogative, the privilege, of her generation. For a while, it looked as if I were succeeding. Then she entered preschool—and oh, how the mighty fall.

Within a week, Thomas the Tank Engine had been shoved to the bottom of the toy box. She had memorized all the names and gown colors of the Disney princesses—I didn't even know what a Disney princess was. (With good reason—while Disney had long made movies based on fairy tales, they were not referred to as "princess" films until 2001, with the launch of what is now a twenty-six-thousand-plus product line that earns an annual five billion dollars globally.) Meanwhile, the supermarket checkout clerk would greet Daisy with, "Hi, Princess!" The nice lady at the drug store, offering her a free balloon, said, "I know which color you'll want," and handed her a pink one without asking. The pierced and tattooed waitress at our local breakfast joint presented her with "princess pancakes" (the menu had said "funny face pancakes"). Finally, the pediatric dentist—the one who charges double because she has a Pac-Man machine in the office—asked if Daisy wanted to get onto her princess chair so "I can sparkle your teeth."

"For God's sake," I snapped. "Do you have a princess drill, too?"

She looked at me like I was the wicked stepmother.

I wasn't sure how to interpret the tsunami of pink and pretty coming at us, but it was clear that something in the culture had changed—significantly—when I wasn't looking. Back in the prefeminist dark ages, when I was a child, I had availed myself of my mom's cast-off tiara now and again—royal play, after all, is as old as King Arthur's court. But I was clearly *playing*. I did not think I was—nor was I expected to be—a princess 24-7, 365 days a year for three years of my life, complete with a closet full of gowns. Nor was I dressed exclusively in pink. My clothes spanned the color spectrum (though my mom, like so many other mothers of blond, blue-eyed children of that era, dressed me largely in blue). It seemed that although girls were making huge strides on one hand—flooding the playing fields, rising to leadership positions in school, going to college in greater numbers than boys—the pressure for them to define themselves through their appearance (or, more particularly, through how they believe *others* evaluate their appearance) had not abated a whit. Rather, it had grown more intense and was skewing younger.

As Daisy grew older, I noticed how ubiquitous the Pepto-Bismol palette was, fusing primping and consumerism with femininity. The Girl Power cri de coeur of the 1990s—which was, in part, the legacy of *Free to Be . . . You and Me*—had morphed into something better termed "Girlz Power." (That "z" is often appended to the names of "sassy" toys like the sexualized Bratz dolls or the Razzbery Lips mall stores that host makeover birthday parties for preschoolers.) Whereas "girl power" celebrated ability over body, "girlz power" tells them that the pursuit of physical perfection is a source—maybe *the* source—of empowerment. It tells them that self-absorption, narcissism, and materialism are the same as self-confidence. Rather than free to *be*, its motto would be free to *buy*. Take the It's So Me! make-your-own messenger bag kit that Daisy received for her seventh birthday. Among the pink iron-on hearts, flowers, and stars were iron-on transfers that read "Brat" and "Spoiled."

"Why do they want me to put spoiled on my purse, Mom?" she asked.

Girlz Power is the impetus behind the recently released Monopoly Pink Boutique edition, which claims to be "All about the things girls love! Buy boutiques and malls, go on a shopping spree, pay your cell phone bill and get text and instant messages." Its success is why, according to the industry tracking group NPD, nearly half of six- to nine-year-old girls now say they wear lipstick or gloss "regularly" and the percentage of eight- to twelve-year-olds wearing eyeliner or mascara doubled between 2008 and 2010. It is behind Wal-Mart's recently released GEO Girl line of cosmetics, aimed at that age group (but don't worry, Mom, it's "eco-friendly!"). I don't know about you, but I don't want my third-grader missing the bus because her concealer isn't properly applied.

Maybe that would all be okay—all in good fun—if the numbers were trending in the right direction. But a survey of more than two thousand school-aged children found that the number of girls fretting excessively about their looks and weight actually rose between 2000 and 2006 (topping their concern about schoolwork), as did their reported stress levels and their rates of depression and suicide. The American Psychological Association links the emphasis on beauty and play sexiness among ever-younger girls with the pitfalls that most concern parents: negative body image, eating disorders, risky sexual behavior, depression, low self-esteem. A 2009 study found that the percentage of girls under twelve hospitalized with eating disorders had doubled.

AND YET, won't girls be girls? Isn't the interest in pink and pretty encoded in their DNA? (For the record, when color first came into the nursery in the early twentieth century, pink, as a pastel version of red, was considered the masculine hue, while blue, with its intimations of the Virgin Mary, was feminine.) *Free to Be* wanted us to believe that gender was a bunch of socially constructed hooey. These days, the pendulum has swung to the other extreme.

In reality, of course, the truth is more complicated. Preschoolers do often seem to be the gender police. That's partly because they don't understand anatomy the way we do: The whole penis-vagina thing doesn't hold a lot of sway with them. To a four-year-old, what makes you a girl is that you wear a dress. If you walk out of the room and come back in a suit, you're a boy. Understandably, that can make a person a little anxious. Psychologists call it "gender impermanence." They express their insecurity by acting out the extremes of gender their culture presents them (claiming that only men can be doctors though their mother is one; insisting on wearing a party dress every day for three months). So their rigidity is natural. But so is "neuroplasticity"—the idea that our inborn tendencies and traits (gender-bred or otherwise) are shaped by experience. A child's brain changes on a molecular level when she learns to walk or talk, laughs or cries. Every activity, every interaction strengthens some neural circuits at the expense of others—and the younger the child, the greater the effect. In that way, nurture *becomes* nature.

That means both that the new hypersegmentation of children's worlds has an innate appeal *and* that it's seriously unhealthy. The pink "no-boys-allowed" versions of Fisher-Price classics like the popcorn popper and the pull-toy phone discourage cross-play at precisely the time it is most important to find common ground. Playing at least some of the time with the opposite sex strengthens girls' spatial skills and improves boys' reading. And children who maintain their cross-sex friendships in early grade school tend to have better dating relationships as teens. It's pretty hard, though, to cultivate that "Friend Like You" when a girl is sitting in her pink dress in her pink room, reading *Pinkalicious*, and playing with her pink Magic 8 Ball.

IN SOME WAYS, then, the lessons of *Free to Be* are as relevant—perhaps even as radical—as ever. Yet sharing it with my daughter has been a mixed experience. Don't get me wrong—she enjoys it. And it makes me smile to hear how that jingly opening tune has insinuated itself into *her* head. But if the more things change, the more they remain the same, the reverse is true as well. We still face the challenge of raising children who can be individuals regardless of gender, race, sexuality, class, and religion yet can also celebrate who they are because of those things; how that challenge is expressed is different. So I found myself, as we listened, having to explain stereotypes to which Daisy had never been exposed and to which I didn't want her exposed: "Mom, what's a sissy?" "Mom, why won't they let that boy have a doll?" "Mom, why does that baby say girls can't keep secrets?" Her dad, I'm abashed to admit, does more housework than her mom, so I'm not sure what she gleaned from Carol Channing's rhyme. She knows moms who are scientists and dads who are bakers and parents of both sexes who stay home.

It may be that at least for some of us, the challenge centers less on the home front than on the popular culture: the marketers and media (new and old) who peddle new gender stereotypes to promote purchase "empowerment." Maybe William can have a doll now, but what happens if he wants to wear nail polish to soccer practice? What if Agatha Fry, after making her pie, pops on her flame-streaked helmet and rides to the park on her silver scooter only to be told by her friends—with their pink scooters and helmets—that hers are not for girls?

Perhaps it's time for a new version of Free to Be . . . You and Me—something equally catchy, equally fun, equally revolutionary. You could even keep some of the songs with a little tinkering ("Two mommies are people," anyone?). I wonder whether today's parents would embrace such a project.

As I mulled that over, I asked my daughter, now eight, what she thinks of Free to Be. "I like it," she answered. "I like the stories. Also the songs."

"And what would you tell someone the album is about?," I pressed.

She thought for a moment: "I guess that boys and girls aren't that different?"

I smiled. It's a start.

On Square Dancing and Title IX

MIRIAM PESKOWITZ

Square Dancing

It's 1972. While Marlo Thomas and her artsy friends were in New York City recording *Free to Be . . . You and Me*, I was eight years old and stuck in the gender culture of second grade at the Lee Avenue Elementary School on nearby Long Island. Our town was only forty minutes away by car (without traffic), but it seemed worlds away. Memory No. 1 is a conversation I had with my friend, Anthony, in which I am relieved to learn that boys are the ones who are supposed to ask girls out on dates. Anthony tells me this bit of information, having learned it at confraternity class, where the Catholic kids at my school went on Wednesday afternoons while the rest of us enjoyed a blissful extra hour of free play. The truth is, he could have learned it anywhere; it's not like it was a secret. He tells me this, I think, because the looming school square dance was making him very nervous. He was shy, as I was. I was relieved to take in what Anthony told me, because I couldn't imagine summoning the courage it would take if I had to ask someone out on a date, even though at age eight, dates seemed very far away.

Memory No. 2: our family's square-dancing story. That same year, Title IX, formally known as Title IX of the Education Amendments of 1972, was enacted by Congress, and over the next few years, it was implemented in public schools nationwide. The new law said that no one in the United States would be excluded from participation in any education program or any activity that received federal funds, nor would they be denied the benefits of such programs, nor be subject to discrimination within them. The legal language wasn't specifically about sports, but it came to be interpreted that way, especially because girls had long been excluded from and discriminated against in school sports programs.

Because public schools received taxpayer money, Title IX required them to figure out how to provide equal sports opportunities for boys and girls. It's a long process, one we're very much still in the process of working out, campus by campus. Forty years later, the vast majority of schools are still out of compliance with Title IX. But that's another story. Let's get back to the early 1970s, when *Free to Be* was released, and the principal and assistant principal at my elementary school had to meet with the phys ed teachers and come up with a Title IX plan.

My school was hardly a hotbed of radical feminism. It was decided that instead of offering girls an actual, fair chance to play baseball or soccer, the phys ed program would comply with the new law by offering square dancing to both girls and boys.

That's right. Square dancing.

I thought it was horrid and stupid and a terrible idea. That's because we were told that the square dance would begin with the boys walking over to the girls' side of the gym to choose their partners. I'm pretty sure that the congressional minds and feminist lobbyists behind Title IX did not have this scenario in mind when they drafted their legislation. In any case, the principal and the phys ed teachers thought it was a fine idea, and no one in my parochial town protested the situation. The schools in our neighborhood offered up religious prayers each day after having us salute the American flag and say the Pledge of Allegiance, which also didn't follow federal law. This was not the kind of place from which a feminist or liberal legal defense fund was going to emerge.

"What new form of gender torture is this?," I must have wondered as the square-dance music filled the gym. I was the daughter of a feminist mom, and I was shy, too. Couldn't they just give us some bats and balls and send us out to the fields to play? Were boys clamoring that they'd been excluded from square dancing for centuries and needed legal resolve? I think not. Luck was with me, though. Anthony and I arranged ahead of time that we would be partners for as long as the square-dance torture went on. We were both relieved.

I didn't tell my mom. She would have freaked, and that would have only made a bad situation worse.

She did learn about the square-dancing disaster four years later, when it was my brother's turn. Four years into Title IX, the school was still making do with square dancing. One evening at home, my soccer-playing little brother was stressed out and sad over what he faced the next day: the fearsome task of trotting over to the girls' side of the gym and summoning his courage to ask a girl to dance.

When my mom found out what was going on, she freaked. I told you she was predictable that way. Good thing I was already in junior high, where she had recently pitched a battle so I could take wood and mechanical shop in addition to home ec. By then I could appreciate her skills. In good activist form, seething with righteous anger, she wrote out her objections to the square-dancing scenario. The letter was addressed to the school principal, and the envelope was sent into school the next day. Knowing her, it's likely she followed up with a phone call before the principal even finished his morning coffee.

The officials at my school wouldn't give up their square-dancing solution to Title IX. But my mom was a force to be reckoned with. In response to her complaint, they agreed to change the rules for choosing square-dance partners. They didn't do anything truly progressive, like offer coed kickball, or just assign partners and take the asking part out of square dancing. Instead, they decided that boys and girls would take turns asking one another. They tiptoed around the gender of the "ask." One day boys asked girls. The next day, girls asked boys. On Day 3, boys and girls were sent into the middle of gym and told to just find themselves a partner. It was a small change, and maybe not one that made much sense, but it was a change, and that's important.

Making a feminist change is personal and intimate. It means putting yourself and your loved ones on the line. It can give you a feeling of headiness, a sense of accomplishment, and the glory of solidarity. It can also feel uncomfortable and unsettling and can make your palms sweat and your heart race. It can feel like something that separates you from your community. That said, when the will is there, many gender-based changes are actually quite easy to achieve. What's needed is a twofold willingness: (1) not to conform and (2) to express a positive vision and a process. When, as an adult, I wonder why women sometimes have a hard time making feminist change, I remember the second-grade girl I was, hoping just to get through the torture of square-dancing week without being the kid whose mom makes a big fuss.

Freedom

I first listened to *Free to Be* around the same time that my elementary school was torturing me with square dancing. I read the lyrics and sang along in my bedroom. The album signified to me everything that my small town wasn't; it let me know that not too far away was New York City—a place I could get to on the train (though not alone when I was eight). A whistle could blow, and we'd be off to a place where people knew about the new kind of world that my feminist mom and her friends sometimes talked about. I liked being reminded of that world. I wanted in.

Free to Be was about the intimate, personal things we do and are. About how they are entangled with sorry old ideas about what it means to act like a girl or a boy, a woman or a man. There were the things my mom complained about, like housework. There were the lessons that she and other well-meaning adults tried to convey, like *It's okay to be yourself.* They'd tell us that, even when every child every- where knows it isn't true, that it's really better to be just like everyone else so you'll fit in and so no one will tease you. *Free to Be* gave the well-meaning adult some cultural backup. It offered me the promise of freedom, which helped a great deal.

Free to Be told me that there was a way out of my boring and old- fashioned little town. There were people thinking about things that mattered, people being creative. It told me that like every kid who grows up different in a small community, if only I could survive, there'd be a way out.

In *Free to Be*, things get better. In "William's Doll," everyone teases William for his doll love. No one, kid or adult, understands. Then Grandma shows up. She cares, and she's wise. She not only brings William a doll but gives it to him in full view of everyone at the dinner table that night. She calms down William's dad, who's upset by the doll-boy equation. Grandma gets it. She advocates for William. Dad eventually gets on board, and so, too, do the other kids, whose taunts turn from sing-songy tease into admiration for William's "cool" new doll! Adults advocate, and the world's meanness disappears.

Visualize the TV special's opening sequence. The kids are on the merry-go-round, going round and round on their horses. We hear the *Free to Be* anthem: "Take my hand. Come with me, Where the children are free. Come with me, take my hand, And we'll live . . ." The actors' credits pop up, and when that's done, the kids and the horses break free of the carousel base and head happily into the setting sun. Didn't we all want to join the posse of painted horses running free?

Bubble Letters

Fast-forward thirty-three years, to 2005, and a classroom of first- and second-graders at my daughter's supposedly progressive elementary school. Each day starts with Choice Time. Every morning, as I get my daughter settled in her classroom, I notice that the girls gather around a table near the coat cubbies. The teacher has stacked a pile of personal-sized white boards and some colorful markers. The girls settle in to spend Choice Time chitchatting and writing their names on the white boards in big colorful bubble letters. Meanwhile, the boys hightail it to the back carpet, where several chess boards have been scattered, and set themselves up at games.

Girls = Bubble Letters
Boys = Chess

It doesn't take a rocket scientist to identify a problem here. Hearing me rant about this on the playground, several other parents try to convince me that scribbling bubble letters is equal to or even more valuable than playing chess; it's just what kids like to do. When I express my concerns to the teacher, she acts surprised. She assures me that in her twenty-odd years of teaching, no parent or student has ever complained that boys were starting their day with brainteasers while the girls began their day with the vacuousness of bubble letters. I'm not a rocket scientist, but I am trained in women's studies and feminist analysis. I decide to take a stand and explain to the teacher why it's wrong and what could be done to fix the situation. That's what most of us don't do. Even as adults, it's easier to rant to each other. To complain. When's the last time any of us saw something in need of fixing, something local and intimate and close, and went ahead and had the conversation or wrote the letter or in any small way took a stand and suggested a specific change? It's harder than it seems. Most of us run from any form of interpersonal conflict where we have to see the person the next day and the day after that.

There's another thing. When a gendered condition is confusing and pervasive, and when it persists for decades, it starts to seem normal. That's when we tend to go into denial and tell each other that it's just the way things are. That's what the teacher did. Her immediate response was to deny that there was a problem in her classroom. Then she claimed it was natural and positive. The girls *chose* to dabble in bubble letters. They were simply doing what they wanted to do. Likewise for the boys playing chess. All was good.

We cheat ourselves though, and we cheat the children, when we say that choices have nothing to do with the world they're being raised into. That's because very often all it takes to outsmart gender stereotypes is a little creative thinking and a little gumption. Why not assign all children random partners and projects? Why not plan the morning so all kids get a chance to try everything?

After I nudged again and again, the teacher eventually taught all the children in the classroom how to play chess. Some girls started to choose that as their morning activity. The next year, in third grade, when at recess the boys played football and the girls stood off to the side of the playground, my daughter knew what to do to change the situation, and I'm proud of her. She asked her classroom teacher for help getting in the game. The classroom teacher worked with the phys ed teacher to teach all the kids the rules of football and how to throw and catch. Then my daughter and some of the other girls started to play.

It doesn't take much to glide off the merry-go-round and create a little more freedom in the world. A few words and some courage, and you'll start to feel like you're on a wooden horse that just jumped the carousel and now runs on its own muscle and breath.

Growing up with Feminism/Feminism Growing Up

In 2007, I published *The Daring Book for Girls*, which spent fourteen weeks on the *New York Times* best seller lists and has been translated into Chinese, Dutch, German, Hebrew, Icelandic, and many other languages. Nearly two million copies of *The Daring Book* and its *Double-Daring* sequel now sit on bookshelves in girls' bedrooms everywhere. The book has turned up in places as culturally different as a Burger King Happy Meal, a PBS pledge special, and German talk shows about whether girls can play the traditional instrument called a didgeridoo, thanks to a controversial chapter added by the editor of the Australian edition.

Unlike *Free to Be*, which targeted kids of both sexes, the *Daring Book* was written especially for girls. Our publisher had already published

The Dangerous Book for Boys—and had already announced that girls didn't need a similar book for themselves. My coauthor and I proposed *The Daring Book for Girls* as an intervention, as a "Girls, too" project that was important and necessary. Boys were being encouraged by the hundreds of thousands to get outside and be adventurous. Girls needed to be in on that, too. The *Daring Book for Girls* didn't announce itself as a feminist intervention. Our feminist critics tended to stereotype the book as too girly, as all cartwheels and handclap games. Either those readers missed the pages where girls made wooden scooters, learned the joys of power tools, and wielded lacrosse sticks, or power drills and hammers have already become the new icons of girlhood.

The Daring Book for Girls was also my personal answer to my second-grade square dancing and to my daughter's second-grade bubble letters. It is, as Judith Warner noted in the *New York Times*, a paean to the 1970s, but it's not nostalgic, and here's the twist. The opening chapter is about basketball. The first paragraph tells the reader about Title IX and its promise that girls can play sports. In *The Daring Book for Girls*, girls can learn and do anything. They can read tide charts, change car tires, and hike, play softball, or have a backyard campout. Girls can make clubhouses and forts. A girl can read herself into the active world of female pirates, spies, and the lives of ancient queens and historical figures such as Abigail Adams. She can play in traditionally "girl" ways. She can play in traditionally "boy" ways. She can mix it up and play any way she chooses. The spirit behind *The Daring Book* is possibility. Across the pages strut girls and women who worked the Underground Railroad. Who ran cattle across the vast Oklahoma plains. Who won Nobel Prizes and who led the major nations of the world. Who spied for the Allies during World War II. Maybe it's the chance to create a big huge outdoor papier-mâché sculpture that will stand because you went to the hardware store and bought some wood, nails, and chicken wire as well as a canister of boat-quality sealant to protect it when you're done. Maybe it's reading inspirational stories of nineteenth-century cowgirls who set out because they wanted to tame horses and own land or leave behind abusive husbands. *The Daring Book* was written out of the belief that curiosity, knowledge, and skills matter for women and girls who want to make their mark on the world today.

The Daring Book isn't preachy and explicit about girlhood and feminism and gender, though the book's intention is certainly to expand what it means to be a girl, to make girlhood more interesting and curious, and to support those awesome girls who are already very daring. The TV version, if you will, would be a "do-it-yourself" show where I demonstrate making snow globes and papier-mâché bowls and offer five tips for basketball while chitchatting happily about the empowerment of women and girls.

Here's the thing about writing books for children. When we speak about feminism to adults, we tend to talk about negatives and things gone wrong, about dismal problems in need of urgent solutions. When we speak or write for children, we tend to skew positive and humorous. Books for children convey life lessons and wisdom with little irony or self-consciousness. If *Free to Be* had been written for adults, it would have been labeled sentimental or worse and ignored.

That's why a retrospective on *Free to Be* seems both helpful and hopeful now. Most of us still don't feel like we've been set free of our carousels. More than the usual feminist lists of problems and solutions, *Free to Be*'s cheeriness still has the power to make our hearts sing. It's a kind of feminism and a gender vision that is generous and likable and fun, all the things that feminism is usually accused of lacking. It is head and heart spun into a positive mix. Listening to it, watching, you feel your own strength building. You know that the world is much bigger and freer than you thought and that you have a place in that marvelous hugeness.

"William's Doll" and Me

KARL BRYANT

Unlike many kids of my generation, I didn't wear out a *Free to Be . . . You and Me* album on my kiddie record player, nor do I have a tattered and treasured copy of the book on a shelf or in a box somewhere. Granted, at ten years old when the record debuted in 1972, I was a little outside the target demographic (my eight-year-old brother was closer to the age range the stories spoke to). However, age aside, there were other reasons why the book and record might have been kept from my childhood home.

No, I didn't grow up in a conservative, overtly antifeminist household. My family held some at least vaguely left-leaning values, especially concerning "social issues." There were both Democrats and Republicans among us, but no Phyllis Schlaflys. Instead, most of us thought that "women's lib"—at least the egalitarian-focused liberal feminism with which we were most familiar—was reasonable, fair, and good. Along with this mild commitment to (or at least tolerance for) some forms of feminism, my extended family was not exactly a study in egregious gender stereotypes: my dad and uncles were soft-spoken, sometimes referred to as "gentle" men by my aunts, whereas the women on both sides of my family struck me as leaders rather than followers. What's more, my parents were well versed in postwar parenting approaches that touted a new answer to the question of what kids should be when they grow up ("anything as long as you're happy"), where children's self-actualization became the hallmark of successful parenting. We seemed like the kind of family where *Free to Be* would be welcomed in with open arms. Except that for many years my parents had received expert advice directing them away from many of the messages found in *Free to Be*.

Some of my earliest memories are of wanting to be a girl. I expressed this in many ways—through the toys I asked for, the clothes I dressed up in, the games I played, and my fantasies for the present and the future. My parents started out tolerating this as "just a phase," but when my desires, behaviors, and identifications hadn't diminished by the time I started kindergarten, any tolerance was overshadowed by deep concern. It turned out that by being born in Southern California in the early 1960s, I was within striking (and driving) distance of what was then a hotbed of research on "childhood gender variance." At the time, a small coterie of researchers and clinicians at UCLA were developing a new area of expertise by studying and treating children who did not conform to standard notions of what it meant to be boys and girls. Through a family friend, my parents learned about psychiatrist Richard Green, then a young rising star and already a leading figure in this new area.[1] We started seeing Dr. Green every other Saturday morning, where through play and talk therapy I would learn subtle and not-so-subtle lessons about how boys were really supposed to act. I didn't know it at the time, but I was part of a long-term study designed to track the adult outcomes of profound forms of childhood gender variance. Dr. Green (and others) wanted to know how boys like me turn out when we grow up, especially concerning adult sexual orientation and gender identity. Would I be homosexual, heterosexual, transsexual? A cross-dresser, bisexual, or something else altogether?

Whether or not my parents discussed *Free to Be*, it's a fair guess that they would have had some hesitations about introducing it into our household. One goal of the time spent at UCLA was that I more clearly and normatively experience and express myself *as a boy*. The kind of expert advice my parents were getting, and the journey they'd begun when they started somewhat ambivalently down a path that included therapy for their gender-nonconforming son, meant that the messages in *Free to Be* might not have been exactly what they were looking for.

Nonetheless, I did come into contact with *Free to Be*. It was too much a part of the social landscape of childhood in the United States during the 1970s for me to remain unaware of it for long. I don't remember exactly where or how I first came across *Free to Be*. Maybe we played the record and learned the songs while visiting my cousins. Maybe I saw the book when I was over at a friend's house. We might have even watched the television special at home when it first aired in 1974. But, one way or another, I did encounter it.

Free to Be is repeatedly described (in the original introduction, in retrospectives, and in news reports) as a collection of stories that replaces messages about what kids *should* be with messages about what they *could* be. It did this by challenging the gender stereotypes that were (and mostly still are) prevalent in the cultural products that saturate children's lives. As a result, *Free to Be* included many portrayals of gender-nonconforming girls and boys, men and women—that is, people doing things that aren't typically or traditionally associated with their presumed gender. In other words, people kind of like me! From mommies and daddies with unconventional occupations to athletic princesses who chose adventure over marriage, *Free to Be* often challenged gender stereotypes through individual expressions of ostensibly nontraditional genders.

"William's Doll" is one such story. Adapted in *Free to Be* from Charlotte Zolotow's 1972 children's book,[2] it introduces us to William, a young boy who wants a doll of his own to "hug and hold." For this, he is taunted by his older brother and other boys, who call him a "sissy" and a "jerk." William's father, also initially antidoll, has a solution: He gets William a slew of sports gear. It turns out that William excels at and enjoys all these "things a boy would love." Yet he still wants a doll. Finally, along comes William's grandmother, who buys him the doll, explaining to William's father that a doll is just fine for William, "'cause some day he is gonna be a father, too."

Not surprisingly, this was the one story in the collection that most caught my attention. As a gender-nonconforming child, I was able to identify in some ways with a character like William. It's true, I wasn't all that interested in having a *baby* doll that I could "wash and clean and dress and feed." What I really wanted was a doll I could dress up—maybe a Barbie (who was never going to show up in *Free to Be*). Even so, here was a boy who wanted a doll, said it out loud, was reprimanded for those desires, yet in the end prevailed and got what he was after all along. In some ways, it seemed like *William's Doll* was written specifically for kids like me!

William's Doll and *Free to Be* were just two examples of a larger phenomenon. When Marlo Thomas went looking for children's stories yet found few that met her expectations, she discovered firsthand something that feminist scholars were learning through more systematic inquiry: Existing children's books forcefully reinforced traditional, stereotypic notions of gender. The same year that *Free to Be* was first released, a now classic study found that portrayals in prizewinning children's picture books reinforced traditional gender stereotypes.[3] Boys and men were active, independent, self-confident leaders who found camaraderie in their male friendships. Girls and women, conversely, were passive, immobile, pleasing, helping, and reliant on men.

Men and boys were praised for achievement and cleverness; women and girls, for their attractiveness. Occupations and social roles also reflected traditional gender stereotypes. Grown women, for example, were universally portrayed as wives and mothers.

This overabundance of traditional representations inspired Marlo Thomas to conceive *Free to Be*; it inspired others as well to create representations for children that worked to undo gender stereotypes. Beginning in the early 1970s, feminist-inspired writers, illustrators, editors, and even entire presses created a miniboom of new "nonsexist" children's books.

Motivated in part by my own experiences reading *William's Doll*, a few years ago I carried out a systematic study of children's stories about gender nonconformity that were part of this boom of "nonsexist" literature produced in the wake of second-wave feminism. There was plenty for me to look at—books about athletic girls, dancing men, sportswriter moms, and of course boys who had (or wanted) dolls.[4] I found these books through indexes of nonsexist children's literature, the kinds of resources to which feminist educators, librarians, and parents might have turned.

Yet as I examined these books comprehensively, I also found that they tacitly reinforced traditional ideas about gender even as they tried to promote alternatives. This was especially the case in stories about boys, but the phenomenon also appeared in stories about girls. For example, girls' gender nonconformity was most often tolerated or valorized when it served others' interests. Girls' gender nonconformity was permitted or even welcomed when it served immediate and basic interests (for example, in wilderness stories where girls' skill at "men's work" like hunting could help keep people alive),[5] or in situations where there weren't enough boys on hand (for example, where a ball-playing girl could fill out a school baseball team).[6] Other times, a girl's competence at gender-nonconforming behaviors was used to shame or encourage boys to be more manly ("If a *girl* can do X, shouldn't you be able to, too?").[7]

By contrast, boys' gender nonconformity was tolerated or valorized when either the boy or the gender nonconformity itself was masculinized. For instance, in one story, a boy dancer's father can tolerate ballet because it "is certainly good exercise for athletes,"[8] and in the well-known *Oliver Button Is a Sissy*, Oliver's father (who strongly disapproves of his son's gender nonconformity) allows that Oliver can take dance lessons "especially for the exercise."[9] Other times, a boy's skill and success in masculine-coded endeavors, such as baseball, worked to offset his gender nonconformity, as in dancing.[10] And in some stories, the struggles associated with being a gender nonconformist (being teased, getting in fights) served to prove a character's masculinity, as illustrated when Doug, who is teased and physically bullied mercilessly for being a ballet dancer, fights back even when outnumbered and overpowered. When the ordeal ends, the bully ringleader tells Doug, "You're no sissy. You put up a good fight."[11]

The child characters in these stories had their own ways of explaining their gender nonconformity, too. Whereas girls overwhelmingly explained it as an active refusal of the traditional female role (and thus as their own refusal to adhere to traditional gender norms), boys sometimes explained their gender nonconformity as a "second choice" that they were forced to make because of their lack of skill, capacity, or competence to succeed at more "properly" gendered behaviors. Girls critiqued a gender system that they found to be fundamentally unfair (and where they saw traditional "women's roles" as limiting, silly, drudgery, or boring); boys used an individualist mode for understanding and explaining their gender nonconformity. The upshot was that none of these stories about boys included a critique of traditional notions of masculinity, whereas stories about girls overtly critiqued traditional notions of femininity.

While this meant that gender expectations themselves were being critiqued and expanded for girls and women, that critique and expansion came at a price: Things that had been stereotypically associated with women (such as housework or motherhood) were sometimes denigrated in the process of expanding other options for women; this denigration often happened in the process of attaching positive value to girls' and women's gender nonconformity. There was little room for girls to enjoy "girly" things or to have aspirations associated with traditional notions of femininity. This aspect of *Free to Be* and other "nonsexist" children's literature has sometimes been critiqued in a liberal humanist vein for the way that it limits girls' *choices*; however, such an approach also risks undervaluing what have traditionally been considered forms of "women's work" and "ways of being." And for boys and men, there was little in the way of critique at all; instead, gender-nonconforming behaviors were redefined as actually adhering to traditional gender expectations.

"William's Doll" shared some of the features of the broader body of children's literature I've been describing. In the story, we are repeatedly reassured of William's masculinity via the skill he exhibits and the pleasure he takes in sports as a boy; we're also assured, at least implicitly, of his heterosexuality via the future that is mapped out for him as a father. It's made clear that William is a "real" boy and will become a man. This same reassurance is also expressed in Free to Be's "Parents Are People," where we are told that mommies can be just about anything except "grandfathers . . . or daddies" and daddies can be anything except "grandmas . . . or mommies." Maybe not so surprisingly, then, my initial reactions to the story left me feeling uneasy. Why should William first have to take part in and enjoy "boy's stuff" like baseball, I asked myself, in order to get his doll? Later, I wondered why William's desire for a doll had to be justified by linking him with a future as a father, where William was at least tacitly heterosexualized.

My desire for a doll represented for me something completely different. It was but one example of a profound, pleasurable, and sometimes painful identification with girls, women, and femininity. There was very little, it seemed to me, suggesting any feminine identification in William. Instead, William fit into the trend in the broader nonsexist children's literature from the time where masculinity was shored up and traditional forms of femininity were implicitly devalued. As a decidedly and self-consciously feminine child who was deeply ashamed of this fact and yet also struggled somehow to be proud of it, I sensed that despite the promise conveyed in its title, "William's Doll" wasn't really about kids like me. In some respects, the story even felt like a betrayal.

So, in retrospect, do I believe that "William's Doll," Free to Be, and the broader set of related children's literature, should be seen as failures? No, I don't think so. During the 1970s, "William's Doll" and the Free to Be project as a whole were breaking new ground: They are examples of early, notable attempts to attach positive value to gender nonconformity through mass-produced cultural products. Up until that time, there had been virtually no conscious attempts in this realm to represent gender nonconformity except in pathologizing, stigmatizing, or otherwise denigrating terms. Today there are listservs and peer support groups for parents of gender-nonconforming children; advocacy organizations and annual conferences for transgender and gender-variant kids and their families; children's books with genderqueer characters; TV shows and news reports (sometimes sensationalist, sometimes sensitive) about kids with a range of gender identities; and so on—in other words, a host of representations and an emerging social support network for gender-nonconforming children. When *Free to Be* was first conceived, *none* of this existed. And in some ways, work like *Free to Be* helped pave the way for the kind of thinking, organizing, and advocating that exists today. Yet early "affirmative" representations of marginalized groups that have previously been negatively portrayed—or not portrayed at all—are up against a daunting and almost impossible task. There's an incredible burden on such representations. They animate the expectations or simply the hopes of people who may have never seen more than a hint of their true experiences represented. So maybe it's not surprising when such attempts sometimes fall short of such high expectations.

What's more, *William's Doll*, *Free to Be*, and similar books from this era are limited by the vision of social change that was at the heart of these stories. While the stories are very obviously about gender, the world they imagined was really about a "gender-blind" society, where equality and justice would be achieved largely through getting *beyond* gender. This perspective often meant that the notion of gender nonconformity (or even gender writ large) was effectively erased. For example, in a story about a group of girls who are creating a "tomboy" club, one mother objects that a tomboy club is "old-fashioned" because girls can do anything that boys can do.[12] This kind of narrative not only presumes a level of gender equity that did not yet exist in reality but also erases any notion of gender nonconformity or, worse, makes it seem retrograde. The impetus behind such visions of social change—to which many progressive-minded people still hold—was ultimately to make gender irrelevant so that it ceased to be a primary vector through which inequality was produced. Given this model for achieving equality, it's not surprising that *William's Doll* and other children's stories produced in a similar vein did not fully validate the lived experiences of being a gender-nonconforming child.

In writing this essay, I went back to the various versions of *William's Doll* and *Free to Be* and became familiar with them again for the first time in several years. In so doing, I've found myself reconciling with William, if not completely with "William's Doll." Yes, it's true that William is presented as a masculine boy who wants a doll. And yes, it's true that the final justification for getting the doll is linked to later fatherhood and presumptive heterosexuality. But it's the *grandmother* and the voice of the *author* presenting these perspectives, not William. When real-life kids digress from others' expectations about their presumed gender, it also often gets "narrated" as trivial, a phase, as somehow *not* about a profound sense of one's own gender identity or embodiment. But the fact that adults spin children's gender nonconformity in such ways doesn't tell us much at all about kids' interior lives or about the meanings and pleasures that they attach to their actions and desires. And maybe that's true of *William's Doll*, too. While others both torment William and provide explanations of who William is, there's very little that we hear directly from William. The one thing we do know is that William wants a doll and doesn't ever give up on that desire. That's a part of William's story well worth remembering and honoring today.

If we heard William speak today, maybe a different story would emerge. Instead of a world where gender no longer mattered, maybe gender and its relevance to our lives would be imagined in multiple forms and in ways that resist reproducing inequalities. Instead of reassurances of William's masculinity, maybe we'd hear about feminine identifications, including the pleasures and pains that are at the heart of so many people's complex gendered experiences. Certainly William still dreams of being "free to be," but perhaps in a slightly different cast and hue than the story written forty years ago.

When Michael Jackson Grew Up

A Mother's Reflections on Race, Pop Culture, and Self-Acceptance

DEESHA PHILYAW

This is not the essay I set out to write. The essay I set out to write was about how I was a year old when *Free to Be . . . You and Me* was first released in 1972 and didn't hear of it until I was an adult. And about how as a black girl growing up in the South, I really could have used *Free to Be*'s empowering messages because I didn't get the memo about being comfortable in my own skin and about how I could achieve anything. As a result, my world was small, my confidence slight. It took being a voracious reader and going away to college to make them larger and sturdier, respectively. I was going to write here about how despite this inauspicious beginning, despite a childhood in which family, friends, and my constant companion, TV, all taught me that white and lighter skin was better than my own brown skin, that straight, blond hair was preferable to my black-girl hair—how despite these roots, I have blossomed into a self-accepting, antiracist parent. I wanted to talk about how I've taught my daughters, ages seven and twelve, to reject cultural messages that promote whiteness as a beauty ideal, to reject supremacist lies, and to embrace their blackness. I planned to write about my kids' reactions when I showed them the clip from the *Free to Be* TV special featuring Michael Jackson singing "When We Grow Up" with Roberta Flack. I was all set to jot down in my notes that a-ha moment when my savvy middle-schooler grasped the irony of the lyrics "I like what I look like . . . We don't have to change at all," being sung by a young man who later changed his entire outward appearance and who in doing so seemed not to like himself very much at all.

Well, a funny thing happened on the way to writing *that* essay: My children flipped the script on me. Now, I could still write everything I mentioned, and technically it would be true. But the heart of it—my understanding of how my children have conceptualized race, pop culture, and self-acceptance—would have missed the mark.

What I didn't (and don't) want to debate here is whether or not

Michael Jackson's skin changes were attributed to vitiligo, as he claimed publicly. I also don't want to conjecture as to how he specifically felt about being black. According to some reports, he underwent surgery after surgery to remove all traces of resemblance to his abusive father. Regardless of his motivation, I can safely make the point that Michael Jackson didn't grow up to like what he looked like. He underwent dozens of appearance-altering procedures that had nothing to do with medical necessity—among them, rhinoplasty, cheek implants, and the remodeling of his jaw. In one of the last pictures taken of him prior to his death in June 2009, the outer ring of one of his ears was missing, likely the result of having the skin and cartilage removed to rebuild his nose after it was damaged by repeated surgeries.

Unlike me, my daughters are not beholden to the essay writer's burden of proof. They are free to call it the way they see it: "Michael Jackson was trying to turn himself white." Like others of their generation, they "discovered" Michael Jackson in the wake of his death. They were already familiar with Jackson 5 hits like "ABC," but I had to make the connection for them that the cute brown kid who sang lead on that song had grown up to become the white-looking, über-talented entertainer the world mourned. We looked at YouTube photo montages of Michael over the years, the Pepsi commercial mishap, his physical transformations. They danced along to *Michael Jackson: The Experience* on the Wii, and listened to *Thriller*, the best-selling album of all time, in heavy rotation in their dad's car in the months immediately following his death. They were almost as mesmerized by the album as I had been during the 1980s.

Our respective generations inform our experience of Michael Jackson. While my girls enjoy his music and showmanship, they aren't die-hard fans. They don't know the awesomeness and timelessness of the *Off the Wall* album. I was eight when it was released. *Thriller* came out three years later, and like a lot of girls, I fell in love with Michael Jackson because of it. I played that album nonstop, dancing madly to "Wanna Be Startin' Something," declared myself a PYT, and really, really wanted to be the lady in someone's life. When I was twelve, Michael claimed the King of Pop crown with his unforgettable performance—he moonwalked!—on the *Motown 25* television special. But when I was thirteen, *Purple Rain* came out, and in the ubiquitous "Prince or Michael Jackson?" debate, my hormonal heart belonged to His Purple Nastiness, Prince.

When Michael Jackson died in 2009, I was no longer crushing on Prince, but the best word to describe how I felt about Michael is *weary*. The changing, damaged face, the child abuse allegations made against him, the drugs—he was unrecognizable to me in a multitude of ways just at the moment of my children's discovery of him. They didn't know about the abuse charges or his excessive plastic surgeries. Pictures told the story of the latter; I haven't mentioned the former to them. Aside from knowing that he died of a drug overdose, their experience of Michael Jackson remains simple: He was an amazing singer and dancer.

Similarly, both my concept of race as informed by pop culture and my children's conceptualization are weighted by the times. Growing up in the 1970s and 1980s, television was king and a central focus of my life, but I never saw the *Free to Be* TV special. It didn't cross my path until the mid-1990s, when I was teaching elementary school. The song "Free to Be . . . You and Me" is mentioned in a book I read with my fifth-graders, *Bridge to Terabithia*. It's fitting, as the music teacher in the book who introduces the students to the song is an open-minded free spirit within an otherwise conservative community. But like that teacher, *Free to Be* was an idealistic voice in the wilderness and a mere drop in the bucket compared to the enormous vats of media Gen-Xers like me consumed through the late 1970s and 1980s. Media that did not affirm little black girls living in the South. My friends and I didn't just want to be one of Charlie's Angels; we had to be blond Farrah Fawcett's character. We wore white towels on our heads to make it so. TV show after TV show, white face after white face, the math was obvious: white = pretty and popular and funny and desirable and smart and rich and heroic. And I wasn't white.

In my real life, *Free to Be* also could not compete with a white boy in my sixth-grade gifted class referring to Brazil nuts as "nigger toes" and the subsequent silence of our white teacher, who was in earshot but who wouldn't make eye contact with me. It couldn't compete with comments like, "She's dark, but she's pretty," spoken by my mother to describe someone, as if "dark" and "pretty" didn't coexist in nature. My mother was not light-skinned herself, and this fact made her comment all the more confusing to me as a child. It saddened me as an adult.

My maternal grandmother came of age when the racial terrorism of lynching was an ever-present threat for southern blacks. My mother remembered drinking from "colored" water fountains. I attended elementary school in a predominantly white area of town, to which all the black students were bused from our predominantly black neighborhood. My mother and my grandmother taught me about racism's ugly manifestations. They taught me a kind of enemy-until-proven-friend racial wariness toward white people. They taught me history. Unfortunately, however, they also internalized some of the very racism they warned me against. They placed a premium on being white or light-skinned, neither of which I was. Unintentional lesson: It was not okay for a white person to see me as inferior, but it was okay to view myself that way. Heavy stuff for a kid.

So, yes, maybe I could have been helped along by the you're-wonderful-just-the-way-you-are message of *Free to Be*. Or maybe not. Maybe the other voices around me, however discordant, would have drowned out Michael Jackson and Roberta Flack.

With all that baggage in tow, I became a mother. I bought toys, books, and other media that would affirm and celebrate my daughters' skin color and natural hair. We read "colorized" children's classic stories in which the characters just happened to have brown skin, cornrows, and beads with braids. I didn't shy away from tough questions like, "If our ancestors are from Africa, how did we get here?" and "Is Grandma white?" (Their paternal grandmother is light-skinned.) Since birth, their friends have come in all colors. We talk about equality, social justice, and treating people the way we want to be treated.

Lest it sound like I'm patting myself on the back, I'll own up to some instances of what you might call a kind of antiracist parenting paranoia (though I prefer "hypervigilance," thank you). Like the time when one of my daughters declared that she wanted to be white when she grew up and then burst into tears when I told her she couldn't. I thought I was going to have a coronary until I got her to explain that she wanted to grow up and be brave like Leigh, our babysitter, who had mentioned that she didn't cry any more when she got her shots at the pediatrician. Leigh was a dead ringer for Britney Spears. Thus, my preschooler equated whiteness with being a teenager. Thankfully, that was easily cleared up.

Having learned nothing from that experience, I nearly crashed my car a few years later when one of my daughters announced that she would be happy to play with any of her new kindergarten classmates "except that brown girl"—the only other brown girl in the class. After having a mini-meltdown, I did what I should have done from the very beginning: Ask my child *why* she didn't want to play with that brown girl. Instead of "because she's brown" and thus bad (my fear of fears), I got, "Because she threw sand all over me in the sandbox."

My children don't play "Spot the Negro" (like I do) on TV shows and movies or in large, predominantly white group settings—counting the number of blacks, if any. After all, there's a generation between theirs and the one in which black people would stop what they were doing and run to the TV to see a black person, any black person, on it. My children don't have to settle for mass media affirmation crumbs. Yet I never wanted them to look to media to determine their self-worth in the first place. But I believed it could happen. I believe that, through a sort of osmosis, they could internalize messages about themselves— their appearance, their abilities—based not only on what they saw but what they didn't see. When you don't see yourself reflected in positive ways, you draw not-so-positive conclusions about yourself. It had happened to me.

So even though there are more black faces in the media my children consume than in the media I encountered when I was a child, I limit their media intake and closely monitor what they do watch. I've also supplemented their media "diet" with DVDs of shows from my past, like *Diff'rent Strokes* and *The Facts of Life*. It's telling that my children's experience of these shows also differs from mine as a child. Arnold makes them laugh out loud, and the show's adoption theme resonates because one of my children is adopted. That *Diff'rent Strokes* features a family created through *transracial* adoption specifically is not remarkable to my children; they personally know four such families. And yet the whiteness of Mr. Drummond and the blackness of Arnold and Willis defined the show for viewers like me in the late 1970s to mid-1980s when it ran.

If *Diff'rent Strokes* affirmed me because it featured kids who were brown like me, *The Facts of Life* went a step further. This show featured a black *girl*. Even though Tootie didn't have the best story lines, I still gravitated toward her. I once dreamed that Kim Fields, the actress who portrayed Tootie, lived next door to me; I awoke to disappointment that it was only a dream. (Incidentally, I also loved Fields's cheesy Michael Jackson fan song, "Dear Michael.") By contrast, as far as my kids are concerned, Tootie blends in with the rest of the Eastland girls. It's sex, not race, that draws them to this show. I had forgotten how many of the episodes dealt with sex, sexuality, and even issues like date rape. Hence the name, *The Facts of Life*.

With regard to contemporary pop culture, my kids were part of the backlash against Justin Bieber before it was fashionable. To my knowledge, there's no celebrity they've ever wanted to "be like." My middle-schooler once wrote a full-page rant about why "Parents of America!" were remiss in allowing their daughters to play with the sexualized Bratz line of dolls. So I should not be surprised that my kids' little-black-girl blues aren't like mine. But I wasn't at all prepared for their reaction to the "When We Grow Up" segment and our subsequent conversation about Michael Jackson and liking oneself.

The lyrics of "When We Grow Up" are the thoughts of two children resolving not to change so that they can remain friends "forever and ever and ever and ever and ever." They affirm that they like themselves and each other just the way they are. I asked my kids what they thought of the song and got a collective shrug. They were interested, though, in the respective ages of Michael Jackson and Roberta Flack. (For the record, they were sixteen and thirty-seven, respectively, both dressed as children.) Then came the observation (from my middle-schooler) that Michael Jackson had indeed changed himself when he'd grown up—and that he'd done so to appear white.

From my seven-year-old: "That's just stupid."

Middle-schooler: "It is stupid. He can change what's on the outside, but it's just a waste of money and time. He's still black deep down inside."

"What does that mean?," I asked. "To be black, deep down inside."

"It means it's your heritage," my middle-schooler said. "You can never change where your parents and your ancestors come from." Her younger sister nodded her head.

And there it was. My children associate blackness with heritage, genetics, place. While they are aware in age-appropriate ways of racism and supremacist ideas in media (also deemed "stupid"), they haven't absorbed media messages that to be black (or a girl) is undesirable or lesser or any number of stereotypes, as I did as a child. Overall, they are far less likely than I was to take cues from media about what's popular and acceptable. Their blackness isn't open for discussion or devaluing. It just is.

Roberta Flack, Michael Jackson, and Marlo Thomas during filming of *Free to Be* television special, 1974.

THIS REVELATION, in all its simplicity, effectively killed the essay I thought I was going to write, the one about how my children were fighting the good fight and winning in the battle for their self-image vis-à-vis pop culture. They are winning; they just don't see themselves in a battle. They are growing up behind a fortress of confidence and self-worth, and they are better armed than I ever was. I pray that this stronghold carries them through the upheaval of their teen years and beyond.

But I wonder about Michael Jackson's children. What did Michael teach them about self-acceptance and beauty? What did he teach them with his words, and did they see his personal behavior as belying those words? In their carefully guarded universe, did he allow his children to see photographs of him as a child? Did they ever ask him why he changed? Now that they are old enough to see for themselves (at least one of them is reportedly on Twitter), I wonder what they would make of seeing their father as a brown-skinned, fuller-nosed, Afro-ed teenager, singing about liking himself and not changing.

I believe that as a parent, I cannot teach my children to love their hair if I don't openly love mine. I can't teach them that their skin is neither a barrier nor a burden if I'm not comfortable in my own. I can't teach them a single thing about their worth and all they can achieve if I don't believe in my own worth and abilities as well as in theirs. When it comes to outcomes for our children, parents are powerful influencers.

But that power is not absolute. By seeking to empower children, *Free to Be* recognizes their free will. Children have the freedom to disregard their parents' teachings and go their own way, for better or for worse. I did. In some ways, Michael Jackson did. No doubt my kids will, too. Nevertheless, we're obligated as parents to equip our children, as best we know how, to thrive in the world. What my children teach me over and over again, however, is that they see the world through the lenses of their own experiences, not mine. Just as lynchings and "colored" water fountains were someone else's sepia-toned flashbacks in my childhood lens, the desire to "be white" because pop culture places a premium on whiteness is a foreign, "stupid" concept to my children. And I'm glad that they are just free to be.

Whose World Is This?

COURTNEY E. MARTIN

When I was young, my mom was more fun than other moms. She jumped on the trampoline and made snow angels with us, but she was still momlike when we needed her to be—rubbing her huge, soft hands over our bellies when they got butterflies. My dad was tall, and there was nothing I loved more than looking at the sidelines during one of my soccer games and seeing that he'd appeared in his navy blue suit with a big smile on his face to see my brother and me play. My mom worked, too, but she didn't wear a suit, and I had no idea what she did. Something involving lots of groups of women with permed hair and dangly earrings. Either my mom or Rita, the best babysitter in the world, was home with us after school, and then my dad came home a few hours later and let me stick the shoe trees in his fancy leather wingtips while he hung up his wrinkled suit.

When I was growing up in a middle-class home in a tree-lined neighborhood in Colorado Springs, Colorado, just as the 1980s turned into the 1990s, *Free to Be . . . You and Me* fit my worldview perfectly. I can still picture that super hot-pink album cover, the bubble letters dancing across the front in bright yellow, blue, and red; the cartoon kids of every color twirling, diving, and doing handstands. I would pull the big black record out of its sleeve, set it carefully on my dad's record player, and gently place the needle down. As the sound started to pour out of the fuzzy speakers, I'd lie back on the carpet and let my cat, Licorice, curl up on my tummy as I listened to Marlo and Diana all their friends tell me about the wonderful world we were living in.

Before I was both cursed and blessed with a complex social consciousness, I could wholeheartedly buy into the lyrics I heard. My favorite song was "Parents Are People," in part because there was nothing I loved more than my parents. And just like the song said, girls could do anything boys could do. I was clear on that much. When my brother, Chris, and I played together, his GI Joes and my Barbies sometimes met head-to-head on the shag carpet in the attic playroom. I once punched Chris in the face, just to see how it would feel. He never, ever hit me back. We both played basketball and soccer. We both went to Camp Shady Brook. Chris even took ballet when he heard that NFL football players were doing it.

Of course "William wants a doll." So did my best friend, Bennett. In fact, he was more scared then I was when my big brother created a haunted house using peeled grapes for eyeballs. Even when Bennett cried, I could tell him that it was okay, because that's what *Free to Be . . . You and Me* said:

> It's all right to feel things
> Though the feelings may be strange
> Feelings are such real things
> And they change and change and change.

It seemed as if the big message behind my *Free to Be . . . You and Me* record was that everyone was fine just the way they were. I liked that idea, even if it didn't seem true at school on Monday, where Jon-Jon, the Filipino kid who was adopted by Mr. Fielden, got teased a lot for being so quiet, and Aisha, the one black girl in the class, was definitely not invited to anyone's birthday parties or after-school clubs.

Once sixth grade rolled around, it suddenly seemed as if it really *wasn't* fine for people to be just the way they were. Megan Hinton and I showed up to the first day of school wearing matching white miniskirts with big purple flowers on them that we'd bought with our allowance at Contempo Casuals. The skirts were cut for teen girls with hips, so there were little puffs of material sticking out at our thighs. People were jealous nonetheless. Lauren Kinnee and Jenny Clark were suddenly *weird* because they still liked to play imaginary games on the playground and Sarah Chambler didn't even have a television so she had no idea what was going on. That was really *weird* too, not having a television. "Weird" had become our new favorite word.

Things got more complicated from there. By the early 1990s, when I was starting to brave junior high, *Free to Be . . . You and Me* became cruelly quaint. There was nothing freeing about identity at North Junior High School. To the contrary, everyone seemed incarcerated by their own insecure sense of who they *should* be. Gina, with her fan bangs and big hoop earrings, defined what it meant to be a popular Mexican girl—sweet until angry, than fierce as hell; focused on boys, not school. Justin, with his military crew cut and his Florida jerseys, reinforced the notion that white guys could escape ridicule only if they were stoic, arrogant, and, of course, athletic. Jen—who just a year before had been *weird*—now wore body suits and baggy jeans. She'd decided that she'd rather be sexy than overlooked.

I showed up on the first day of seventh grade wearing an Esprit pantsuit and by the end of the year I was decked out in green jeans and zip-up flannels. I tried to shed the goody-two-shoes image while retaining some of my sweet-girl charm. I would listen to hip-hop music, like everyone else, but I would still get good grades and go on extra credit field trips with the biology teacher. Megan became the Queen Bee, and I was her loyal sidekick. If she said it was important that we sneak out and TP Patrick's house, I was prepared to do so. If she wanted to put makeup on me before we went to the movies with a big group of jerks, I was grateful.

It felt as if everyone—at least everyone popular—was either a ring-leader or a follower, with nothing in between. There were all sorts of unspoken but indisputable rules about what was cool and what wasn't, what was allowed and what wasn't tolerated, and the worst thing was that they were always changing. At North Junior High, we were not free. We were bound by a complicated code of acceptable and unacceptable outfits, emotional expressions, interests, and de-sires. There were very few models of brave authenticity.

I do remember one. Rachel, whom we all called Snoopy, was—as I understand it now—transgendered, but as I understood it then, she was a girl who pretended to be a boy. Snoopy had short hair and a rattail, a puffy Raiders jacket, and black jeans that sagged well below her ass. She smashed her breasts down with multiple sports bras. She wore her gender-bending style with such organic bravado that it somehow passed under the radar of all the judges and juries posted up in the hallways of North Junior. Snoopy was Snoopy. She tran-scended categorization. In fact, Snoopy was even more free than the imaginary kids in *Free to Be . . . You and Me*, which promised, "In this land, every girl/Grows to be her own woman." In Colorado Springs in 1992, it turned out, some girls grew up to be their own men.

That may have been the first indication that I had outgrown *Free to Be . . . You and Me*. By this time, all the songs about boys and girls, men and women, daddies and mommies seemed ill fit for the world I was newly inhabiting, a world where some people didn't have daddies and where mommies, contrary to the lyrics of "Parents Are People," couldn't "be almost anything they want to be" as a consequence of various injustices, addictions, or plain bad luck. *Free to Be . . . You and Me*, more than anything, was about a new sort of feminist tolerance: Let everyone inhabit the roles they feel most at home in, regardless of tradition. That was still radical—even in the early 1990s. But it still wasn't enough.

Though I didn't have a fully formed systemic analysis at the time, I could look at my own parents' marriage and see the ways in which their ideals got trampled by institutions. My parents had promised one another they would coparent equally, yet when push came to shove, my dad's law firm would never allow—either in policy or by cultural permission—for the kind of flexibility he would need to follow through on his end of the deal. My mom's employer—herself—had been socialized to compromise, care take, problem solve. (I was aware by then that she was a clinical social worker and also the cofounder of the Rocky Mountain Women's Film Festival.) Thus began a common story that ended in a parenting arrangement that looked very similar to the one that both my mom and dad swore they wouldn't emulate. Sure, mommies *could* have jobs, but whether they were forced into them (in the case of lower-income arrangements) or out of them (in the case of higher-income arrangements) was never discussed on the album.

Not that *Free to Be* was anywhere near our radar screens at this point. Rather, the pervasive soundtrack at North Junior High, bumping down every hallway and animating every lunch break, was hip-hop. Dr. Dre's "Nuthin but a G Thang." Snoop Dog's "Gin and Juice." Common's "Used to Love H.E.R." In fact, Nas's "The World Is Yours"—one of my favorites at the time and to this day—could serve as sort of a grittier, grown-up version of some of *Free to Be . . . You and Me*'s themes. As Nas writes his rhymes, "all the words pass the margin," transcending tired rap conventions and stereotypes of who he—a boy from the Queensbridge housing project—should be. He glorifies himself as "the wild, golden child" and asks, "Whose world is this?" Answer: "The world is yours."

Josh, my boyfriend in eighth and ninth grades, a conundrum of characteristics himself, worshipped Nas's music. His record, *Illmatic*, was the first thing Josh ever bumped in his snow white Cadillac with red leather interior, gearshift on the steering wheel, Jesus piece around his neck. He also loved Enya and Nebraska football and sunflowers and *Lonesome Dove*, but Nas gave him a certain kind of insight into the experiences of minorities, like him, in the exalted big city. To be Hispanic in Colorado Springs was "ghetto"; to be black in Queens may have been "ghetto," but it was also romantic. Josh used to sneak out of his house and walk a couple of miles to mine in the middle of the night. I'd meet him in the backyard with a comforter and we'd kiss and talk till the sun came up, under the cover of the trampoline. The world was indeed ours.

It was audacious for Nas—the son of a jazz musician and a postal worker, a dropout by eighth grade—to claim the whole damn world was his. Every measurable indicator—educational attainment, economic class, family cohesion—told an entirely different story. But Nas was determined to tell his own story, to write his own life, to claim his own liberty through lyricism.

Hip-hop spoke to social injustice in a way that *Free to Be . . . You and Me* never could. Both were about individual expression, but hip-hop was steeped in the culture that created it, a time and place where the crack epidemic of the late 1970s and early 1980s had smoked out any delusion about the legacy of slavery. Yes, we are each born with the inalienable right to become who we are truly meant to be, *but many are swathed in poverty and prejudice from the beginning*. Hip-hop managed to glorify individual resilience in the face of institutional violence. It painted a picture of creative freedom but still acknowledged the enduring chains.

This was an especially compelling analysis to me as I ached through my adolescent years and my world got wider and wider. While my elementary school had been largely filled with white kids from economically secure families, my junior high and high schools were as diverse as the United States at large—barring a few peculiarities of our particular geographic context. Hip-hop was the music of the moment as well as a way into understanding the complicated demographic notes that were starting to fill my days. I started hanging out with boys who stood in circles and freestyled stories about their lives and dreams. Sometimes it felt like hip-hop was the only way into their largely disguised and machismo-protected inner lives.

Where hip-hop failed—miserably, over and over again—was gender. The freedom to transcend economic or racial categories was accompanied by an inverse rigidity and staleness when it came to gender roles. A sort of souped-up masculinity—defined by money, violence, and the bodies of beautiful women—dominated every song, every video, every album cover. That left girls like me—burgeoning feminists fascinated with suffering—between rap and a hard place. *Free to Be . . . You and Me* and my own dynamic mother had taught me that women deserved just as much mic time as the guys, and yet I mostly only heard the hyperbolic lyrics of half of my generation. There were a few shining exceptions, but they were inevitably marginalized. At house parties on Saturday nights, a girl might hope that her boyfriend would weave her name into a freestyle rhyme but never that she might add her own voice to the cipher.

Why? If mommies could be "ranchers, or poetry makers, or doctors or teachers, or cleaners or bakers," why couldn't teenage girls be lyricists? *Free to Be . . . You and Me* claimed that "some mommies drive taxis, or sing on TV," so why couldn't we rap? Was it our own internalized oppression that kept us from joining in? Were we socialized to be perfect girls, too afraid to screw up in front of the guys? Or was it just too hard to become what we'd never seen? That was what *Free to Be . . . You and Me* was all about—giving both boys and girls clear models of nontraditional masculinity and femininity, and by doing so, freeing them up to become whatever they were meant to become.

But it was a product of its time and place, a moment when even having a job was still seen as controversial (for higher-income women, that is) and the idea of a man doing housework was still a novelty. *Free to Be* was created for young children and was therefore understandably devoid of some of the sharp complexities that made other cultural critiques—like hip-hop—so salient a few decades later. And while the *Free to Be* cover's multicolored cartoon kids welcomed a diverse audience of listeners, the harmonious world imagined in the songs and stories didn't reflect the economic injustices and racial inequalities that shaped the lives of even the littlest boys and girls.

It turned out that neither the bright-pink cover of *Free to Be . . . You and Me* nor the cover of Nas's best-selling album, *Illmatic*—a hazy cityscape with Nas's sweet child face superimposed over it—really painted an accurate picture of life as I saw or experienced it. But no matter. Both encouraged me to write my own story anyway—and perhaps more important, to problematize any simple telling of someone else's story.

Free to Be . . . You and Me was like the primer on defying expectations, questioning received wisdom, being perpetually driven to ask, "But why has it always been that way? Does that way still work? Is that really true for everybody?" And hip-hop, in so many ways, was my advanced degree. It cultivated deep, abiding empathy in me for those who are still caught up in the enduring systemic injustices that shape so many lives. It fostered not pity but a kind of awe for the artistic response that oppression inspired in so many of my peers coming from homes without college guides and carpool schedules. And for this—my curiosity and my humility, my freedom and my empathy, my privilege and my conscience—I am eternally grateful.

Marlo and Me

BECKY FRIEDMAN

When I was growing up in the suburb of Chelmsford, Massachusetts, during the 1980s, Marlo Thomas came into my home every day and sang to me about the wonder of being a kid in the world, what it meant to be a good friend, and the possibilities that lay ahead for me as a girl and later a woman. I wish I could say that Marlo was a treasured babysitter or family friend—but she wasn't. I connected with Marlo and her spirited messages by playing *Free to Be . . . You and Me* on my brown and orange portable Fisher-Price record player.

That iconic vamp of the banjo, followed by the cheerful beat of the tambourine as the New Seekers sang the title song, sent me spinning around my bedroom: bare feet scuffing yellow carpet, long brown hair whipping around my face, and arms tossed high in the air as I sang along to the music—imagining that I was one of those kids in a land where the river runs free . . . where I was free to be *me*.

And wasn't I? My parents didn't enforce rigid gender roles for me and my brother. Okay, chores were gender-specific (the idea that I would touch the lawnmower sent a chill down my spine, while my brother was never asked to set the table), but my parents generally embraced any ideas I had about who I wanted to play with or what I wanted to play. One of my favorite pastimes was sorting baseball cards and playing Transformers with my best friend, Jeremy.

As a matter of fact, thanks to my mother, not a single Barbie doll could be found among my playthings. At the time, my mom joked to her adult friends that she didn't want her daughter to have a doll with a larger cup size than she had, but as I got older, I sensed there was something more to it than that. My mother herself was in a very traditional marriage, where classic gender roles played out in my parents' partnership: My mother cooked dinner for us every single night, while my father handled the finances. But, I wondered, was there an outspoken feminist lying beneath my mother's mild-mannered librarian exterior?

I revisited the topic with my mother when I was in college. I was writing a paper on the evolution of the Barbie doll and wanted to determine if my mom was keyed in to a set of firmly held feminist values or if she just got tired of buying all of those tiny outfits with the little rubber shoes that were always getting lost. "I didn't want you to have the idea that women were hard and plastic," she reflected back. "I wanted you to think of women as warm and soft and loving. Plus, those high heels that Barbie wore were murder on the Achilles." It turns out, I wasn't the only one who was absorbing the messages of *Free to Be . . . You and Me.* My mother had her own ideas about raising an independent young woman based on her own experiences: "Mommies are people," after all.

So when I turned on *Free to Be . . . You and Me,* it was already in many ways reflecting the values espoused by my parents at home. But at school? The boundaries were more rigid. I found myself struggling. It wasn't math or science or even gym that had me examining the expectations placed on a young girl of my age; it seemed far, far more important than that. It was recess.

Every day at recess, the boys would play tag and the girls would stand on a nearby log, imitating the cheerleader types we saw on television. The girls would never play tag. Because everyone knew girls weren't fast, right? I wanted so badly to be out there running with the boys! Hell, I wanted to be *faster* than the boys, but I was painfully aware of the unspoken law of the playground that bound me to that log and kept me questioning my emerging relationship with my own gender identity. I went back to *Free to Be . . . You and Me,* anxious to find an answer.

I found it in the story of Atalanta retold through Marlo's lens. Atalanta was a girl who wasn't interested in marrying a boy, she was interested in *beating* a boy in a race! If Atalanta was a fast girl, then maybe it was okay if I was, too. I'll never forget the day I stepped off of that log and onto that field. I ran my heart out and caught up to Jason, the fastest boy in third grade. I grabbed his shirt, took one look at his incredulous face, shrugged, and walked off the field. I'd proven it to myself, and that was all I needed.

Twenty years later, in 2009, when I was training for the marathon, I listened again to Marlo's story of Atalanta—this time to remind myself of the joy of running and the power of speed. On the back of my shirt, I ironed the letters "Follow *That Girl!*," the first of many attempts to keep the spirit of that album with me and capture the inspiration and motivation I've been able to derive from Marlo's work.

After college, I moved to San Francisco and started teaching at a private, progressive preschool staffed with teachers who were always in search of the latest in educational philosophies and teaching techniques and who were supported by parents with the resources to back up those explorations.

As a teacher, I sought to create a classroom where kids would thrive, develop the skills they needed for kindergarten, learn to treat to each other kindly, and get a sense of themselves as people in the world. The books on my bookshelf represented the spectrum of male and female roles; the dolls were not only varied in gender and color but also anatomically correct. The block corner had dress-up clothes nearby to encourage the melding of the traditional "boy" world and "girl" world. The art corner was home to big and active art projects, the kind that would cause the little boys in my class to come running. And at the listening center? My very own copy of Free to Be . . . You and Me, of course.

Anyone who has worked with preschoolers knows that traditional gender stereotypes inform most of what you see played out in a classroom. In general, little girls want to play princess in the dress-up corner, color with all of the colors in the crayon box, and spend hours negotiating play with their friends, all while subconsciously navigating the complex structures of the social world. Boys like to wrestle each other—constantly.

Conversely, even at that young age, you find kids who are already exceptions to the rule. There was a little boy in my class who came into the classroom every day and made a beeline to the dress-up corner to wrap himself in his favorite pink tutu. Never mind the death stares from the ballet-loving little girls anxious to do their twirls swathed in tulle, this little boy wore that tutu the entire day, every day—and damn if he didn't pull it off! However, even in this, a progressive preschool in one of the most progressive cities in the country, the parents were concerned. What business did a little boy have wearing a tutu? Did this mean he was gay? Or wanted to be a girl? Or did he just have an avant-garde sense of fashion? I scurried back to my apartment and looked frantically for my old copy of Free to Be . . . You and Me. For if ever there was a time to hear "William's Doll," this was it. I was reminded that kids were always struggling to communicate with adults without the benefit of an emotional language at their disposal. And I was reminded that it was the adult's job to understand what the child needed and to partner with other adults in that child's life to help him or her get it. And in Marlo's world, it could all be done through song! I was ready to talk to the parents and support that little boy. Over the span of several decades, Marlo had joined me in San Francisco, and she was still making her voice heard.

AFTER A FEW YEARS of teaching, I was ready for a change. After helping groups of four- and five-year-olds find their place in the world, I needed to find mine, too. And the only place I could think to look was New York City, a place with abundant opportunities shoved into shoebox-size apartments. I would pack up my life and move out of my comfort zone. I needed to find my way. Sound like a familiar story? Someone in my family thought so, and within weeks of my announcement, I received a package in the mail.

The package was from my father's youngest brother, my favorite uncle, Jack. When the package arrived, I eyed it warily: Uncle Jack has been known to send things that seem initially entertaining but are soon relegated to the back of my closet: things like the "boyfriend" pillow for me to cuddle up to when I'm single (the antifeminist implications of that gift can be explored at another time), a toaster that doubles as a radio, and an alarm clock that looks like a stick of dynamite.

What did Uncle Jack have up his sleeve this time? I slowly unwrapped the package and found myself with the DVDs of Marlo's groundbreaking television series, *That Girl*, with a handwritten note taped to the cover: *Required Viewing*.

Every night, as I sat in the middle of my rapidly emptying apartment, tossing things haphazardly into boxes, I'd pop a new episode of *That Girl* into the DVD player as a source of laughter, distraction, and comfort. I saw Ann Marie leave her secure nest in Brewster, New York, and move into an apartment all on her own. (Admittedly, I knew my future apartment would likely be half that size and crammed with a roommate but no matter, I still found it comforting.) I watched Marlo find romantic independence (Oh, Donald!) and career satisfaction, all on her own terms. Could I do that too? Here Marlo was again, stepping in as a guiding force in my transition to a new life.

What was it about *That Girl* that felt so personal and so inspirational to me? On the surface, it seems unlikely that a television show depicting a young woman in the 1960s, just escaping from under the thumb of her protective parents and living in a time when the rule

Marlo and Me   225

book for women was completely different, would appeal to a young woman in the here and now. But have things changed that much in the coming-of-age process? As I watched Ann Marie each night, something about her journey felt familiar.

Because even now I struggled with what everyone else's expectations for my gender were: I was hypersexualized by my male friends starting in middle school, reduced to a few distinct body parts while watching girls my age regain their power by sublimating their intelligence, their personalities, and their opinions in favor of a giggle and a bat of the eyelashes. I was eager to identify myself outside of my relationship to men—not as a "daughter" or a "girlfriend" but simply as a person—while maintaining my sense of femininity and uniqueness. And wasn't that exactly what Ann Marie was doing? Ann Marie was brave, curious, exuberant, and—most important—unapologetic. In one episode, she gets a part on a soap opera as a villain, a bad girl. When Donald's mother meets Ann Marie for the first time, a chill hangs in the air. It goes unexplained until it comes out that Donald's mother has been watching the soap opera and hasn't been able to separate Ann Marie from her character. This is played for laughs, but to me it said something real: For a young woman coming of age, the pressure was to be "good," but Ann Marie had the courage to be something more than just "good": She could be herself. As she found love, explored boundaries with her parents, and charged after her chosen career, Ann Marie defied gender stereotypes while still embracing what it meant to be a woman. Like her, I didn't want to be just any girl; I wanted to be *that* girl.

After a year and a half living and working in New York, I found my way into my dream job, working as a writer in children's educational television. Finally, I could blend the philosophy of my teaching days with the confidence and career focus of *That Girl*. The first program on which I worked, *Super Why!*, was an animated show aimed at teaching preschoolers how to read. Four little superheroes (with reading powers supplanting regular powers) would fly into classic fairy tales and rescue the heroes, often fracturing the stories in service of their mission. The Big Bad Wolf became the Small Good Wolf, the Princess ate the pea rather than sleeping on it, and so on.

My classroom had just expanded to include children from all over the country and all over the world. I was cognizant of the profound responsibility serving this larger audience implied. I felt responsible

for the messages we were sending children about who they could become, just like Marlo did when she created *Free to Be . . . You and Me.*
That's right, me and Marlo, just two regular ladies working on groundbreaking media for children across the globe.

I wanted to show girls that they could be powerful. I imagined that
little girls could watch Princess Presto wave her magic spelling wand
and imagine that they could be princesses *and* superheroes. I hoped
that girls would see Wonder Red and picture themselves as bad-ass
roller-skating superheroes who could wear cute pigtail-braids under
their skating helmets if the spirit moved them. As we created more
episodes, my (female!) boss focused on twisting hero/heroine-based
stories like *Rapunzel* and *George and the Dragon*, giving classic princesses
a new attitude. Rapunzel didn't need to wait around for that prince to
climb up her hair: She got out her ladder and climbed on down from
that tower! And George didn't need to waste his time battling that
dragon: Our princess was perfectly capable of rescuing herself! One of
my favorite episodes was an original story about a princess who (get
this!) wanted to be *funny.* Can a woman be *funny* and *feminine?* In our
story, she could. After all, Marlo's iconic persona has always blended
lighthearted humor with impeccable style.

As my career expanded, I wrote more and more until I was promoted to story editor. When I got word of this new boost, I raced back
home and watched the bonus features on my *That Girl* DVDs. I became
fixated on a documentary about who Marlo Thomas was off camera
and about her struggle to give women a voice. I remember a compelling interview where she talked about advocating to hire women
writers and a female story editor on *That Girl.* Marlo asserted the importance of having women telling women's stories. I felt a renewed
sense of importance and a deeper connection to her. She went from
being some far-off ideal to, well, a peer in some ways. Both of us were
women asserting ourselves in the big, bad (male-dominated) world of
television. She put her support behind a female story editor, and I *was*
a female story editor! I watched that documentary over and over, finding power in seeing myself in Marlo—and a little bit of Marlo in *me.*

Currently I'm working as a writer and story editor on a new animated show that is based on the legacy of Fred Rogers and will begin
airing on PBS in the fall of 2012. The show is aimed at young preschoolers who are expanding their social-emotional knowledge, the foundation for their future cognitive growth. Once again, I find myself faced

with the wonderful challenge of creating stories that will showcase the characters' strengths and sensitivities within the larger preschool population. Stories that children can watch and find themselves in one of the characters, whether they're a princess-loving girly-girl, a baseball-card-collecting boy, or a baseball-card-collecting girly-boy who wants to play tag while wearing his tutu. Each time I sit down in front of the empty page, I think about what I would have wanted for myself as a preschooler, what I wanted for my preschool students, and what I want for my future children. And what I want for them, quite simply, is this: a land where you and me are free to be.

Free to Be on West 80th Street

DOROTHY PITMAN HUGHES

During the years when *Free to Be . . . You and Me* was created, I was living in New York City and working to help bring about social change. I had moved from Georgia to New York in 1957, when I was nineteen years old, just as the civil rights movement was expanding the fight for racial equality, human rights, and social justice. I became involved in many community and political organizations, including the Congress of Racial Equality (CORE), where I worked as a fund-raiser. During the 1960s, two new movements were forming in Manhattan: the antiwar movement and the struggle for women's liberation. I later became involved in these movements as well.

In all my work as an activist, I have focused mainly on children. When I saw the toll taken by the Vietnam War, I was concerned not only about the soldiers but also about the children whose fathers were fighting and sacrificing their lives. Some of these kids did not even have a bed to sleep in. I immediately went to work to try to solve this problem. This involved me fully in the antiwar movement and in the fight for racially integrated child care in New York City.

Working women desperately needed child care services. I knew many women in the late 1960s and early 1970s who were working at any job they could get and leaving their children at home. The kids were not left totally by themselves. Children often were taking care of other children; twelve-year-olds were taking care of four-year-olds. Twelve-year-olds were doing the cooking, cleaning, and clothes washing—the things a full-grown person would do. They could do it, but I did not think it was safe to have children taking care of babies.

I started a child care center in my home, and when that proved too small, I started looking for a larger place. The only place that I could get with a big enough room that was also inexpensive was in the Endicott Hotel on West 81st Street. In the late 1960s, the Endicott was one of the largest welfare hotels, a place of ill repute. I remember that there were always winos sitting around out on the stoop. I got them to help clean up the street in front of the building. I persuaded them that they should create a better environment for the children in their community. Soon they started to hide whatever they were drinking when anyone from the center was on the street.

I did what I could to make this community-based center a success, even if I had to pick up furniture off the street to fill it. In fact, I got a call one morning that someone had seen me collecting furniture and wanted to donate ten thousand dollars to the center. A woman with young children who lived on the same street had seen what I was doing and wanted to help. I could offer her friendship and support in exchange for her contribution. Once we started building community support, we became more successful at fund-raising and eventually were able to buy our own space on West 80th Street. At first I used my income from singing in nightclubs to help pay for the center. Soon I was able to go from charging very little to offering free day care with city and state funding.

In addition to providing day care and child care services, we focused on job skills training for women and on providing food and housing resources for families. In 1972, the year the *Free to Be* album appeared, I organized a large group of children and day care workers to occupy New York City mayor John Lindsay's presidential campaign headquarters to protest his limitations for day care eligibility, which would have destroyed the racial and economic integration of our West 80th Street Day Care Center and similar centers.

When Gloria Steinem heard about what I was doing at the child care center, she came by to talk and write about us for *New York* magazine.[1] Through Gloria I was introduced to the larger women's movement. At that point, we thought we could make child care and children's welfare a part of the feminist movement and make social change.

Some people questioned me about why would I join the women's movement. I answered, "Why not?" I was a woman without human rights. An expression of sisterhood from Gloria resulted in more speaking engagements for us, and that helped create a decent income for my family. I also got more financial support for the day care center and youth program.

As Gloria and I spent time on the lecture circuit, I began looking differently at freedom. Sometimes when we would meet, there would be a focus on sexism or racism or classism, but what was special was our diversity, racially and economically. Gloria's attitude of sisterhood meant that she always gave me credit for my experience, ideas, and actions. Together, we definitely made a difference.

During those years when we concentrated on sexism, we created rap groups where we talked about our feelings and what we could do to change the way things were. In these rap groups, also known as consciousness-raising sessions, we shared our experiences and focused on how the personal was political. At one point, I attended the same rap session as Marlo Thomas, and it was there that I was introduced to her project, *Free to Be . . . You and Me*. When Marlo explained her children's album, I understood the need for it. From all my experiences caring for and working with children, I know that social change has to start with them. *Free to Be*'s message of respect, dignity, and equality for all people was the same message that Gloria and I spoke about when we traveled together.

Marlo saw a chance to show how education at the beginning of life could enlighten thousands. She knew that the diverse cast of performers that she chose would get the attention of all racial, ethnic, gender, and age groups. From the beginning, I did not consider *Free to Be . . . You and Me* to be an album or film for children only. Like the child care center, it was about a family-training program, a community-training program, and even a job-training program. It was a way to change adults' attitudes and improve their skills, too. For example, the song "Parents Are People" taught children and adults that all kinds of jobs are worthy of respect.

I was pleased when my community day care center on West 80th Street was selected as a location for filming the *Free to Be . . . You and Me* television show in 1974. Some children from our center were selected to participate in the children's group sessions during the filming. My daughter, Patrice, and some of her friends were included in a segment where children appeared in a group conversation about families. Sadly, there were cuts to the film. Some of the day care youth and their parents were upset that they all did not make it into the television show as it aired. But I believe that the children from the center gained personal confidence from listening to the record and from being filmed that day. They sat with Marlo and talked, and that setting surely had an impact on them. And I believe that my concerns about all forms of discrimination made it into the television show.

The children from the West 80th Street Day Care Center are in their early forties now, so I decided to reach out to those that I could find to see what they might remember from this time. Patrice Pitman Quinn, my daughter, is an actress and jazz singer who has lived in Beverly

Hills for twenty-five years. Lea Carla is also a singer in Los Angeles, and Jonathan Tipton Meyers is a producer. They all fondly remember the day care center as a place that had real diversity. They recall *Free to Be*'s message that "Sisters and Brothers" of all races can live together in harmony. They know that they heard that they were free to be whoever they wanted to be. When I asked Delethia Marvin what she remembered about *Free to Be*, she said, "I never felt that I was not loved. I was born in the 1960s, and growing up in the 1970s was about embracing yourself as a black person. I grew up in a multicultural environment at home where my mom is African American, and I had a white stepfather. In my early years, I was taught to be myself and to feel good in my own skin. My best friend was Jewish; we played well together. At West 80th Day Care Center, there seemed to be persons from all racial and cultural groups." The children depicted in *Free to Be . . . You and Me* showed an understanding of friendship, curiosity, love, and social, racial, and class difference. This is what we tried to create at the West 80th Street Day Care Center as well.

But I also had to deal with major differences between myself and some of the characters and stories in *Free to Be*. I saw a comparison to my experience in the story "Ladies First" and how it represented the privilege of the main character. Just like in our feminist rap sessions, sometimes I did not understand the white women's perspective. I remember silently thinking sometimes: *How can women complain about having wall-to-wall carpeting, staying home, caring for the children, and being put on what they called a pedestal while the man of the house worked and brought in the money?* I remember wishing that I could have wall-to-wall carpets. I wished I didn't have to work every day and sometimes nights. I wished I didn't have to worry about money. I would have liked to go shopping for my children and myself and not worry about spending more than fifty dollars. I had not fully understood why being male made any difference, because both white women and men determined economically what the people I represented were worth.

In my work as an activist, I was always facing questions of racism, sexism, or both at the same time. For example, in 1964, when I worked at CORE's national office, I organized a benefit at the newly built Lincoln Center with all proceeds going to CORE, yet my salary was a fraction of what my male coworker earned. I initially felt that the difference was the result of racism, because my coworker was a white male. Joining the feminist movement also helped me to understand what was happening to me as a woman and as a black woman. Wherever I worked for social, political, or community organizations or even individual domestic jobs, it was always a double whammy. I was always going to be black and a woman. It wasn't just racist stereotypes or images that resulted in my or any black woman's oppression. It was the combination of racial injustice, sexism, and economic inequality.

As I look around today, I'm shocked at the lack of respect shown to those who have spent years working to bring about equality. There are women who don't realize that we opened doors for them to be in corporate America, and there are African American men who are news correspondents who without us would not be working in the media yet seem not to know of our struggle. Watching *Free to Be . . . You and Me* again took me back to that time when we worked on what we could do to create social change. I believe we helped a generation of young people learn to be civil with each other and to respect the rights and dignity of others. *Free to Be . . . You and Me* is still appropriate for people, old and young, who missed it when it first came out. Its message of respect and equality still needs to be heard.

A Free Perspective

PATRICE QUINN

I am the middle daughter of Dorothy Pitman Hughes, an activist and community organizer (like President Obama, I like to say!). My mother was the founder of the West Side Community Alliance and the West 80th Street Day Care Center in New York City. From the age of six months until I went away on scholarship to prep school, I was educated and cared for through community-controlled day care, community schools, and after-school and summer programs organized and run by my mother and the people of our community.

My father was white, from Ireland; my mother, black, from the rural South. This made me a mixed-race African American, as were many of my classmates at our community schools. Interracial marriage was a real social taboo when my parents were married in 1963, and their relationship reflected the depth of commitment to the ideal of equality held by many people involved in the freedom movements at that time.

In our neighborhood in the middle of Manhattan, there were families who had emigrated from Puerto Rico, the Dominican Republic, and elsewhere in Latin America, Europe, and the Caribbean as well as white and black families from along the East Coast. We were an extremely diverse community—racially, ethnically, culturally, and economically. Within several blocks of my mother's day care center lived some of the wealthiest people in the country, including John Lennon and Yoko Ono. Among my classmates on the Upper West Side were children from every position on the economic spectrum—from "old money" rich to recipients of state welfare. Most of the families at the center, however, were poor and underserved. In fact, the day care facility, first started in our apartment, was located for several years in the basement of a local welfare hotel. Many of the teachers and organizers at the center were parents, family members, and neighbors. Some of the parents were single mothers, but many of the fathers were out of work.

In 1969, Gloria Steinem, a dear friend of my mother's and, like my mother, one of the lights in my life, wrote beautifully in *New York* magazine about my mother and her work. The article describes how a "neighborhood" became a "community" through the vision and organizational genius of a young black woman from the South who brought together people who had been strangers to one another in a troubled New York neighborhood (now one of its most exclusive) and got them to work under the simple, just proposal that our real needs should and could be met. To my mother's mind, the need for food, shelter, child care, education, meaningful work at fair wages, and relationships that acknowledge and affirm the truth and fullness our being were the birthright of all people and perfectly within our means to achieve.

If the day care and community center had had a motto, it could easily have been *Free to Be . . . You and Me*. These must be six of the most powerful words in the universe. They not only represent the consciousness promoted by the album and television special but also reflect the ideas behind the civil rights, Black Power, antipoverty, and women's movements of the 1960s and 1970s as well as the Occupy resistance movement spreading across the world today. Here, I offer my personal reflections on what it means to have grown up in an environment where the entire emphasis was on the importance of being "free to be."

As I peruse my Facebook news stream and talk with people about the most recent movement for freedom from corporate repression and domination, I am struck by how difficult it seems for many people to understand why economic parity is central to the very idea of freedom. Perhaps it relates to our society's general unwillingness to face and talk about the facts, the legacy, and the pervasiveness of its opposite: slavery. Over the years, I have often felt as if I were from another planet. And in a way, I am.

People often can feel and point to the mechanisms of their enslavement, whether it's rooted in racism, sexism, classism, consumerism, or other factors. But many people seem to have a harder time identifying what it means to be "free." I believe that you don't really know freedom until you experience it. And true freedom doesn't really exist if it's only for some and not for others. When I was growing up, I was lucky to get a good taste of freedom, thanks to my mother and other members of our community, and thanks to Gloria, Marlo Thomas, and the other producers of *Free to Be . . . You and Me* and the social movements that surrounded it.

At one point, one of the parents in the neighborhood enrolled her children in the day care center and donated more than a hundred thousand dollars toward its new, state-of-the-art building. I imagine that like many of the other parents—jobless black and brown men, women working three jobs a day for lunch money—she understood something about enslavement, whether by economic system or by patriarchal culture. I imagine that she also knew something about freedom. And I know that all of the parents, many of whom moved out of work as maids, laundresses, and other less desirable occupations and above the poverty line through the programs at the center, were willing to learn. This woman must have been familiar with the concepts of charity and philanthropy. But more important, she counted herself and her children as a true part of our community, and she saw particular value in sharing at this level and in the freedom of access, movement, and control it represented for everyone.

We children benefited from the love of all kinds of people. We had playdates and sleepovers with each other and attended meetings with our parents at each other's houses. I remember trying to explain fried green plantains to my mother: "They're like little round breads." I wanted her to cook me some Puerto Rican food. There were white children on welfare, black children of professors and Hollywood stars. Our teachers were grateful and proud to be teaching each one of us and could not have wished anything for us they wouldn't wish for their own, because we were their own.

From the perspective of a child who is enjoying hot meals (cooked by an amazing chef from Louisiana who was also the grandmother of at least six kids at the center), learning and playing beside her counterparts and watching all the parents work together, there is no case for any prejudices or "isms." They're simply impossible to sustain in the presence of this kind of intimacy. Many people still have difficulty understanding my mother's vision for literally raising children as "Sisters and Brothers" and for including families in the concept of child welfare, including economic empowerment as a necessary part of any service to the poor, and insisting that people's dignity need not be diminished in the process of having their needs met. Many laws regarding funding for community programs enforce separation on the basis of income.

This kind of diversity, coupled with community control, contributed greatly to the center's success in terms of the consciousness and the public good it produced. Real diversity fosters and respects open, agile minds. It notices and makes use of everyone's contributions and doesn't overlook them on the basis or race, sex, or class. It produces community members who do not derive their sense of security or power from numbers or sameness or even agreement. We lived, worked, and grew together and found our basis for communication with each other at a deeper level. The ground for our relationship was the fact that we were all there together.

This is why "Sisters and Brothers" is the most meaningful song to me from *Free to Be*. As children we listened and sang along with the Voices of East Harlem. They also sang, "Ain't We Lucky Being Everybody's Brother." A song has personal meaning to you when you realize you have a vested interest in those ideals and when you are a part of the work being done to fulfill those ideals. As children, we participated regularly in freedom marches on Washington, D.C. We stuffed envelopes inviting the community to rallies and meetings, and we attended them. We sang those songs with pride because we understood ourselves to be brothers and sisters, and with hope because we knew that not everyone shared the same understanding.

In 1974, we also participated in the filming of part of the *Free to Be . . . You and Me* television special at the center. I was one of the children present when Marlo Thomas interviewed a bunch of us about family life. We're all seated in a circle under a geodesic dome on the orange, carpeted floor in one of the classrooms at the center. Although you may glimpse me, and you may see the back of the cornrowed head of my best friend, Lisa (shaped into a crown by my Aunt Mary), and you can see the alert body of my other best friend, Lisa's brother Tino, legs akimbo, and his sweet, dimpled smile, you never hear from us.

I remember being distinctly aware that we were the only black children in the group. And when it was aired I felt disappointed, as most children would, at being excluded from the final version, whatever the reasons might be. I remember mentally trying to sort out whether those reasons had to do with what we said, how we said it, or what we looked like. I remember thinking that Tino's comments had been so lovely—about loving his sister—and that it might have been important for the viewing public to see this expression of familial love coming from a black boy. (This was before *The Cosby Show*, and, as the child of revolutionaries and as a future artist myself, my consciousness was already tuned toward getting these messages out.) I was proud of Tino and disappointed that the world would not hear what he said. But then I remember questioning whether our way of relating was somehow evidence of our not "deserving" to be a part of the larger society that generally rejected us and our parents.

While I benefited a lot from *Free to Be . . . You and Me*, I never for a second believed that it wasn't all right to cry or that parents weren't people, that girls couldn't run in races and boys couldn't play with dolls, or any of that stuff. To see the genius of performers like Rosey Grier, Roberta Flack, Diana Ross, Harry Belafonte, and Michael Jackson alongside that of Marlo and Alan Alda and Mel Brooks represented what my life really looked like. Since I was a child, I've regarded the *Free to Be* television special almost as a pamphlet or a calling card for our lifestyle and ideals at that time and place. *Hey, this is how we live, this is how we think. We want to include you and respect you and love you. We see you, we don't see things in you that don't exist and we see all the things in you that do.*

When we went outside our neighborhood, we had a sense that we were visiting the "outside" world and that we weren't necessarily beloved children in this world. In our community, our teachers and adults loved us, respected us, and listened to what we had to say. We understood to some degree how rare our situation was. I remember meeting children who had just moved to town and kids from other neighborhoods and being surprised at what appeared to be a lack of trust among them. They often had tendencies toward cheating, stealing, and fighting. They also had to deal with power struggles within their families, and sometimes they tried to impose those power struggles on us.

But we weren't raised with competition. We weren't raised to respect status or the status quo. We were allowed and encouraged to question authority, and we saw our parents and teachers do it every day. We also saw our parents tolerating and enjoying difference and always learning. And we were lucky to have special experiences like singing with Pete Seeger at a concert at Carnegie Hall. It sounds almost glamorous now, but back then, it was just one of the ways we participated in making a world we could live in.

We were taught to express ourselves, so it isn't surprising that many children from the community are now artists. I'm still in contact with many of them (including Erica Gimpel, Jonathan Tipton Meyers, and Leah-Carla Gordone, daughter of Pulitzer Prize–winning playwright

Charles Gordone) all of whom—like the creators of *Free to Be*—have committed their lives to serving, teaching, learning, and sharing the message of love and peace through the arts.

I took the whole production of *Free to Be* to heart, and I was inspired in every way by the presence of the performers in the show, especially their excellence. They let me know that it was possible to sing these kinds of songs, tell these stories. They were my models and teachers.

I've often been called a "utopian" or a "pollyanna." A friend of mine once said, "I don't think people really understand how serious and effective you are because you're so happy!" That's funny, because it's actually a serious thing to envision freedom for all people—even as it does put a smile on your face.

As a middle and high school teacher, I love to witness my students becoming friends with one another. My students often marvel at how "all" of them become friends, even the ones whom "no one" would ever have imagined they could "like." To me, that is the definition of freedom. It looks like love and appreciation for the endless and wonderous subtleties we find in the presence of others. Freedom is found in friendship, in the connection between "brothers and sisters." Freedom is a lack of rigidity that allows us to perceive subtleties and respond to them. I'm grateful for the freedoms I've uncovered in my life and equally grateful that I've known where to look for them. The commitment to other people's freedom has guaranteed my own.

One of my students asked me, "Ms. Quinn, do you really think you can dance and sing your way through life?" My answer: "I don't see why not."

Peace.

When We Grow Up

TREY MCINTYRE

The broadcast premiere of *Free to Be . . . You and Me* was so important to my family that we had to invent the VCR. We arranged a borrowed reel-to-reel video camera from my dad's school and set it up on a tripod across from the TV set in my mom's new third-floor apartment. We had to watch silently so that our voices wouldn't be recorded in the background, the first of many times I would watch that tape. From that first viewing, I watched it with a strange reverence. I didn't really know why it was important, but there was no mistaking that it was. *Free to Be*, I have come to understand, represented a cultural shift that extended ideas of progressive feminism and equality to child rearing, a lightning bolt shift away from the repressive images of the 1960s we see re-created on *Mad Men* today.

For me, though, there was no sudden shift. As a four-year-old boy, I was being carried along the fast-moving river of my parents' recent divorce, living and negotiating between two households, learning the clinical details that differentiated boys and girls, being afraid of the dark, meeting my mom's new husband and my dad's new girlfriend, and trying to get my mom to let me eat Count Chocula for breakfast. My mom was a pioneer of midwestern feminism, and I started kindergarten as one of the inaugural class at Emerson Open Alternative School, a bold experiment for Kansas at the time. We didn't sit at desks, there was no homework, I called my teachers by their first names, there were no grades, and I was responsible for creating and upholding my own goals. On the first day of school, we sang *Free to Be . . . You and Me* at an assembly, and I already knew all the words. The beginning of my life was steeped in the constant awareness of each person's unique value and the unrestricted potential that lies within every individual.

As I grew, however, I began to realize my unconscious conflict in relation to this progressive worldview. What began as surprised annoyance eventually became a disconnect with the world around me. The ideas of *Free to Be . . . You and Me* were simple and clear and easy for a four-year-old to understand. But real-life circumstances were proving contrary to the utopian world of equal possibility in which I was taught to believe. At times, it was difficult to for me to relate to my father, who was struggling with the traditional values that he had learned growing up in a small Kansas town and that didn't fit with the way the world was changing in the 1970s. Sometimes it felt as if I was learning to speak two different languages. In one home, I spoke the careful, balanced, and at times restrictive language of gender neutrality (where we said "humankind" instead of "mankind," and where women were "women," not "girls"). In my other home, more traditional language was the rule.

In other ways, too, I entered the world unequipped because I wasn't coming from the same mind-set that other kids seemed to have. I was a very creative and artistic kid, and even in my open alternative school, the expectation was that all boys should first and foremost excel at sports. The school provided ample opportunity for me to pursue any artistic endeavor that motivated me. I spent much of my time creating children's plays to perform for the younger grades, but when lunchtime came, I threw myself into playing soccer, wanting to be a part of things, but the other kids rejected me because I didn't excel at it. Even now, I hesitate to write about it because on some level, I believe the idea that I'm not a man if I can't kick a soccer ball.

Looking back, it is amazing to see the progress we have made as a society and how absurd some of the contrasts are between now and the 1970s, but it is also striking that people still feel the need to apologize for the revolutionary thinkers who helped make this kind of change possible. For example, I recently watched an episode of a television talk show where they were celebrating the changing role of women on television and specifically the contributions of Barbara Walters. Two female cohosts flanked the male cohost as they screened clips from the show's history, and they looked back in amazement at the fact that they once featured what were essentially Playboy Bunnies on the program. One of the female cohosts struggled mightily to find words to define the historical shift, and when backed into the corner because there was no other word for what she was getting at, she apologized before saying the word "feminism." And when the male cohost made a joke to keep the mood light, they bubbled and cooed for him. It was clear to me that many women in high positions still think it's necessary to downplay women's progress and make their presence palatable for the men in the room.

Today I am a ballet choreographer and run a dance company where I seek to provide a balanced, equitable, empowered environment for dancers as artists. The ballet world is perhaps one of the most fraught professions in our society because the gender imbalance is so insidious. When the dancer becomes professional, what begins as a child-adult relationship where the child is almost always silent in communication turns into an adult-adult relationship where that dynamic remains the same. There are more women than men who pursue this profession, so it is more competitive for them and the message to do only what they are told is reinforced every day. Traditional partnering and classical ballet storytelling is almost always the story of a fragile maiden and how she is saved by her prince.

In creating a dance company of my own, I thought I could create a new version of the utopia that had nurtured me as a child. The shocking consistency, however, is that even when handed the keys to an environment of equality, many of the female dancers in the company have had a hard time taking them. Even among dancers from more modern and progressive backgrounds, the impulse to be dutiful and silent instead of a confident and equal partner remains compelling. I have come to realize that the societal dynamic of an authoritarian male leader and a passive female follower is still a huge driving force in our culture. We live in a world where both men and women still struggle with achieving or even desiring equality in gender roles.

During the summer of 2009, my dance company, the Trey McIntyre Project, had the fortune of returning to the Jacob's Pillow Dance Festival in the Berkshires of Massachusetts to perform. During one of our performances there, the house manager let me know that actor Alan Alda was in the audience. I asked her to please invite him backstage afterward. Meeting him was like hearing a voice that was a part of me my whole life, but under the surface—like the way the leaves of a tree sound rustling outside your window. You don't always notice it for what it is, but it is always there, and it becomes a part of your experience. I know him, of course, for his iconic role on M*A*S*H and many other memorable performances, but it was the hole I burned through the Free to Be album that made his presence most felt in my life. When we met that evening, he was gracious and wonderful and surprised me with the fact that he was accompanied by another member of the creative team that had produced Free to Be, Letty Cottin Pogrebin. He was almost giddy to discover that I was, in his words, a "Free to Be kid."

It was a full-circle moment for me to be an adult, creating my own art, performing for the same people who had entertained me as a child and who had now come to watch my dance company as spectators.

The Free to Be Foundation has graciously allowed me to interpret the material of *Free to Be* as a dance piece that I will begin choreographing in the summer of 2012. In the meantime, I have cultivated the first seeds of the creation process by enlisting the help of costume designer and my longtime collaborator Andrea Lauer. Andrea was also a "*Free to Be* kid," and the album had a similarly important influence in her life. In fact, her college major focused on feminist studies and the social ramifications of clothing design, which led to her career path. As we began to conceive how the dancers in this piece will dress, we discussed our experiences with the *Free to Be . . . You and Me* material and its impact on our life experiences. As a result of these conversations, we plan to dress the six dancers in the hyperstructured, restrictive clothes of the 1960s, clothes that are starkly formal in contrast to the casual norms of today. Underneath that clothing, the dancers will wear the bright, eccentric patterns of the 1970s (inspired by the colorful drawings on the album cover) on unitards fabricated into shapes inspired by the cut of swimsuits. Over the course of the piece, the dancers will shed the more restrictive clothing to reveal a freer, truer, more childlike version of themselves. Eventually they must reconfigure back into their adult costume, but when the clothes are put back on, they no longer fit properly. The remainder of the piece is spent negotiating the grayer, more complicated path of human relationships, one that is neither utopian nor safely old-fashioned but actually multilayered and complicated.

I'm never quite sure what a piece is going to be choreographically until I'm in the studio, facing a group of dancers. But I plan to try to reconcile some of the conflicts I felt growing up with one set of ideals and then discovering the world to be very different. Although at first I had avoided the possibility of using the song "William's Doll," I was eventually drawn to the parts of it that it are filled with friction and substance. Therefore, the song is now at the forefront of the piece. I'm choreographing it as a trio for three men, dressed in the prescribed, structured suits of the 1960s, dancing with a competitive aggression that will serve in stark contrast to the open, nurturing message of the song. In another section I'm creating, using "Dudley Pippin and His No-Friend," one of the men breaks off and dances about his loneliness, exploring the depth and multifaceted experience of all people, regardless of how strongly they may hold on to a particular cultural identity. I am just beginning to conceptualize these different sections, but for each of them, the creative process is the same. I begin by setting up an idea somewhat like a puzzle, a way of being or a question that I want to explore; then I go into the studio and search for the answers. The more rich and multifaceted the questions, the more interesting, surprising, and truthful the process and outcome.

Making dance has always been the way I have figured out the complexity of the world. I get to play out what is incomplete in my life with other people in a kind of poetry that goes beyond words. It makes me realize that the greatest gift that I received from *Free to Be* is the understanding and belief in the boundless potential of human creativity. Prejudice can essentially be viewed as a lack of creativity—or a failure of imagination, an inability to see someone in any other capacity than a preconceived expectation of them. I know that regardless of my dancers' struggles with their roles in the world, I have the capacity to make room for and be hopeful for what is possible in them, to nurture what is undeveloped rather than limit them by what I think I might already know. The legacy of *Free to Be . . . You and Me* has been a tremendous blessing, and I continue to be enriched by an upbringing that was about openness, creation, and human potential.

The Price of Freedom

TAYLOE MCDONALD

I recently spent some time stomping around the woods, reflecting on how *Free to Be . . . You and Me* has influenced my life. I felt oddly troubled by this opportunity, and I couldn't put my finger on why. Somewhere between the dirt road and the marsh, the answer came to me. It's because living authentically in such a way that my outward behavior matches my deepest inner values has always come with a price; it has never been free. In no particular order, deciding to be true to myself has cost me nights of sleep, friendships, family relationships, church membership, my marriage, and my house. The poems and songs of *Free to Be . . . You and Me* were lighthearted and funny, but they planted the seed of the serious idea that everyone has the right to be fully human, to make their own choices, and to live out those choices with dignity. This seed eventually grew into a strong belief that has caused me all sorts of trouble. I can be whatever I like, as long as I'm willing to pay.

I grew up in the Bible Belt of the South in the 1980s, where the ethos of privilege and martyrdom lived together like odd housemates. Hypothetically, a woman could do whatever she wanted to do, but what woman would want to become a doctor or a business executive when it was the will of the Lord himself that she find her deepest satisfaction in a life of servitude to her husband and children? All the mothers I knew "stayed at home" and, despite their privileged position, seemed busy and irritable. Moms played tennis at the country club and ran errands. Dads went to work in the morning and drank scotch and soda when they came home. Girls cleared the table from the meal mom cooked every night. Boys took out the garbage once a week.

It was into this context that the message of *Free to Be . . . You and Me* sang out to me when I was a child. My mom and I belted out its soundtrack every morning on the way to school as it played from the stereo of her blue Dodge Maxivan. "A person should wear what he wants to / And not just what other folks say. / A person should do what she likes to / A person's a person that way." Though evidence for this kind of freedom was scarce, something about reciting these confident, rhyming words made my second-grade self feel stronger. I may have forgotten the message for a while, but it never left me: I get to be a person. Not someone else's idea of what kind of a person I should be, but a person who thinks for herself and does what she likes. There is a cost for such a life, but its alternative—to let others do my thinking for me—always costs me more.

My college experience offered many opportunities for learning this lesson. In 1993, while at the University of Florida, I broke family tradition and decided to—horrors!—drop out of my sorority. My grande dame of a grandmother insisted that my choice was "the worst decision of my life." I tried to help her understand that I wasn't interested in paying for membership in an organization so that I could have friends. There are many ways to pay for friends, though, and sorority dues were the least of them. I had just joined the church my older brother introduced me to as a freshman. Sunday morning guilt at church for Saturday night fun was what was really intolerable about sorority life. In hindsight, I see that what my grandmother wanted for me was to have the protection of a tribe that could offer enduring friendships through college and beyond. Her belief that a sorority was the best source for this kind of support was far more feminist than my own thinking at the time. The fear of disappointing God was stronger than the fear of disappointing my grandmother, so I left the sorority and became more deeply involved with church life.

At that church I was taught that the Bible held all the answers for how to be close to God. Who wouldn't want to be close to God? Also, I didn't want to piss him off. The Evangelical Free Church I attended focused on the exegetical study of scripture. We didn't read the Bible; we dissected it. We researched the original Hebrew and Greek in order to understand context and meaning. We cross-referenced other uses of the words we studied to glean what our personal Lord and Savior was trying to tell us. I actually believed that if we, as church congregants, could literally be on the same page, we would all be close to God and to each other. Peace, love, and harmony. Sigh. When we studied the role of women in the church, I questioned why we refer to the Holy Spirit exclusively as "he" since the Hebrew word is gender-neutral and the Greek word used in the New Testament was always feminine. My questions weren't appreciated.

More painful was when the wife of the pastor suggested I find a different church since I wasn't able to accept the teaching that women were to be submissive to their husbands. At a church wedding shower later that year, a friend of the pastor pointed me out to all the guests as the "enemy."

It would be easy to dismiss these losses as being well worth losing, but the approval of a matriarch and the protection of a rich social network are not small things for a twenty-year-old to lose. We have strong reasons to follow the pack; our ancient ancestors often died when ousted from their tribe.

Four years later, on graduation day from the university, I skipped my commencement to walk down a different aisle when I married a fellow member of that church. Five years later, after a very rough pregnancy, our son was born. I happily quit my job as a director at a not-for-profit organization so I could be a stay-at-home mother. I knew mothering would be difficult, but I also believed mothering was my spiritual calling—one especially ordained and blessed by God. I had no idea how utterly incompetent I would feel in this new role. Our son was chronically ill with ear infections and other mysterious health problems. Germs that other children quickly bounced back from would often land him in the hospital. My boy was suffering, and there wasn't a thing I could do about it. I felt utterly inept at my high-est calling.

Instead of questioning the traditional paradigm in which I was living, I redoubled my efforts and tried to be what I thought a good Christian wife and mother should be: active in the church, a maker of a beautiful home, a perennial bride who was sexually available when-ever my husband might need to "cleave" unto me. I wanted to create a home that would serve as a garden of clean, calm order, a refuge amid chaos. I planned nutritious and colorful meals and served them at a well-set table. I believed that if I could create a beautiful aesthetic and a warm atmosphere, the sharing and discussion of ideas with my husband would certainly follow. How I wish I had remembered Carol Channing's ditty about sharing the housework! Instead, to help me be happy and satisfied with housework, I subscribed to flylady. net, which sent emails several times a day with helpful reminders: Go clean the sink! Sort the laundry! Dust the horizontal surfaces! The logo of the site featured a rotund fairy-woman festooned in a lavender tutu with matching wand and wings. My house was clean, the meals were served, and issues—including the medication I had begun tak-ing for anxiety—were not discussed so much as commented on at that well-set table. "I don't know how I feel about having a medicated wife," my husband commented. It would be another eight years before I asked myself how I felt about being married to someone who would offer that response.

I still hung onto the myth of Happy Christian Womanhood. What I needed was another tribe. I joined MOPS, Mothers of Preschoolers, a ministry for stay-at-home mothers where groups of young mothers sat around tables decoupaged in various "Fruits of the Spirit" to discuss how to be better wives and mothers. We became better wives and mothers mostly by making crafts. I was at the grape table and was given a purple three-ring binder to keep my craft handouts in order. Women with advanced degrees from Ivy League universities were instructed on how to make bookmarks from wire and beads, a seven-layer terrarium in a mason jar, a replenishing facemask out of mayonnaise. We brainstormed ways of making our husbands feel loved when they came home from work. For a few hours I felt fairly satisfied that I had the gem idea of the day—greeting my husband as he came home from work with the song "For He's a Jolly Good Fellow" with our son on my hip; yet I couldn't figure out why I would weep when we prayed out loud and in unison for mothers who were lonely.

And so it went.

And the day came when the risk to remain tight in the bud became more painful than the risk it took to blossom.—ANAÏS NIN

You don't get a blossom without the messy business of gardening.

One Tuesday evening, after an exhausting day of mommying, a conversation with my husband turned into an argument, and for the first time in our marriage I screamed: "I am *so* goddamned angry!" And then I heard my voice telling him to leave.

For weeks I considered the proverbial soil of my life. I assessed the weed population in my marriage and considered plucking what little vegetation was left. I considered the costs and benefits of starting over against the costs of upkeep and fertilizer. In the end, I decided to keep working on my marriage. My husband and I started therapy together. I discarded my role as victim and began a journey to reclaim the power I had given away.

But what a mess gardening is. Loose soil spills to the ground, wedges between toes, stubbornly sticks underneath fingernails. The whole process is a baptism in mud. The mud is where I began the task of loss assessment. The illusions with which I had surrounded myself slowly began to unearth themselves. I was deeply unhappy and had been for a long, long time. I was deeply angry, too. I was furious that no one had told me about the deaths I'd die when I became a Christian Wife. A Mother. Who was this woman whose skin I was living in? When had she decided she was willing to die? And for what? For whom?

I spent the next five years answering these questions.

I decided that I would no longer be a member of an organization whose members collectively described themselves as cleaning implements used on dirty floors. I unsubscribed to the cleaning website and hired a house cleaner. To pay for the cost of the service, I invested in a good camera and started a business taking photographs of friends' children.

I experimented with printing and painting over the photos using a variety of media and techniques. At the art store, I discovered fat tubes of paint labeled "heavy body" in colors I'd never seen before—Pyrol, Deep Crimson Hue, Carmine. The possibilities that called out from walls lined entirely with paintbrushes mesmerized me. I had known for a long time that the metaphorical pansy that was my life had died, but what I didn't know yet was that the symbolic bud of the blossom would manifest in my paintings as a lush, scarlet poppy flower.

I decoupaged gold leaf onto my canvases and poured shiny resin over the lush blossoms. My paintings were picked up by one gallery, then another. Soon, I was represented by several galleries across the country and was working full time in the studio. Because I focused on process over product in making my art, two words were always on my mind: I wonder. This wonder led me to all kinds of exciting discoveries in my artwork and in every other area of my life.

I wonder what would happen if I used copper on my canvas? I wonder what I would believe if I wasn't afraid believing it would send me straight to hell? I wonder why I feel guilty all the time? The universe is filled with things to be curious about and offers so many ways to live out the possibilities. The canvas was a safe place to begin the questioning process, and it was only a matter of time before those questions would expand from the canvas to my beliefs and to my personal life.

After ten years of marriage, I announced that I could no longer attend the church where my husband was serving as the children's minister. It had become too painful to have the feminine divine ignored and dismissed every Sunday. We both tried to make space in our marriage for our differing beliefs, but that space grew to an unbridgeable chasm between us.

I realize that being free to be me means that I have a right to make a decision and also a right to change my mind. This past spring, after thirteen and a half years of marriage, I told my husband I wanted a divorce. When he wouldn't agree to move out of our home, I found a job, moved out, and bartered art for my divorce attorney's fees. For the first time in my life, I am living independently and autonomously. And this is why my healthy nine-year-old son and I listen to the *Free to Be . . . You and Me* soundtrack every morning on the way to school: Choosing to be fully human and fully alive is a sacred act of faith that undoubtedly costs a great deal. I want my son to know that though this freedom has a high price, it's one worth paying. A person's a person that way.

Lessons and Legacies—
You're Free to Be . . . a Champion

CHERYL KILODAVIS

When I speak at universities and organizations around the country about my children's book, *My Princess Boy* (published in 2010), I am doing so as an advocate for the acceptance of gender difference. I'm a published author, but I enjoy being introduced as a mom. Being a mom is hard. It involves a skillful balance between living your own authenticity (after years of finding it) and learning about who your child is becoming—supporting your child's innate being. We begin motherhood by planning all the great experiences that we hope will happen for our children: first steps, first friends, first crush—a lot of firsts, then college, life outside of the home, and extended family. Then, somewhere along the way, we are blindsided by the fact that our children become—well, they become themselves. We are proud but scared, happy but sad, secure but shocked.

When my younger son, Dyson, was almost two years old, he proclaimed he wanted to wear dresses and jewelry and proceeded to design and create his own fashions as well. He said, "I *am* a princess boy, Mommy!" Dyson's comfort with himself and his identity has always been supported and accepted by his brother and father. However, my journey toward acceptance has been a longer process.

I spent one full year modeling insensitive and bullying behavior in my house by redirecting Dyson away from all things pink and sparkly, including dolls and dress-up, and toward doing and playing with "boy" things. Then my older son, Dkobe, at just six years old, showed me what a true champion is by pulling me aside and stating, "Why can't you just let him be happy, Mom?" I will never forget that moment. My son's words forever changed my life and our family's lives. It became painfully obvious to me that the problem of accepting this young human spirit was mine. It was time for me to change my views and embark on a lifelong journey to acceptance. I figured I had about ten more years before my children left the nest, so I would need to begin the process immediately to truly accept their individuality.

I spent every possible evening with my dad at the ballpark, and I fell in love with professional basketball—only to quickly learn there weren't any professional girl teams. I played soccer, too. I was kicked out of ballet—"She's too rough!" yelled the teacher—and was bored in gymnastics.

I played cards and games with my mom all the time, perfecting my wins, hating my losses, and becoming a fierce competitor. I was a strong team player, a winner, and I often dreamed about a life as a strong woman, making money with a briefcase in hand. I loved business so much that in second grade, I ran a secret playground tutoring business at my Catholic school and took a cut on the connection. (It was really a cheating ring, but I believed I was connecting buyers [those bad at math] and sellers [those good at math].) I spent a day in the principal's office and missed out on some great class perks because of my secret "business." Neither the nuns and sisters nor my parents were impressed with my early stab at small-business ownership.

Although I was born with a business edge, I harbored a social justice tornado within me. I now look at pictures of myself sporting a tough fashion look but always crossing my hands over my heart, a gesture that I think showed my soft side and my caring, loving intentions. In all cases, I was, and still am, mixed. Not really biracial, mulatto, or one drop of black (as it was called back then) but mixed—in race, culture, and life. I never landed 100 percent on anything other than doing the right thing for unfortunate and unlucky people. Even as I gained access to the popular crowd through sports, looks, or grades, I remained in the middle and often defended the underdog. I didn't like that people were categorized and compartmentalized, that people were judged by looks, by abilities, by color. I hated when someone was treated badly, and I always risked my "coolness" for them. So in the middle I remained.

I can recall my first experience of not fitting in and how crushing it felt. I was four years old, and my dad had taken me to the park. I was on the swing set with a boy my age, and we were laughing at swinging so high. He asked me if I wanted to play with him, but before I could answer, his father whispered something in his ear. The boy turned to me and said, "What nationality are you?" I remember the big word and quickly got off the swing and ran to my dad. I said, "Daddy, quick, what nationality am I?" I recall itching for an answer, the right answer.

My Princess Boy is a nonfiction story about acceptance. The book is designed to spark and continue a dialogue about unconditional friendship—teaching children and adults how to embrace and support children for who they are and how they wish to look. Many times, parents have told me how much *My Princess Boy* reminds them of *Free to Be . . . You and Me*. While I did not grow up listening to *Free to Be*, Marlo Thomas and I seem to have been cut from the same cloth. Like Marlo, I too was frustrated when I could not find a book for my son (and she for her niece) that taught the positive side of being accepted for who you are. Both of our stories—and many stories in between—show how basic and fundamental levels of acceptance can change lives.

When I think back to my own childhood, I realize how much I would have learned from *Free to Be . . . You and Me*'s gentle wisdom. I was born in 1970, an only child of a Caucasian mother and African American father. On my mother's side, my grandpa was an orphan, and my grandma was the last child of nine; both were very poor. On my father's side, my grandfather had a farm in Alabama with no plumbing. Back in the Northwest, I was raised in a loving home with our fair share of challenges—racial, cultural, and financial. I always felt different. I was a light-skinned only child who went to a private Catholic school, although my parents weren't Catholic. I was one of three black students in the entire school and spent time at houses that were bigger than gymnasiums and were owned by wealthy families. My parents taught me about my black and white race and the depth of both cultures and to be proud of them. They also taught me how to live spiritually, tapping into a core of self-awareness and sensing what feels truly right and wrong. But the world I lived in seemed critical, abusive, and tough—one where my interests never quite measured up to those of other girls and boys around me, where choosing one religion appeared to exclude another, and where the quest to achieve financial security felt more like suffocation than a life-affirming goal.

As a little girl, I remember being strong, not liking dresses or dolls, and doing what the boys did—and often doing it better. I was the first girl on a city all-boys Little League baseball team (often pitched around so I wouldn't hit home runs), and I could tear apart and put back together a dirt bike like no other. Throughout my childhood, I rode my bike in the woods, doing wheelies on trails, climbing trees, and hating when it was time to go home. When we could afford it,

I badly wanted to play with this little boy; I enjoyed how we laughed together. We connected, just as kids innately do. My dad leaned over, looked me straight in the eyes, and said, "You go tell him you're an American." I ran back. "I'm an American." The father looked at me, then looked at his son and said, "No, she's a nigger." They left. I was four, and I had the wrong answer. My spirit was crushed.

My parents raised me as an independent self-starter; I heard daily that I was loved and could do and be anything—even when the neighborhood boys told me I couldn't. My mother and grandmother are still strong, independent women who show me that success is achievable (and tout clearly that it's a woman's success). My father taught me everything from loving others to good manners to checking the oil and fixing a spare tire. Society portrayed a different image for me, though. I remember feeling frustrated when reading books where the man was always the doctor and the woman was always the nurse. I never saw a book with a female CEO or company president, which was how I saw myself. (My fourth-grade drawings consistently depicted me wearing suits and carrying a briefcase.) I remember never seeing a positive, light-skinned, mixed African American and Caucasian female in any books I read. I was fourteen when *The Cosby Show* premiered, featuring Denise (portrayed by actress Lisa Bonet), who looked just like me. But I remember feeling deflated, thinking that I didn't have siblings like she did, or any doctors or lawyers in my family, like Bill Cosby's fictional family did. Looking back now, I believe that show introduced to me to the possibility of a multicolored family who could achieve anything—including two top married professionals.

Free to Be . . . You and Me has had an indirect impact on me as a mother and an author. With its strong themes of respect and acceptance, *Free to Be* helped set a foundation for *My Princess Boy* to be successfully received by adults who at one time also felt the wrath of being different. In many ways, the experiences of mothers like myself—and children like my son—are similar to the need for acceptance and pride that families felt back when Marlo Thomas's collaborators sang about everyone's right to be "free."

Despite the steps I've taken to accept gender expression, I can't ignore that I still feel a bit uncomfortable when *My Princess Boy* dresses in what we label as "female" clothing. If we are honest, we can agree that differences often cause some discomfort. We all have deep, often unconscious perceptions of how males and females should look and behave. The challenge is to ask ourselves why it bothers us and who it is hurting. Who decides how we can or should express ourselves? This is a journey we must all take—digging into our own self-awareness and reevaluating stereotypes and perceptions of what we think we believe. There is a real hypocrisy that allows a woman to wear jeans or pants while a man, shy of a kilt or beautiful robe in traditional ceremonies, is stigmatized and often has his sexuality questioned if he chooses to wear pretty clothes or dresses. Forty years ago, *Free to Be . . . You and Me* helped uncover the beauty of differences. Songs like "When We Grow Up" are still relevant because we haven't yet accepted people's differences. And we haven't yet accepted ourselves. We sing "I like what you look like, and you're nice small/We don't have to change at all." But so many of us do think we need to change to fit in.

I wrote *My Princess Boy* as a tool to help people like me, a recovering bully, begin a fundamental conversation about accepting diversity. From my experiences visiting preschool classrooms and talking with students, teachers, and parents, I've seen how quickly children can learn to coexist with each other. What is surprising is the swift change that happens around middle school, when kids make mean comments about those who are different—smaller, larger, a different color, living with different abilities. This is when real exclusion begins. Why? Because at this age, kids really begin imitating adults, and too often, the behavior we model is that of a bully. Let me ask you: How many of us have isolated someone at a staff meeting? How many of us have yelled at someone in a parking garage? How many of us have talked secretly about a teacher behind her back? Another family? And how many times were our children present during our outbursts on a "bad" day at home?

When our kids engage in cruel and bullying behavior, the outcome can be unthinkable—children taking their own lives because they are not accepted for who they are. We need to find ways to honor those people who are making positive change—doing something, saying something, speaking up for the bullied. They are saving lives right now, just as you read this. Champions aren't bystanders—they're willing to speak up and take risks for the greater good of acceptance. Have you been a champion today?

Epilogue

LAURA L. LOVETT

As much as historians love to tell stories of beginnings, one of the most important things about *Free to Be . . . You and Me* is that it has continued. The contributors to this book have described why they created *Free to Be*, how *Free to Be* influenced their lives, and how changing times have altered what we discover in those songs, stories, skits, and poems from the early 1970s. For some, the continued attraction of *Free to Be* may signal that the work of the women's movement remains unfinished; the pervasiveness of princess culture today makes the messages of *Free to Be* not only relevant but urgently needed. For others, the messages of acceptance and equity in *Free to Be* reflect a narrow focus on gender roles that has been reinterpreted by subsequent activists to keep up with new issues that complicate the old stories about "the pinks and the blues." Of course, there is room for both points of view; broadening the call for acceptance does not push aside gender but instead reveals how complexly gender is interwoven into our lives.

The creators of *Free to Be* understood this complexity, and they continued their efforts after 1974 when the television special premiered. Just as they had worked to overturn gender stereotypes that did not reflect reality during the early 1970s, later in the decade and into the 1980s, Marlo Thomas, Letty Cottin Pogrebin, and some new collaborators, including Christopher Cerf, turned to stereotypes about the family that disparaged every nontraditional family as a "broken family" and stigmatized children whose families did not fit the traditional ideal. *Free to Be . . . a Family* debuted as a record and a book in 1987, followed by an ABC television special that aired in 1988.[1]

Free to Be . . . a Family was developed during a time when the American family was used as a vehicle to debate social change. The American family has a history of being held up as a nostalgic icon that makes social reforms and new governmental policies seem less radical. So it is not surprising that in the 1970s, a particular ideal of the family was used as part of a backlash against the civil rights movement, the women's movement, and the antiwar movement. For instance, in 1977, James Dobson founded Focus on the Family to defend and promote the biblical institution of the family through a short radio program that aired primarily on Christian broadcast stations. Dobson and many others of that era believed that the family was in crisis because they held onto a patriarchal ideal of the family based on a male breadwinner and a dependent wife.[2]

Even though this ideal had been enshrined by the media throughout the 1950s and 1960s, this "Ozzie and Harriet" form of the family was in fact very short-lived and even at its peak only represented around 60 percent of American families.[3] It certainly did not extend to the quarter of the population living in poverty, who did not benefit from the postwar economic boom, and to many minority families, who were actively excluded from suburban communities. At the same time, the rising divorce rate meant that the number of female-headed households and the number of women in the workforce were increasing substantially.[4] Combined with the counterculture of the 1960s, economic change and high divorce rates in the 1970s created incredible anxiety among experts and legislators who worried about a perceived decline in parental authority and the absence of fathers from middle- and upper-class families.

Some of these policy makers associated absent fathers with poor and African American families, where female-headed households were more common. These officials feared that a decline in paternal involvement in white middle- and upper-class families meant that those families would soon resemble poor and African American families. In 1965, Daniel Patrick Moynihan, an assistant secretary of labor in the Kennedy and Johnson administrations, was charged with developing policies for the War on Poverty. In his resulting report, he famously labeled the African American family a "tangle of pathology," claiming that the legacies of slavery helped create African American families where women had too much authority. Moynihan argued that this trend toward matriarchy should be reversed by making African American men economic breadwinners and parental authorities. For Moynihan and others, reconstituting a patriarchal African American family was the solution to the rapidly increasing numbers of women-headed African American families living on welfare. While Moynihan may have been well intentioned in his contribution to the War on Poverty, his report contributed to the chorus that saw any deviation from the "traditional" family as a "broken" family.[5]

Marlo Thomas reading *Free to Be . . . a Family* in a classroom, 1987.

By 1980, this stigmatizing language of "broken families" resonated with and troubled Marlo Thomas, who became a stepmother when she married the popular television talk show host Phil Donahue, who had five children from a previous marriage. Soon after the completion of the first *Free to Be* television show, Marlo and Letty Cottin Pogrebin began to discuss their follow-up project with a group of researchers at the Carnegie Council on Children. Together they devised *Free to Be . . . a Family* as a direct response to the nuclear family norm.[6] In one of her 1977 reports on the project, Pogrebin explained, "If *Free to Be, You and Me* established the worth of the individual and the right of every person to fulfill her or his fullest potential, *Free to Be a Family* will celebrate 'together people'—people together in various combinations—and will recognize children's right to warm, loving support from diverse 'family' units, which are not necessarily or exclusively the two-parent nuclear household."[7] *Free to Be . . . a Family* sought to affirm a range of families and to decenter the definition of a traditional family to assure that all children felt as though they belonged to a whole, valued family unit. Pointedly noting that only about 7 percent of U.S. households featured a "traditional" family structure with a stay-at-home mother, an employed father, and their own biological children, Pogrebin remarked that the audience included "two-paycheck families, stepfamilies, blended families, extended families, adoptive families, single-parent families, foster families and others that have no label at all."[8] From this observation, Pogrebin, Thomas, and their collaborators created a new book to address a broad range of themes, including divorce, remarriage, adoption, sibling rivalry, and family life on welfare.

Like the first *Free to Be* project, *Free to Be . . . a Family* used songs, stories, and other vignettes to convey its message to adults and kids alike. They revisited sketches like the "Boy Meets Girl" dialogue, but this time audiences discovered that the baby boy was adopted. Adoption was also the topic for a comic book section that described the parents of Clark Kent, a.k.a. Superman, telling their son about his adoption after he landed in a field in a rocket ship from outer space. Some of the same authors and artists came back as the project developed during the 1980s under the editorial direction of Christopher Cerf, a producer from *Sesame Street*. Many new contributors helped flesh out the diverse themes of the second project. Norman Stiles, for instance, retold Cinderella by making the stepmother quite nice, while Emily Kingsley, a seasoned writer for *Sesame Street*, extended the book's embrace to include disability in her poem, "Like Me," in which a father and son talk about a new kid in school who has Down syndrome.

This was a brave vision. The first *Free to Be* volume included clear attempts to explore issues of race and class, (especially evident in Lucille Clifton's story, "Three Wishes"), but *Free to Be . . . a Family* went further in its effort to destigmatize the experience of receiving welfare benefits when it included the story "Doris Knows Everything," by Whoopi Goldberg. The story is extraordinary in how it reframes welfare myths being used to chip away at programs designed to benefit the poor. While Ronald Reagan would retell the myth of the Cadillac-driving "welfare queen" beginning in 1976, laying the groundwork for Bill Clinton's 1996 determination to "end welfare as we know it," Goldberg's piece intentionally destigmatized the receipt of government benefits. Visiting a welfare office, a little girl encounters someone who works at her school and a friend whose mother plays in the symphony and has been laid off. Unlike the narrative created by the all-knowing Doris, the woman helping with benefits did not "have fangs or warts or glasses," no one in the office ate out of garbage cans, and the building was not dark or cold. This literary attempt to humanize welfare recipients and normalize the receipt of benefits challenged the conservative effort to denigrate the welfare system and people who benefited from it, which had resulted in steep cuts to federal aid programs aimed at improving the lives of those in need.

Curiously, the *Free to Be . . . a Family* television show that aired the next year, in 1988, departed significantly from the material in the album and book. Instead of addressing tensions surrounding the American family as it was variously constructed and construed, the television show went global. Using the new technology of a live satellite link between television studios in the United States and the Soviet Union, the show created a global blended family between children in two rival nations in the ongoing Cold War. The children, who had previously become pen pals, were able to talk and laugh with each other and appeared along with a few performances and skits added in for variety. By so deliberately shifting the focus, the *Free to Be . . . a Family* television show, like *Free to Be . . . You and Me* and even the *Free to Be . . . a Family* book and album, was a product of its time. Nevertheless, both projects continued to speak to an American society struggling with issues of difference, equality, and acceptance at many levels ranging from the personal to the national to the international.

A quick Internet search "for the phrase "Free to Be" reveals how much has changed in the decades since original the *Free to Be* project began to reframe how we understand gender roles. For example, the Internet domain name Freetobeme.com belongs to a Canadian religious organization, New Direction for Life Ministries, whose website promises to help men and women who "experience unwanted same gender attractions."[9] Launched by an evangelical group that advocates bridge building between what it describes as a Christian community and those it defines as "outside the heterosexual mainstream," this website makes a targeted appeal for compassion and loving toleration from an audience that may not initially be so accepting.

A similar domain name, free-to-be.net, belongs to a Northern California–based organization that has been preaching abstinence from sexual activity until marriage to American youth since 1992 with the help of almost four million dollars in federal monies, including a U.S. Department of Health and Human Services grant credited with enabling the creation of the website.[10] The Northern California ACLU requested that this "Free to Be" organization discontinue its provision of "abstinence only" education in forty public school districts in Sonoma.[11]

Neither of these organizations had anything to do with the original *Free to Be* project, but both played on the idea of freedom, claimed a spirit of acceptance, and aimed to redefine social expectations. Accepting those who are not heterosexual as Christian allies or encouraging teenagers to defy stereotypes about permissive sexual behavior is tolerant but nonetheless promotes a conservative social ideal. These recent appropriations of "Free to Be" pit themselves against a "mainstream" that they define as problematic, a mainstream rooted in notions of freedom that they see as "excessive." This is a very different notion of freedom than what animated *Free to Be* during the 1970s. The original project countered gender and racial stereotypes that did not reflect the diversity of children's experiences and so limited their potential for development in a "free land"—a land that would embrace many kinds of gendered behavior. Today's "Free to Be" websites have shifted the focus away from gender roles (whether boys can cry or girls should work) to sex and sexuality. From a historical point of view, this shift reflects contemporary battles over "family values" that took place in the media and the culture at large in the decades following *Free to Be*'s debut.

The family values debate went national in 1992 when vice presidential candidate Dan Quayle took on the supposedly corrosive family ideals presented by the popular television show *Murphy Brown*, whose title character decided to have a child and raise him as a single mother. In his speech, Quayle linked this TVs show's influence to the "poverty of values" that he saw underlying the Los Angeles riots that took place the same year. For Quayle and other conservative commentators in the 1990s, the "traditional family" of the 1950s had been an antidote against both social and economic ills. Returning patriarchal authority to men as breadwinners would reestablish the "values" needed to maintain a stable society. Many advocates of "family values" believe them to be synonymous with what they understand to be Christian values. These advocates opposed abortion, premarital sex, cohabitation, feminism, and same-sex marriage. More recent opponents of same-sex marriage argue that the government should encourage traditional families composed of a male and a female parent because children in two-parent households are better off academically and psychologically than children raised by single mothers. Most research indicates that same-sex parents do as well as parents of the opposite sex when it comes to positive outcomes for their children. The idea that same-sex marriage will undermine traditional marriage and so increase the divorce rate constitutes a key political debate in the early twenty-first century.[12] As divergent as the issues in the family values debates may be, they all contribute to the salience and regulation of sexuality in our contemporary discussions.

The creators of *Free to Be* were aware of how issues of sexuality and gender intersected in their project, but during the 1970s, sexuality did not dominate public conversations that were still concerned with fighting fundamental stereotypes based on gender and race. Contemporary concern over sexuality does not mean that we are no longer fighting prejudices and discrimination based on gender, race, and disability. As the essays in this collection reveal—and as virtually any parent or school-age child can attest—gender stereotypes are still real and powerful influences in our society. Sex and sexuality happen to be at the forefront of political struggle right now, just as women's rights and the family took their place in the "culture wars" of the 1970s and 1980s. As such, advocacy of a rich spectrum of sexual expression joins the struggle against the "cultural sledgehammers" of polarized gender roles, racial stereotypes, and caricatures of disability. At their core, the *Free to Be* projects express more than claims for individual expression; they also reflect a continuing struggle to build a more just and equitable society. This is why *Free to Be . . . You and Me* remains both historically significant and socially relevant today.

Appendix

The Songs, Stories, and Skits of
Free to Be . . . You and Me
A Content Overview

LORI ROTSKOFF & LAURA L. LOVETT

EDITORS' NOTE: This section offers an alphabetized overview of many selections from *Free to Be . . . You and Me*. Nearly all of the pieces discussed here appeared on at least two of the original productions (album, book, and television special), and they represent the project's most popular and influential contributions. Space does not permit us to include many poems and stories added to the *Free to Be* book in 1974 or to reprint all the verses or complete song lyrics. For a comprehensive review—and for a full, multisensory experience of *Free to Be*'s content—there is no substitute for the original material.

"Atalanta"

"Atalanta," written by Betty Miles, is a feminist retelling of a Greek myth. Appearing in all three *Free to Be* productions, "Atalanta" combines a focus on women's athleticism with a strong statement about female independence.

In the original myth, Atalanta is left to die by her father because he wanted a son. She is suckled by a bear and raised by hunters. When she is rediscovered by her father, he wants her to marry. She agrees, but only if someone can beat her in a footrace. Melanion enters the race after getting help from the goddess Aphrodite, allowing him to win the race and marry Atalanta. In *Free to Be*'s retelling, Atalanta agrees to the race and spends her time training to run fast. A townsman named Young John enters the race, he and Atalanta turn out to be a good match, and the race ends in a tie. When they reach the finish line together, they become friends but do not marry. Instead they part, each to travel and see the world. "Perhaps they will marry and perhaps they will not. But one thing is for certain, they will live happily ever after," the story concludes.

"Atalanta" highlighted the conviction that girls should not be raised to view marriage as life's crowning achievement. Young John shares this vision, telling the king, "I could not possibly marry your daughter unless she wished to marry me."

The story also destigmatized women's athleticism and celebrated women's sports the same year that Title IX passed. This was a time when women staged a sit-in strike at the start of the New York City marathon to protest differential treatment for female athletes. In the 1970s, street harassment often made it difficult for women to run in public. (Sportswriter Gloria Auerbach commented that "on a visit to New York City in 1974, I armed myself against a barrage of verbal assaults every time I ran the five blocks to Central Park.")[1] In this context, Free to Be's "Atalanta" granted women and girls permission to run, to compete, and to win.

The story also depicts Atalanta as highly intelligent and studious. She is handy with tools, has a passion for science, and yearns to explore new places. One illustration contributed by printmaker Barbara Bascove depicts Atalanta peering toward the heavens through a telescope while surrounded by books, maps, and other objects symbolizing math and astronomy.

Some critics argue that "Atalanta" subtly puts pressure on girls to push themselves too far or to think that they must excel at both sports and school-work to feel good about themselves. (Judith Stadtman Tucker, for example, connects "Atalanta" to a trend of perfectionism among girls and young women in the wake of second-wave feminism and critiques the story for implying that girls must perform better than boys merely to be perceived as their equals.)[2] Many others, however, describe "Atalanta" as wholly positive and inspirational. In any case, the story has influenced countless girls' attitudes toward healthy competition, fitness, intellectual curiosity, and independence.

"Boy Meets Girl" and "Let's Hear It for Babies"

This comedic dialogue is one of the most popular sketches in the Free to Be trio. Cowritten by Peter Stone and Carl Reiner, the skit takes place in a hospital maternity ward and features two diapered newborns who share a wickedly adult sense of humor and a desire to find out what sex they are. In the script, the spoken parts are designated as "high voice" and "low voice"; on the audio and visual productions, they are voiced by Marlo Thomas and Mel Brooks. The conceit of the skit is that the audience "knows" the sex of each baby (by the actors' high and low voices) but the babies themselves do not.

"I'm a baby," proclaims the deep-voiced infant. "What do you think I am, a loaf of bread?," the high voice responds. Thus begins a conversation in which each baby tries to guess his or her sex as well as that of the other baby, using clues that adults (and probably older children) can recognize as typically gendered characteristics. The high-voiced baby assumes that the low-voiced baby is a girl because s/he is afraid of mice, while the low-voiced baby insists that the high-voiced baby is a boy because s/he is bald. The mystery is solved when a nurse comes to change their diapers, exposing the tell-all physical evidence. "Well, it sure goes to show you," the high voice declares, "you can't judge a book by its cover."

In the television special, the babies' parts are enacted by puppets created by the innovative puppeteer Wayland Flowers. Each puppet wears a yellow infant gown, color-coding the gender neutrality favored by those who shunned pink and blue as symbols of rigid gender norms. The skit dramatized the idea, endorsed by many second-wave feminists, that biology isn't destiny. By keeping the news of the babies' "real" sex a secret until the end, the skit toys with conventional stereotypes and proposes that listeners challenge them. And yet, the skit's gender politics were far less radical than those of some feminist theorists, who believed that children should be raised to appear in an androgynous manner throughout their youth. Included in this group were Cornell University psychologists Darryl and Sandra Lipsitz Bem, who taught their children to perceive biological sex and gender identity as distinctly separate entities. Even as the actors' knowing voice-overs questioned traditional notions of masculinity and femininity, they nonetheless reinscribed prevailing assumptions about two stable gender categories—"boys" and "girls"—presumed to be linked to one's biological sex.

The "Boy Meets Girl" skit, in turn, spawned a new segment for the TV special, "Let's Hear It for Babies," featuring a multiracial chorus of additional puppets, all wearing yellow gowns, who sing and dance in a musical revue recalling blockbuster Hollywood extravaganzas by Busby Berkeley during the 1930s and 1940s. The appearance of the puppets visually underscored the project's effort to imagine a more racially and ethnically inclusive and gender-blind society.

"Circle of Friends"

The *Free to Be* television special is filled with visual circles, suggesting intimacy and companionship. From the opening scene of a merry-go-round where the horses and children break out of a rotating caravan, metaphors of circular connection figure strongly throughout. For example, one scene features a conversation circle enclosed within a circular domed play structure with Marlo Thomas at the center. Rings or circles open the scene for "William's Doll," "Atalanta," and "Ladies First," while the anthem "Sisters and Brothers" is danced around an outdoor play ring.

These themes are reinforced by the song "Circle of Friends," composed as a round by Bruce Hart and Stephen Lawrence and sung by Kris Kristofferson, Rita Coolidge, Marlo Thomas, and others at the end of the show. Filmed in front of a brick fireplace with a coffee table brimming with food, glasses, and candles, it is a lovely moment meant to convey the importance of social bonds and supportive relationships. While at one point Marlo sings a lyric noting that "sometimes you live on the highway and sometimes you're flying above," the round's chorus reassuringly repeats that "love goes around in a circle, and friendship begun doesn't end."

"Don't Dress Your Cat in an Apron" and "My Dog Is a Plumber"

This pair of playful poems by Dan Greenburg are recited on the album by Billy De Wolfe and Dick Cavett, respectively. Using personified animals instead of people, both rhymes question norms about the things people should like, do, or wear on account of their sex. Greenburg's animal characters allowed him to create gender ambiguity more easily and in so doing to drive wedges between a person's sex, their gender roles, and what they do well.

For instance, in "My Dog Is a Plumber," being a plumber is assumed to make the dog male, but his desire to play with a play kitchen suggests that perhaps he could be a girl. In "Don't Dress Your Cat in an Apron," we are told not to dress a horse in a nightgown "just 'cause he can't stay awake" or to outfit a whale in galoshes "if he really prefers overshoes." Instead, we learn that it's okay to resist common expectations about outward appearances, dress, and personal comportment. The last stanza of this funny rhyme, in fact, offers a profound and serious message—one that has resonated with audiences in its simple, eloquent recognition of human individuality: "A person should wear what he wants to/And not just what other folks say./A person should do what she likes to/A person's a person that way."

"Dudley Pippin and the Principal"; "Dudley Pippin and His No-Friend"

Two "Dudley Pippin" stories were reproduced from an earlier children's book published in 1965 by Phil Ressner. The *Dudley Pippin* book sympathetically told the story of a young boy who is wrongly accused of tipping over a sand table at school. Voiced by Billy De Wolfe, Bobby Morse, and Marlo Thomas, the story is told as a lead-in to the song "It's All Right to Cry" on the album. Animated for the television special, "Dudley Pippin and the Principal" gives children—in this case a young boy—permission to express their emotions even when doing so leads to tears.

The second excerpt, omitted from the book and television special, "Dudley Pippin and His No-Friend," returns to the theme that boys and girls can play together. One of the *Free to Be* producers' goals was to give children tools to imagine how to get along, play, and work together, and this story represents that vision.

"Free to Be . . . You and Me" (Title Track)

Free to Be. . . . You and Me's title track, with music by Stephen Lawrence and lyrics by Bruce Hart, is among the most beloved songs on the album. The song was recorded by the British-based pop band the New Seekers, whose blend of rock and folk influences attracted many fans beginning in 1969. Their song "I'd Like to Teach the World to Sing" was a worldwide smash in 1971, and their spirited sound made them a perfect fit for a melody and lyrics bursting with optimism and promise.

"There's a land that I see/Where the children are free./And I say it ain't far/To this land, from where we are": In just four lines, children are invited to picture themselves within an imaginary space "not far" from their own community—a land where they can feel "free." Invited by the cheerful voices of trustworthy grown-ups ("Take my hand. Come with me . . ."), young listeners enter a metaphorical "green country" symbolized by a river and bounded by a "shining sea," a landscape that connects the beauty of nature with creativity and personal autonomy.

"Girl Land"

This song, featured on the album only, was written by Mary Rodgers and Bruce Hart and sung by Jack Cassidy and Shirley Jones. The song juxtaposes male and female attitudes about a fictional amusement park, Girl Land, where "good little girls pick up after the boys." In the voice of a carnival barker, Cassidy informs listeners that Girl Land is a place where "you go in a girl . . . and come out a lady." But he also laments that Girl Land is now closing. Jones's verses retort that the place was "never much fun" for girls.

As an allegory of the impact of feminism on traditional gender roles, "Girl

Land" represents the patriarchal ideal being dismantled by the women's movement. Like Rodgers's adaptation of the story "Ladies First," the cultural imperative of dressing and acting like a "lady" is figured as a sign of women's subordination in the broader society. Now that Girl Land has shut down, "good little girls" no longer have to grow into compliant "ladies" who will cater to men's wishes. Instead, the song implies, feminism has replaced this outmoded park with a place where "You'll do what you like/And be who you are." Once this new park is created, everyone will forget that Girl Land ever existed.

Some reviewers commented that the song's eerie-sounding tone and adult-oriented themes were not pitched at a level appropriate for most young listeners. It was not adapted for inclusion in the television special in 1974. Nonetheless, it exemplifies how *Free to Be*'s creators translated feminist ideas about outmoded feminine conventions into a musical medium.

"Glad to Have a Friend Like You"

Carol Hall wrote the words and lyrics to this song that expands on the theme of boys and girls playing happily together. Reversing pairs of rhyming names, "Jill and Bill," "Pearl and Earl," and "Peg and Greg" appear in verses that describe sets of fun activities for children, such as fishing, making up secret codes, and concocting ice cream out of snow.

The most important part of these shared activities, the song suggests, is that they create a solid friendship bond. The lyrics built on the central assumption among advocates of nonsexist child rearing that children "learn" gender equality by interacting with children of both sexes through imaginative play. Each refrain is followed by a chorus celebrating this bond: "Glad to have a friend like you/Fair and fun and skipping free/Glad to have a friend like you/And glad to just be me."

The song also struck a subtle anticonsumerist note. In contrast to advertisements endorsing commercialized toys that prescribed children's play experiences or, as in the case of Barbie dolls, encouraged purchases of additional fashion accessories, Hall's lyrics evoked "old-fashioned" moments of simple enjoyment and gave children ideas for designing their own play narratives using pillows, furniture, and other household objects.

"Helping"

This clever short song with music and lyrics by Shel Silverstein presents pairs of boys and girls working together to accomplish goals: "Agatha Fry helped make a pie, and Christopher John helped bake it/Christopher John helped mow the lawn, and Agatha Fry helped rake it." Sung by comedian Tom Smothers, half of the famous 1960s comedy team the Smothers Brothers, the joke is in the second pair of helpers: "Zachary Zugg took out the rug, and Jennifer Joy helped shake it./And Jennifer Joy she made a toy, and Zachary Zugg helped break it." The funny concluding line presents a kind of inverted moral, saying that even with the best of intentions, things don't always work out the way we want them to. And it's okay: "Some kind of help is the kind of help/That helping's all about./And some kind of help is the kind of help/We all can do without."

Shel Silverstein, known as "Uncle Shelby" in his children's author persona, has often reflected social concerns in his work. His books, including the best seller *The Giving Tree*, and his collections of poems, including *Where the Sidewalk Ends* and *A Light in the Attic*, are considered classic works for children.

"Housework"

Renowned lyricist Sheldon Harnick, famous for writing the lyrics to *Fiddler on the Roof*, penned the monologue "Housework" for the album. Recited by the inimitable Broadway actress Carol Channing, this fiercely funny thought piece also appeared in the book, illustrated with cartoon images of a woman dripping with sweat as she tries to keep up with the racing rate of the tasks at hand. The feminist message of the monologue was twofold. First, it argued that domestic work should not fall exclusively on women's shoulders. Its solution to the problem that housework is "just no fun" is to propose to listeners: "Little boys, little girls/If you want all the days of your lives/To seem sunny as summer weather/Make sure, when there's housework to do,/That you do it together." This conclusion offered a child-friendly version of Pat Mainardi's manifesto "The Politics of Housework," first published by the New York women's liberation group Redstockings in 1970. Mainardi sought to overturn sexist social arrangements that sanctioned men's relegation of domestic chores to women, asserting, "Participatory democracy begins at home."[3]

Second, the "Housework" piece functioned as a cultural critique and tool for media literacy. Beginning with a contemplative "You know, there are times when we happen to be/just sitting there quietly watching TV," Channing challenged the media's insistence, prevalent since the post–World War II era, that waxing floors and polishing furniture represented the pinnacle of fulfillment for housewives. Through a clever send-up of how television commercials sold both cleaning products *and* traditional gender roles, "Housework" encouraged young listeners (and their parents) to question advertisers' dubious claims that connected personal happiness with a clean, shiny home.

Many listeners enjoyed the "Housework" piece, and some may have been inspired by it to divide domestic tasks more evenly by gender. But in response to critical feedback, *Free to Be*'s creators decided not to include the vignette in the television special. Some listeners had criticized the poem for depicting domestic labor as drudgery and for inadvertently denigrating people who perform the necessary tasks of household work, either for themselves or for pay.

"It's All Right to Cry"

Carol Hall's music and lyrics to this song, inspired by the words of children themselves, encourage young listeners to express the full range of their emotions, whether sad, happy, or "down in the dumpy." In the book, the printed lyrics are surrounded by a rectangular montage of black-and-white photographs of men, women, and babies from a range of cultures, races, and backgrounds, each in the midst of what we might call a "sloppy cry." The largest photograph depicts a young adult basketball player sitting on a bench wiping a tear away with a jersey. The photographs from the montage appear in the television show as well.

The producers chose a memorable performer for this song on both the record and television special: Roosevelt "Rosey" Grier, well known by 1972 for many reasons. Once a star football player for the New York Giants, he later joined, in 1967, the formidable defense line for the Los Angeles Rams, where he remained for several years. His rendition of "It's All Right to Cry" conveyed the message that even someone who fits a stereotypical masculine "tough-guy" role at times needs to give voice to pain and sadness. (Incidentally, Grier also engaged in creative pursuits that ran counter to the standard macho image and even coauthored a 1973 book, *Rosey Grier's Needlepoint for Men*.)

Grier was also a competent musician. While some viewers of the TV special assumed that Grier was pretending to play the guitar, he was in fact strumming. Grier added a signature touch at the end of the song: an improvisational spoken line in which he soulfully reassures listeners, "It's all right to cry, little boy. I know some big boys that cry, too."

"Ladies First"

This story, written originally as a poem by Shel Silverstein and adapted by Mary Rodgers, appeared in all three of the *Free to Be* projects. Rodgers's adaptation took Silverstein's rhyme about pushy Pamela Purse who always needed to be first and reshaped the main character in ways that highlight her adherence to codes of feminine dress and comportment and expose her belief that her status as a "little lady" entitled her to special treatment that was actually demeaning.

Rodgers's version of the tale features an unnamed girl who embarks on a jungle expedition with a group of explorers. Voiced by Marlo Thomas, she calls herself as a "tender sweet young thing," wears perfume and white gloves, and speaks in a coquettish voice. Her endless refrain is "Ladies First." Soon enough, the explorers come upon a pack of hungry tigers who are happy to comply with her demand for "Ladies first, ladies first." The story ends, "And so she was. And mighty tasty, too."

In the feminist imagination that inspired this adaptation, the selfish protagonist—the main character offered up as an object lesson in ethical behavior—is cast as an ultrafeminine "little lady." The girl's appearance reinforces the flawed aspects of her inner character: her shallowness, impatience, and self-absorption. By asking for preferential treatment based on the false "power" derived from coquettish behavior, this "tender sweet young thing" got much worse than she bargained for. Her overconcern with beauty—she's given to "admiring herself in mirrors"—also marked her failure to develop an inner character based on more substantial things.[4]

"Parents Are People"

This song, with music and lyrics by Carol Hall, constructs a world of possibilities for children's imaginations, opening with the premise that "Mommies are people/People with children."[5] The same is true for daddies. Beginning the song from the point of view of the child, "When mommies were little/They used to be girls,/Like some of you,/But then they grew" imagines a world in which children truly matter, as do parents' work lives. Continuing to acknowledge the impact of children, parents are defined as women and men who are busy with children and paid work outside the home. A range of jobs and occupations are included for male and female parents. Whether they are playing cello, selling groceries, or seafaring, roles are insistently mixed up between the genders in terms of blue-collar and white-collar work and care work and creative work. People's labor and the time needed to do things (including being "busy with children and things that they do") are affirmed and celebrated.

The song was performed by Marlo Thomas and Harry Belafonte on the album and television special. Visual references to the range of possible jobs are extended in the television show. The television montages repeatedly show the paired singers. For example, Thomas as a police officer stops Belafonte driving a cab, but the roles are reversed in a later vignette. Beyond Hall's working-class positions, such as welders, the television segment added an image of hoboes as parents, with the two actors dressed in ragged clothes and smudged faces, as well as upscale professionals pushing baby carriages. All of these scenarios for parents are played by a singing, dancing, costume-changing mixed-race couple, Thomas and Belafonte, who offer many ways to reimagine all of the things that "A lot of mommies/And a lot of daddies/And a lot of parents/Can do."

"Sisters and Brothers"

With music by Stephen Lawrence and lyrics by Bruce Hart, this lively anthem combines a traditionally African American musical invocation of gospel and rhythm and blues or soul style with a call for the symbolic unity of fictive kinship. "Sisters and Brothers" reverses the usual phrasing of "brothers and sisters" invoked in a southern colloquialism rooted in the religious language of the nineteenth-century evangelical Christian revivals. The regional references ring throughout the song with the refrain, "Ain't we everyone . . .," echoed by "Ain't we lucky (ain't we)?/Ain't we happy (ain't we)?" The song creates an insistently equal vision by repeated reversals of connection: "Brothers and Sisters/Sisters and Brothers/Every father's daughter/Every mother's son." It drives the point of connection home by evoking "Mr. Mister," a phrase often used by enslaved peoples to refer to the white master: "Ain't we happy, everybody/Being everybody's sister?/Ain't we happy, everybody/Lookin' out for Mr. Mister?"

The song was sung by the Voices of East Harlem, an African American performance group formed in 1970. The group included approximately twenty young people aged twelve to twenty in an area of New York City hard hit by fiscal crises, urban rioting, unemployment, and drug trafficking. This young, community-organized group performed gospel and soul music in concert halls and less traditional venues, including Sing Sing Prison, that called attention to specific social problems.

The Voices of East Harlem were gifted singers and dancers, and it appears that they made up the majority of the dancers on a New York playground when the song was filmed for the television special. Additional dancers wearing brightly colored shirts and pants, with occasional kufis and wide belts, jumped from small play platforms and slides to swings and balance beams.

The joyfulness of this ensemble makes it a remarkable answer to the TV show's preceding scene: an earnest discussion between Marlo Thomas and some young children who sit together indoors under a dome-shaped structure and discuss their feelings about having sisters and brothers. She listens as several of the youngsters share complex emotions; some say they love having someone their age to talk to, while others respond that they don't always like their siblings. The problems of minor sibling struggles and rivalries discussed in this scene are answered with the lively anthem that follows: "Ain't we lucky, everybody./Being everybody's brother?/Ain't we lucky, everybody?/Lookin' out for one another?"

"The Sun and the Moon"

This short poem by Elaine Laron concludes the *Free to Be* book; it was also adapted as a song and performed by Dionne Warwick on the television special. Laron, who contributed two other poems to the book as well, was a writer and head lyricist for the educational children's TV series *The Electric Company*. She also produced the popular show *Captain Kangaroo* during the late 1960s.

Laron's poem poses an apparently simple question: Would you rather be the sun, filled with its own radiant light, or the moon, which can only reflect the light of another? Laron's answer, "I'd rather be the sun," makes no overt claims about gender. However, seen in light of prevailing stereotypes that placed women in subordinate positions, the poem offers a subtle but powerful feminist message about self-realization in the context of gender restrictions. The poem was illustrated by fourteen-year-old Lisa Antupit, who depicted a female figure whose smiling face embodied the sun and a smaller, sad, and presumably male figure whose head was rendered in the shape of a crescent moon.[6]

"Three Wishes"

This short story by poet and children's book author Lucille Clifton did not appear on the album but was included in the book and television special. Later printed as an illustrated children's book, *All about Three Wishes* (1976), the story featured two African American friends, a female narrator, Zenobia (Nobie), and a boy, Victor. The story tenderly illustrates some of the difficulties as well as the importance of maintaining friendships, including social connections between boys and girls. In Clifton's uplifting narrative, the support of parents, loved ones, and others in the surrounding community is depicted as a positive influence for children seeking to forge and maintain secure relationships with one another.

"When We Grow Up"

This song, with music written by Stephen Lawrence and lyrics by Shelley Miller, was composed originally for a single female vocalist; Diana Ross recorded it for the album. For the television special, however, the producers dramatized the melody with a pair of actors, a more theatrical and entertaining concept for the visual medium. The TV version pairs a boy and a girl who sing together about the future in a playful fashion. The concerns for each—about personal appearance and performance—are reflected in the questions that the two ask one another: "When I grow up will I be pretty?/Will you be big and strong?" The chorus, repeated several times, states the song's primary message: "Well, I don't care if I'm pretty at all/And I don't care if you never get tall/I like what I look like and you're nice small/We don't have to change at all." On the television special, the parts are sung and enacted by Roberta Flack (who was thirty-seven at the time but dressed in a childlike manner with her hair in pigtails) and a sixteen-year-old Michael Jackson, who wore overalls. As they sing, they take turns trying on dress-up items and smiling at each other through a frame designed in the shape of a mirror.

Shelley Miller's lyrics changed slightly between the album and television version, and the later lyrics were included in the book. On the 1972 album, Diana Ross ponders whether she will "wear perfume and gloves" when she grows up. According to Miller, in the two years between projects, the producers came to see this particular reference to dressing in a "ladylike" fashion as outmoded, so she changed the lyrics to focus on potential career ambitions instead.[7] In the revised version, the characters explore the idea of becoming an astronaut.

In the end, the song suggests that the characters are more alike than different. No matter what their physical characteristics, they share a common humanity and desire to experience joy, pursue activities of choice, and make friends with others: "When we grow up do you think we'll see/That I'm still like you/And you're still like me?"

In hindsight, the irony of the television performance has not been lost on viewers. The last line of the song schools young viewers in thoughts of self-acceptance: "I might be pretty/You might grow tall/But we don't have to change at all." The fact that Jackson went on to spend much of his adult life undergoing radical changes to his appearance speaks to the profound ways in which normative expectations about bodily appearance continue to affect people of all races, genders, sizes, and ages.

"William's Doll"

Mary Rodgers's music and Sheldon Harnick's lyrics provided a musical adaptation of Charlotte Zolotow's acclaimed picture book. Illustrated by William Pène Du Bois, the book was named an outstanding book of 1972 by the *New York Times* and the *School Library Journal* and was excerpted in *Ms.* magazine's "Stories for Free Children" section. The melody and lyrics turned the story into a mini-musical, complete with a problem (William wants a doll), an obstacle (William is taunted and ridiculed by his friends, cousin, and brother), a seeming solution (his father buys many athletic "boys' toys" to distract him), and a happy conclusion (his grandmother buys him a doll and explains that it will help make him a good father one day).

Alan Alda and Marlo Thomas sang the version on the album as well as the voice-over for an animated version on the television program. The song's attention to the work of caring for an infant (such as dressing, diapering, and burping) subtly differentiates the *Free to Be* version from Zolotow's original story. As the song concludes, these skills may be important for developing paternal caretaking skills: "William has a doll!/'Cause someday he is gonna be a father, too."

Notes

"Introduction" by Lori Rotskoff and Laura L. Lovett

1. The marketing of children's gender differences is thoroughly explored in Sharon Lamb and Lyn Mikel Brown, *Packaging Girlhood: Rescuing Our Daughters from Marketers' Schemes* (New York: St. Martin's, 2006); Lyn Mikel Brown, Sharon Lamb, and Mark Tappan, *Packaging Boyhood: Saving Our Sons from Superheroes, Slackers, and Other Media Stereotypes* (New York: St. Martin's, 2009). See also Peggy Orenstein, *Cinderella Ate My Daughter: Dispatches from the Front Lines of the New Girlie-Girl Culture* (New York: HarperCollins, 2011).

2. According to a recent study that polled more than four thousand students and teachers, 28 percent reported that when students were bullied, called names, or harassed, it was because of how masculine or feminine they appeared to be. And 33 percent replied that students were bullied because the tormenters thought the victims were gay, lesbian, or bisexual. See "From Teasing to Torment: School Climate in America," a 2005 survey conducted by the Gay, Lesbian, and Straight Education Network, cited in Charles M. Blow, "The Bleakness of the Bullied," *New York Times*, October 15, 2011.

3. Letty Cottin Pogrebin, "Toys for Free Children," Ms., March 1974, 48–53, 82–85; Women's Action Alliance Records, Sophia Smith Collection, Smith College Library, Northampton, Mass.

4. On the theory and practice of a collaborative approach to recording women's history, see Linda Shopes, "Oral History and the Study of Communities: Problems, Paradoxes, and Possibilities," *Journal of American History* 89, no. 2 (2002): 588–98; Thomas Charlton, Lois E. Meyers, and Rebecca Sharpless, eds., *Handbook of Oral History* (Lanham, Md.: AltaMira, 2006); Sherna Berger Gluck and Daphne Patai, eds., *Women's Words: The Feminist Practice of Oral History* (New York: Routledge, 1991); Barbara W. Sommer and Mary Kay Quinlan, *The Oral History Manual* (Lanham, Md.: AltaMira, 2009).

5. In her book *The Mother Knot* (New York: McGraw-Hill, 1976), Jane Lazarre writes poignantly about this kind of ambivalence, the fierce love she felt for her children as well as the frustration she felt about integrating motherhood with her literary ambitions and need for intellectual development. Another legendary critique of motherhood as a patriarchal institution is Adrienne

Rich's *Of Woman Born: Motherhood as Experience and Institution* (New York: Norton, 1977). For more on this topic, see Lauri Umansky, *Motherhood Reconceived: Feminism and the Legacies of the Sixties* (New York: New York University Press, 1996); Anne Roiphe, *Fruitful: A Real Mother in the Modern World* (New York: Penguin, 1997); Amy Richards, *Opting In: Having a Child without Losing Yourself* (New York: Farrar, Straus, and Giroux, 2008).

6. Leslie Paris also situates *Free to Be* in the context of the women's movement in her contribution to this volume and in "Happily Ever After: Free to Be . . . You and Me, Second-Wave Feminism, and 1970s American Children's Culture," in *The Oxford Handbook of Children's Literature*, ed. Julia Mickenberg and Lynne Vallone (New York: Oxford University Press, 2011). Our own contributions in part 2 of this book elaborate on the roles that children and childhood played in second-wave feminism. For a more general and particularly lucid discussion of children's agency and participation in historical change, see Karen Sánchez-Eppler, *Dependent States: The Child's Part in Nineteenth-Century American Culture* (Chicago: University of Chicago Press, 2005), xiv–xv.

"The Foundations of *Free to Be . . . You and Me*" by Lori Rotskoff

1. Katie Kelly, "Marlo Thomas: 'My Whole Life I've Had My Dukes Up,'" *New York Times*, March 11, 1973; Marlo Thomas, *Growing Up Laughing* (New York: Hyperion, 2010) 303–9.

2. Stephanie Coontz, *The Way We Never Were: American Families and the Nostalgia Trap* (New York: Basic Books, 1992). Between 1940 and 1956, the median age of women at first marriage fell from 21.5 years to 20.1 years; for men, the figures dropped from 24.3 to 22.5 years. The drop in the median age of first marriage is even more striking when comparing figures from the mid-1950s to those of 1910, when the median age for new husbands was 25.1 years and the median for wives was 21.6 years. See www.census.gov/population/socdemo/hh-fam/tabMS-2 (accessed January 25, 2012).

3. On the history of women during and after World War II and the rise of postwar domestic ideology, see Susan M. Hartmann, *The Home Front and Beyond: American Women in the 1940s* (New York: Macmillan, 1983); Karen Anderson, *Wartime Women: Sex Roles, Family Relations, and the Status of Women during World War II* (New York: Greenwood, 1981); Coontz, *Way We Never Were*, 8–41, 180–206; Elaine Tyler May, *Homeward Bound: American Families in the Cold War Era* (New York: Basic Books, 1988).

4. During the 1940s, Levittown's homeowners' contracts and rental leases barred those who were "not member(s) of the Caucasian race." Homebuilder William Levitt defended these racial restrictions as simply in keeping with social custom. Even after the Supreme Court rendered racial covenants unconstitutional in 1948, the Federal Housing Authority continued to guarantee loans only in predominantly white communities, and real estate agents followed suit. See Steven Mintz and Susan Kellogg, *Domestic Revolutions: A Social History of American Family Life* (New York: Free Press, 1989), 178–200; Coontz, *Way We Never Were*, 78–79; Laura L. Lovett, *Conceiving the Future: Pronatalism, Reproduction, and the Family in the United States, 1890–1938* (Chapel Hill: University of North Carolina Press, 2007), 159–60.

5. The history of African Americans on television is explored in the excellent documentary film *Color Adjustment* (1992), directed by Marlon Riggs and produced by Vivian Kleiman.

6. Mary Thom, *Inside Ms.: 25 Years of the Magazine and the Feminist Movement* (New York: Holt, 1997), 180. Leslie Paris also connects *Free to Be* to second-wave feminism in "Happily Ever After: Free to Be . . . You and Me, Second-Wave Feminism, and 1970s American Children's Culture," in *The Oxford Handbook of Children's Literature*, ed. Julia Mickenberg and Lynne Vallone (New York: Oxford University Press, 2011).

7. Marlo Thomas, conversation with author, April 6, 2012; *Free to Be . . . You and Me* (New York: McGraw-Hill, 1974), 11.

8. Amy Erdman Farrell, *Yours in Sisterhood: Ms. Magazine and the Promise of Popular Feminism* (Chapel Hill: University of North Carolina Press, 1998), 89–93; http://ms.foundation.org/about_us/our-history (accessed April 10, 2012).

9. Farrell, 89–93.

10. http://www.ahpweb.org (accessed June 19, 2011); Ellen Herman, *The Romance of American Psychology: Political Culture in the Age of Experts* (Berkeley: University of California Press, 1995), 264–75.

11. Herman, *Romance of American Psychology*, 276–77, 290–303; Betty Friedan, *The Feminine Mystique* (New York: Dell, 1963); Letty Cottin Pogrebin, email to author, October 20, 2011. While second-wave feminists rejected strict Freudian theory as a product and tool of patriarchal culture, they mined positive psychology for theoretical ballast with which to ground their galvanizing politics of gender. For Friedan's discussion of female potential and her analysis of Maslow's theories, see *Feminine Mystique*, especially chapters 3, 13. In 1966, Friedan and other cofounders of the National Organization for Women drafted their mission statement in explicitly humanistic terms: "NOW is dedicated to

the proposition that women first and foremost are human beings, who, like all other people in our society, must have the chance to develop their fullest human potential."

12. For essays that speak directly to the ways in which race and class differences have shaped children's conceptions of personal freedom or their responses to *Free to Be . . . You and Me*, see the contributions in this volume by Dorothy Pitman Hughes, Deesha Philyaw, Courtney E. Martin, Patrice Quinn, and Cheryl Kilodavis.

"How a Preschool Teacher Became Free to Be"
by Barbara Sprung

1. Barbara Sprung, *Non-Sexist Education for Young Children: A Practical Guide* (New York: Citation, 1975).

2. Selma Greenberg, "Educational Equity in Early Education Environments," in *Handbook for Achieving Sex Equity through Education*, ed. Sue Klein (Baltimore: Johns Hopkins University Press, 1984).

3. Lisa A. Serbin, Jane M. Connor, and Cheryl C. Citron, "Sex Differentiated Free Play Behavior: Effect of Teacher Modeling, Location, and Gender" *Developmental Psychology* 17 (1981): 640–46.

"Where the Children Are Free:
Free to Be . . . You and Me, Second-Wave Feminism, and
1970s American Children's Culture" by Leslie Paris

This essay is based on a similar article by Leslie Paris published in *The Oxford Handbook of Children's Literature*, ed. Julia Mickenberg and Lynne Vallone (New York: Oxford University Press, 2011).

1. Letters in Marlo Thomas Collection, New York, New York. Original spellings have been preserved.

2. The *Free to Be* series was the recipient of a Grammy nomination, an American Library Association Award, an Emmy Award for children's prime-time entertainment, and a Peabody Award for excellence in broadcasting.

3. Susan Jane Gilman, *Hypocrite in a Pouffy White Dress: Tales of Growing Up Groovy and Clueless* (New York: Warner, 2005), 26.

4. Letter from A. B., Whittier, Calif., Thomas Collection.

5. On Spock and his response to feminist critiques, see, for example, Ann

Hulbert, *Raising America: Experts, Parents, and a Century of Advice about Children* (New York: Knopf, 2003), 269–71.

6. On scholarship that traces the continuing vitality of 1960s rights movements in the 1970s, see Peter N. Carroll, *It Seemed Like Nothing Happened: America in the 1970s* (1982; New Brunswick: Rutgers University Press, 1990); Peter Braunstein and Michael William Doyle, eds., *Imagine Nation: The American Counterculture of the 1960s and '70s* (New York: Routledge, 2002); Van Gosse and Richard Moser, eds., *The World the Sixties Made: Politics and Culture in Recent America* (Philadelphia: Temple University Press, 2003); Beth Bailey and David Farber, eds., *America in the 1970s* (Lawrence: University Press of Kansas, 2004); Philip Jenkins, *Decade of Nightmares: The End of the Sixties and the Making of Eighties America* (New York: Oxford University Press, 2006); Sam Binkley, *Getting Loose: Lifestyle Consumption in the 1970s* (Durham: Duke University Press, 2007).

7. Binkley, *Getting Loose*, 6; Braunstein and Doyle, *Imagine Nation*, 12.

8. Sydney Ladensohn Stern, *Gloria Steinem: Her Passions, Politics, and Mystique* (Secaucus, N.J.: Birch Lane, 1997), 308–10.

9. Free to Be You and Me Foundation, http://www.freetobefoundation.org/history.htm (accessed April 9, 2009).

10. "Little Miss Muffet Fights Back," *Library Journal* 95, no. 20 (November 5, 1970): 3947; Feminists on Children's Media, *Little Miss Muffet Fights Back: Recommended Non-Sexist Books about Girls for Young Readers* (New York: Feminists on Children's Media, 1971).

11. Women on Words and Images, *Dick and Jane as Victims: Sex Stereotyping in Children's Readers: An Analysis* (Princeton, N.J.: National Organization for Women, 1972).

12. Feminists on Children's Media, "A Feminist Look at Children's Books," *Library Journal* 96, no. 2 (January 15, 1971): 235.

13. Betty Miles, "Harmful Lessons Little Girls Learn in School," *Redbook* 136, no. 5 (March 1971), 168.

14. Elizabeth Fisher, "Children's Books: The Second Sex, Junior Division," in *And Jill Came Tumbling After: Sexism in American Education*, ed. Judith Stacey, Susan Béreaud, and Joan Daniels (New York: Dell, 1974), 121–22. The classic academic study of the period is Lenore J. Weitzman, Deborah Eifler, Elizabeth Hokada, and Catherine Ross, "Sex-Role Socialization in Picture Books for Preschool Children," *American Journal of Sociology* 77, no. 6 (May 1972): 1125–50. See also John Stewig and Margaret Higgs, "Girls Grow Up to Be Mommies: A Study of Sexism in Children's Literature," *Library Journal* 98, no. 1 (January 15, 1973): 226–41. More recent critiques of this generation of scholarship include J. Allen

Williams Jr., JoEtta A. Vernon, Martha C. Williams, and Karen Malecha, "Sex Role Socialization in Picture Books: An Update," *Social Science Quarterly* 68, no. 1 (March 1987): 148–56; Roger Clark, Heidi Kulkin, and Liam Clancy, "The Liberal Bias in Feminist Social Science Research on Children's Books," in *Girls Boys Books Toys: Gender in Children's Literature and Culture,* ed. Beverly Lyon Clark and Margaret R. Higonnet (Baltimore: Johns Hopkins University Press, 1999), 71–82.

15. Numerous feminists cited the politics of Whitney Darrow Jr., *I'm Glad I'm a Boy! I'm Glad I'm a Girl!* (New York: Windmill, 1970).

16. Miles, "Harmful Lessons," 168.

17. Feminists on Children's Media, "Feminist Look," 236.

18. Sandra Scofield, "Is It True Boys Have More Fun?: What Every Parent Should Know about Children's Books," *Redbook* 149, no. 1 (May 1977): 214, 216.

19. On the first major conservative textbook protest, in Kanawha County, West Virginia, see, for example, Frank Lambert, *Religion in American Politics: A Short History* (Princeton: Princeton University Press, 2010), 194–95.

20. Sharon Wigutoff, "The Feminist Press: Ten Years of Nonsexist Children's Books," *Lion and the Unicorn* 3, no. 2 (1979–80): 57–58; Scofield, "Is It True," 216.

21. Ginette Castro and Elizabeth Loverde-Bagwell, *American Feminism: A Contemporary History* (New York: New York University Press, 1990), 238.

22. Margrit Eichler, *Martin's Father* (Chapel Hill, N.C.: Lollipop Power, 1971); Lynn Phillips, *Exactly Like Me* (Chapel Hill, N.C.: Lollipop Power, 1972); Carol De Poix, *Jo, Flo, and Yolanda* (Chapel Hill, N.C.: Lollipop Power, 1973).

23. Naomi Slifkin, "Lollipop Power," *Seventeen* 34, no. 1 (1975): 18. On the history of Lollipop Power, see Kyle Emily Erickson, "The Picture Books of Women's Liberation: Lollipop Power Press' Contribution to a Social Movement" (bachelor's thesis, University of North Carolina at Asheville, 2009).

24. While *Ms.* magazine was not profitable, *Free to Be* was a commercial success. See Stern, *Gloria Steinem,* 307; Anna Quindlen, "Women for Women Only," *New York Times,* March 13, 1978.

25. For the original "Ladies First," see Shel Silverstein, *A Light in the Attic* (New York: HarperCollins, 1981), 184.

26. For 1970s feminist analyses of fairy tales, see Alison Lurie, "Fairy Tale Liberation," *New York Review of Books,* December 17, 1970, 42; Marcia R. Lieberman, "'Some Day My Prince Will Come': Female Acculturation through the Fairy Tale," *College English* 34, no. 3 (1972): 383–95; Karen E. Rowe, "Feminism and Fairy Tales," *Women's Studies* 6, no. 3 (1979), 237–57.

27. Jay Williams's *The Practical Princess* (New York: Parents' Magazine Press, 1969) tells a similar tale of a princess who must outwit both her father and a hungry dragon.

28. Charlotte Zolotow, *William's Doll* (New York: Harper and Row, 1972). *William's Doll* was a *New York Times* Outstanding Book of the Year and the *School Library Journal* Best Book of the Year. On scholarly approaches to the text, see Karin A. Martin, "William Wants a Doll. Can He Have One?: Feminists, Child Care Advisors, and Gender-Neutral Child Rearing," *Gender and Society* 19, no. 4 (2005): 456–79; Ricky Herzog, "Sissies, Dolls, and Dancing: Children's Literature and Gender Deviance in the Seventies," *Lion and the Unicorn* 33, no. 1 (January 2009): 60–76.

29. I have written elsewhere about girls and feminist activism in the 1970s in athletics, the classroom, and popular culture. See, for example, Leslie Paris, "Wearing the Pants: Girls and Second-Wave Feminism in the 1970s" (paper presented at the Society for the History of Children and Youth, 2009).

30. Nanette Rainone quoted in Letty Cottin Pogrebin, "Toys for Free Children," *Ms.*, December 1973, 52.

31. Myra Pollack Sadker and David Miller Sadker, *Now upon a Time: A Contemporary View of Children's Literature* (New York: Harper and Row, 1977), 257.

32. Rachel Blustain, "Still Free to Be," *Lilith* 29, no. 2 (2004), 11.

33. Herzog, "Sissies, Dolls, and Dancing," 68–69.

34. http://metrodad.typepad.com/index/2005/11/free_to_be_you_.html, November 2005 (accessed April 8, 2009).

35. http://www.facebook.com/topic.php?uid=44092522222&topic=6128 (accessed September 7, 2011).

36. For a range of critiques of *Free to Be* and of second-wave feminist arguments about childhood gender relations, see, for example, Susan Douglas, *Where the Girls Are: Growing Up Female with the Mass Media* (New York: Random House, 1995), 298; Kara Lynn Braun, "*Free to Be . . . You and Me*: Considering the Impact of Feminist Influences in Children's Literature from the 1970s," *Journal of the Association of Research on Mothering* 1, no. 1 (1999): 137–44; Angela E. Hubler, "Beyond the Image: Adolescent Girls, Reading, and Social Identity," *NWSA Journal* 12, no. 1 (2000): 84–99; Judith Stadtman Tucker, "Mommies Are People: Revisiting Free to Be . . . You and Me," June 2007, http://www.mothers movement.org/features/07/06/f2b_prn.html (accessed March 11, 2012).

37. Lori Soderlind, *Chasing Montana: A Love Story* (Madison, Wis.: Terrace, 2006), 9.

38. On the movement of ideas from countercultural 1970s children's presses into the mainstream, see Leonard S. Marcus, *Minders of Make-Believe: Idealists, Entrepreneurs, and the Shaping of American Children's Literature* (Boston: Houghton Mifflin, 2008), 272–73.

"'Little Women's Libbers' and 'Free to Be Kids': Children and the Struggle for Gender Equality in the United States" by Lori Rotskoff

1. Mindful of their future historical significance, Ms. editors categorized, filed, and preserved the bulk of the letters they received. They are currently housed in Letters to Ms., Schlesinger Library, Radcliffe Institute, Harvard University, Cambridge, Mass. (hereafter Ms. Letters). "Randi Lewis" was not the writer's real name. I have changed most of the children's names to protect their privacy, in accordance with archive regulations: Real names are used only when a child's letter was published in the magazine.

2. Ms. Letters, Carton 1, File 3 (original spelling preserved).

3. Amy Erdman Farrell defines "popular feminism" as a commitment to improving women's lives and ending gender domination that emanates widely from the realm of popular culture. See Yours in Sisterhood: Ms. Magazine and the Promise of Popular Feminism (Chapel Hill: University of North Carolina Press, 1998), 5.

4. Ms. Letters, Carton 1, File 3.

5. On the various roles that children and childhood have played in cultural history, I am indebted to Karen Sánchez-Eppler's brilliant study, Dependent States: The Child's Part in Nineteenth-Century American Culture (Chicago: University of Chicago Press, 2005), especially the book's introduction. Two important studies of children and teenagers who participated in twentieth-century movements for social change include Gael Graham, Young Activists: American High School Students in the Age of Protest (De Kalb: Northern Illinois University Press, 2006); Rebecca de Schweinitz, If We Could Change the World: Young People and America's Long Struggle for Racial Equality (Chapel Hill: University of North Carolina Press, 2009).

6. Sara Evans, Tidal Wave: How Women Changed America at Century's End (New York: Free Press, 2003), 24.

7. On this point, I am grateful to Leslie Paris for her comments on an earlier version of this essay.

8. Bruce J. Schulman, The Seventies (New York: Free Press, 2001), 160–61; http://www.essortment.com/biography-billy-jean-king-20607.html (accessed April 2, 2012).

9. Mary Thom, Inside Ms.: Twenty-Five Years of the Magazine and the Feminist Movement (New York: Holt, 1997); Selena Roberts, A Necessary Spectacle: Billie Jean King, Bobby Riggs, and the Tennis Match That Leveled the Game (New York: Crown, 2005).

10. Patricia Horing, conversation with author, October 14, 2008.

11. *Ms.* Letters, Carton 1, File 3.

12. Ibid.

13. Arthur and Judith Sharenow, conversation with author, May 21, 2010.

14. *Ebony Jr.* 3, no. 8 (1976).

15. Ibid., 3, no. 10 (1976).

16. *Ms.* Letters, Carton 1, File 3.

17. Ibid. This correspondence includes a letter from Stephanie's mother as well as a copy of the original letter the child wrote to the textbook publisher. The sex of the teacher was not specified.

18. Ibid.

19. Ibid.

20. *Ms.*, April 1973, 8.

21. Ibid.

22. Ibid.

23. *Ms.*, June 1974, 49, 80.

24. *Ms.* Letters, Carton 1, File 3.

25. Ibid.

26. Ibid.

27. Ibid.

28. Ibid.

29. Letty Cottin Pogrebin, *Growing Up Free: Raising Your Child in the 80s* (New York: McGraw-Hill, 1980), 410–13.

30. Ibid., 416.

31. Ibid.; www.lionel.com (accessed January 30, 2012).

32. Letty Cottin Pogrebin Papers, "Toys" file, Sophia Smith Collection, Smith College Library, Northampton, Mass.

33. Ibid.

34. Caroline Ranald Curvan, email to author, December 15, 2008. Interestingly, as an adult, Caroline has worked in theater as a stage manager and technical engineer, a field that requires skills that train play supposedly hones in children.

35. *Ms.* Letters, Carton 1, File 3.

36. Farrell, *Yours in Sisterhood*, 151–62.

37. For two sobering accounts describing the extent to which American society still suffers from sexual inequality, gender discrimination, and media stereotypes, see Barbara J. Berg, *Sexism in America: Alive, Well, and Ruining Our Future* (Chicago: Hill, 2009); Susan J. Douglas, *Enlightened Sexism: The Seductive Message That Feminism's Work Is Done* (New York: Holt, 2010).

"Child's Play: Boys' Toys, Women's Work, and 'Free Children'" by Laura L. Lovett

1. There is a vast literature documenting the complicated relationships of girls, women, and mothers to the iconic Barbie doll. See Miriam Forman-Brunell, "Barbie in 'LIFE': The Life of Barbie," *Journal of the History of Childhood and Youth* 2, no. 3 (2009): 303–11.

2. Letty Cottin Pogrebin, "Toys for Free Children," Ms., March 1974, 48.

3. "What Shall I Wear?" was mentioned as an example of a sexist toy by Letty Cottin Pogrebin in her book, *Growing Up Free: Raising Your Child in the 80s* (New York: McGraw-Hill, 1980).

4. Pogrebin, "Toys for Free Children," 3.

5. Ruth Abram, introduction to *Perspectives on Non-Sexist Early Childhood Education*, ed. Barbara Sprung (New York: Teachers College Press, 1978), 17.

6. Barbara Sprung, "Non-Sexist Education: A New Focus for Early Childhood Programs," *Children Today*, May–June 1977, 2–6. See also Barbara Sprung, "Let's Address Not Redress: Achieving Educational Equity in the Early Childhood Years," *Equal Play* 1 (1980): 4–6; Project T.R.E.E., *Maximizing Young Children's Potential: A Non-Sexist Manual for Early Childhood Educators* (Washington, D.C.: U.S. Department of Health, Education, and Welfare, 1980).

7. Amy Ogata, "Creative Playthings: Educational Toys and Postwar American Culture," *Winterthur Portfolio* 39, nos. 2–3 (2004): 129–56; Gary Cross, *Kid's Stuff: Toys and the Changing World of American Childhood* (Cambridge, Mass.: Harvard University Press, 1997).

8. Ogata, "Creative Playthings."

9. Pogrebin, *Growing Up Free*, 1–6.

10. Sigmund Freud, *Three Contributions to the Theory of Sex* (1905; New York: Dover, 2001). Helen Deutsch's *The Psychology of Women*, vol. 1, *Girlhood* (New York: Allyn and Bacon, 1943) and vol. 2, *Motherhood* (New York: Allyn and Bacon, 1945) brought Freud's theories on women to American audiences.

11. Edward A. Ross, *Social Control: A Survey of the Foundations of Order* (New York: Macmillan, 1922); Laura L. Lovett, *Conceiving the Future: Pronatalism, Reproduction, and the Family in the United States, 1890–1938* (Chapel Hill: University of North Carolina Press, 2007).

12. James B. Watson, *Behaviorism*, rev. ed. (New York: Norton, 1930), 82.

13. Kerry Buckley, *Mechanical Man: James Broadus Watson and the Beginnings of Behaviorism* (New York: Guilford, 1989), 168; Carl Degler, *In Search of Human Nature: The Decline and Revival of Darwinism in American Social Thought* (New York: Oxford University Press, 1991), 153.

14. Mildred B. Parten, "Social Play among Preschool Children," *Journal of Abnormal and Social Psychology* 28, no. 2 (1933): 136–47.

15. Mildred B. Parten, "Social Participation among Preschool Children," *Journal of Abnormal and Social Psychology* 27, no. 3 (1932): 243–69.

16. Parten, "Social Play," 143.

17. Margaret H. Pintler, Ruth Phillips, and Robert R. Sears, "Sex Differences in Projective Doll Play of Preschool Children," *Journal of Psychology* 21, no. 1 (1946): 73–80; Hamilton Cravens, *Beyond Head Start: The Iowa Station and America's Children* (Chapel Hill: University of North Carolina Press, 2002), 241.

18. Eleanor E. Maccoby, "Eleanor E. Maccoby," in *A History of Psychology in Autobiography*, ed. Gardner Lindsey (Palo Alto, Calif.: Stanford University Press, 1989), 8:291–335; Robert R. Sears, Eleanor E. Maccoby, and Harry Levin, *Practices of Child Rearing* (Chicago: Row, Peterson, 1957).

19. Eleanor E. Maccoby and Carol N. Jacklin, *The Psychology of Sex Differences* (Palo Alto, Calif.: Stanford University Press, 1974).

20. Barbara Sprung, communication with author, August 23, 2010.

21. Maccoby and Jacklin, *Psychology of Sex Differences*, 283.

22. Ibid., 302.

23. Pogrebin, *Growing Up Free*, 32–33.

24. Pogrebin, "Toys for Free Children," 49.

25. Ibid., 84.

26. Ibid., 50.

27. Eleanor Bader, "WAA: Agenda, Advice and Toys," *Majority Report*, September 20, 1975, cited in Cynthia Harrison, "Creating a National Feminist Agenda: Coalition Building in the 1970s," in *Feminist Coalitions: Historical Perspectives on Second-Wave Feminism in the United States*, ed. Stephanie Gilmore (Urbana: University of Illinois Press, 2008), 19, 43.

28. Ibid. The WAA was referred to as "the Alliance" by its founders. Brenda Feigen, communication with author, June 20, 2012.

29. Lauri Umansky, *Motherhood Reconceived: Feminism and the Legacies of the Sixties* (New York: New York University Press, 1996); Flora Davis, *Moving the Mountain: The Women's Movement in America since 1960* (Urbana: University of Illinois Press, 1991).

30. Claudia Goldin, "The Quiet Revolution That Transformed Women's Employment, Education, and the Family," *American Economic Review* 96, no. 2 (2006): 9.

31. Barbara Sprung, "Brief Introduction to the Non-Sexist Child Development Project," Typescript Manuscript, Series 112: Folder 17, Women's Action Alliance Records, Sophia Smith Collection, Smith College Library, Northampton, Mass.

32. Sprung, "Non-Sexist Education." The inclusion of race and ethnicity in a project concerning nonsexist education is significant. From its beginning, the NSCD sought a multiracial curriculum. In 1982, when the collection of *Ms.* magazine children's stories was published as a separate book, the stories were presented as "multi-cultural, multi-racial, and hav[ing] a non-sexist point or purpose." This preceded Viola Florey-Tighe's push for multicultural curricula in 1983. The NSCD also added disability in the early 1980s. See "Resource Photos for Mainstreaming," Women's Action Alliance Records.

33. Sprung, "Non-Sexist Education," 3.

34. *A Non-Sexist Curriculum in Early Childhood* (film), Women's Action Alliance Records, Box 312, Item 183; *A Non-Sexist Curriculum in Early Childhood* (tape), Women's Action Alliance Records, Box 312, Item 182.

35. Sprung, "Let's Address Not Redress."

36. Carol Hall, who penned "Parents Are People," went on to write the musical *The Best Little Whorehouse in Texas* in 1978. I doubt, however, that this trajectory was a comment on women's employment options.

37. Nadine Brozan, "Using Toys to Free Children from the Roles Society Dictates," *New York Times*, May 12, 1971.

38. Roger Chapman, "War Toys," in *Culture Wars: An Encyclopedia of Issues, Voices, and Viewpoints*, ed. Roger Chapman (Armonk, N.Y.: Sharpe, 2010), 597.

39. Edward M. Swartz, *Toys That Don't Care* (Boston: Gambit, 1970).

40. Cross, *Kid's Stuff*, 182.

41. "Nabisco Picketed over Monster Toys," *New York Times*, November 16, 1971.

42. Pogrebin, "Toys for Free Children," 49.

43. Ellen Goodman and Fran Gustavson, "Toys That Care: Non-Sexist Teaching Aids, Pre-School–Adult," (1976), Education Resources Information Center, ED 131848, http://www.eric.ed.gov (accessed August 2, 2010).

44. Ron Alexander, "Survey Finds Lack of Nonsexist Toys," *New York Times*, August 1, 1983.

45. Paul Mussen and Luther Distler, "Child-Rearing Antecedents of Masculine Identification in Kindergarten Boys," *Child Development* 31, no. 1 (1960): 89–100.

46. Sprung, "Non-Sexist Education," 21.

47. Karin A. Martin, "William Wants a Doll. Can He Have One?: Feminists, Child Care Advisors, and Gender-Neutral Child Rearing," *Gender and Society* 19, no. 4 (2005): 456–79.

48. Pogrebin, *Growing Up Free*, 292.

49. The son of an evangelical minister, Dobson earned a Ph.D. in child de-

velopment from the University of Southern California in 1967. He worked for fourteen years as an associate clinical professor of pediatrics at the University of Southern California School of Medicine, where he did research on cognitive disabilities and especially the role of a genetic disease, phenylketonuria, as a cause of disability.

50. See Wendy Kline, *Building a Better Race: Gender, Sexuality, and Eugenics from the Turn of the Century to the Baby Boom* (Berkeley: University of California Press, 2001); James Dobson, *Dare to Discipline: A Psychologist Offers Urgent Advice to Parents and Teachers* (Wheaton, Ill.: Tyndal House Publishers, 1973), 10.

51. Dobson, *Dare to Discipline*, 185.

52. Dale Buss, *Family Man: The Biography of Dr. James Dobson* (Wheaton, Ill.: Tyndale House, 2005), 330–31.

53. Judy Klemesrud, "Award-Winning Toys: Nonsexist, Nonracist—and Peaceful," *New York Times*, February 19, 1975.

54. Pogrebin, "Toys for Free Children," 52.

55. Ibid., 53.

"Getting the Message: Audiences Respond to *Free to Be . . . You and Me*" by Lori Rotskoff

1. Personal collection of Marlo Thomas and the Free to Be Foundation, New York; Marlo Thomas, interview by author, December 3, 2010.

2. Nadine Brozan, "A Women's Lib Message for Children," *New York Times*, December 24, 1972.

3. Deborah Jowitt, "Free to Be . . . You and Me," *New York Times*, December 24, 1972.

4. Ibid.

5. Ibid.

6. Letters to *Ms.*, Schlesinger Library, Radcliffe Institute, Harvard University, Cambridge, Mass. (hereafter cited as *Ms.* Letters), Carton 1, Folder 6.

7. *Ms.* Letters, Carton 1, Folder 6. The archive includes a memo noting a discussion at an editorial meeting in response to this letter, in which some editors shared the view that housework is best viewed neutrally and dispassionately. In my research, confirmed during a phone conversation with Marlo Thomas on February 10, 2012, I learned that *Free to Be*'s creators were apprised of these criticisms and believed that while the skit had been popular with many listeners, it was best to omit it from the small screen version.

8. Both clippings in press clippings scrapbook, Thomas Collection.

9. Ibid.

10. Jean Stafford, "Children's Books for Christmas," *New Yorker*, December 2, 1974, 170–75, copy in Letty Cottin Pogrebin Papers, Sophia Smith Collection, Smith College Library, Northampton, Mass.

11. Press clippings scrapbook, Thomas Collection.

12. Ibid.

13. *Ms.* Letters, Carton 1, File 6.

14. *Ms.* Letters, Carton 1, File 6.

15. Letters in Thomas Collection; *Ms.* Letters, Carton 1, File 6.

"Genderfication Starts Here" by Deborah Siegel

1. Lise Eliot, *Pink Brain, Blue Brain: How Small Differences Grow into Troublesome Gaps* (New York: Houghton Mifflin, 2009) p. 14.

2. Sandra Lipsitz Bem, *An Unconventional Family* (New Haven: Yale University Press, 1998); Lois Gould, "X: A Fabulous Child's Story," *Ms.* (December, 1972). The book version of this tale was published under the same title by Daughters Publishing Company in 1978. The full text of Gould's story is reprinted in Julia L. Mickenberg and Philip Nel, ed., *Tales for Little Rebels: A Collection of Radical Children's Literature* (New York: New York University Press, 2008).

3. There have been two recent, highly publicized cases of parents attempting to keep their child's biological sex a secret: a Swedish child named Pop and a Canadian child named Storm. See http://transpedianews.com/?=636 (accessed April 2, 2012).

4. Thomas Rogers, "Delusions of Gender: The Bad Science of Brain Sexism," *Salon*, September 7, 2009, http://www.salon.com/books.feature/2010/09/07/sexism_neuroscience_interview (accessed March 11, 2012).

5. The original Friday night prayer said for a boy is "May God make you like Ephraim and Menashe," and for a girl, "May God make you like Sarah, Rebecca, Rachel, and Leah."

"Can William Have a Doll Now?: The Legacy of *Free to Be* in Parenting Advice Books" by Karin A. Martin

1. Michael J. Geboy, "Who Is Listening to the 'Experts'?: The Use of Child Care Materials by Parents," *Family Relations* 30, no. 2 (1981): 205–10; Sharon Hays, *The Cultural Contradictions of Motherhood* (New Haven: Yale University Press, 1996).

2. Arlie Hochschild, "The Commercial Spirit of Intimate Life and the Abduction of Feminism: Signs from Women's Advice Books," *Theory, Culture, and Society* 11, no. 2 (1994): 1–24.

3. All of the websites were comprehensive parenting websites (that is, not directed at a particular type of child—e.g., spirited or autistic). They ranged from being sponsored by parenting magazines (parents.com) or doctors (askdrsears.com) to having a particular agenda about parenting (naturalchild.com). About half of the authors of the books and web articles are women. There was no apparent correlation between the gender of the author and stance toward gender-neutral parenting. Most authors claim their expertise from their medical or psychology credentials. For methodological and sample details, see Karin A. Martin, "William Wants a Doll. Can He Have One?: Feminists, Child Care Advisors, and Gender-Neutral Child Rearing," *Gender and Society* 19, no. 4 (2005): 456–79.

4. Shelley Butler and Deb Kratz, *Field Guide to Parenting* (Worcester, Mass.: Chandler House, 1999); Laura Davis and Janis Keyser, *Becoming the Parent You Want to Be* (New York: Broadway, 1997); Letty Cottin Pogrebin, *Growing Up Free: Raising Your Child in the 80s* (New York: McGraw-Hill, 1980); Charlotte Zolotow, *William's Doll* (New York: Harper and Row, 1972).

5. Arlene Eisenberg, Heidi E. Murkoff, and Sandra E. Hathaway, *What to Expect: The Toddler Years* (New York: Workman, 1996), 224.

6. American Academy of Pediatrics, *Caring for Your Baby and Young Child: Birth to Age 5* (New York: Bantam, 1998), 143.

7. Benjamin Spock and Steven J. Parker, *Dr. Spock's Baby and Child Care*, 7th ed. (New York: Pocket, 1998), 656.

8. Penelope Leach, *Your Baby and Child* (New York: Knopf, 2000), 530.

9. Bridget Barnes and Steven York, *Common Sense Parenting of Toddlers and Preschoolers* (Boys Town, Neb.: Boys Town Press, 2001), 53–54.

10. http://www.naturalchild.org/advice/q59.html (accessed 2011).

11. John Rosemond, *Parent Power: A Common-Sense Approach to Parenting in the 90s and Beyond* (Kansas City, Mo.: Andrews McMeel, 1990), 151–52 (emphasis added).

12. http://family.go.com/raisingkids/child/dev/expert/dony67fahypersensitive/ (accessed 2002); http://family.go.com/raisingkids/child/dev/expert/dony109sensitive/dony109sensitive.html (accessed 2002).

13. http://www.naturalchild.org/advice/q59.html (accessed 2011).

14. Spock and Parker, *Dr. Spock's Baby and Child Care*, 40.

15. http://www.parentsplace.com/expert/family/qas/0,10338,240331_115624,00.html (accessed 2002).

16. http://www.drspock.com/article/0,1510,8248,00.html (accessed 2002).

17. http://www.parentsoup.com/experts/preteens/qas/0,7813,448544_150350,00.html (accessed 2002).

18. Spock and Parker, *Dr. Spock's Baby and Child Care*, 38.

19. Leach, *Your Baby*, 530; Rosemond, *Parent Power*, 153; Paul C. Reisser, *Focus on the Family Complete Book of Baby and Child Care* (Wheaton, Ill.: Tyndale House, 1997), 11.

20. Eisenberg, Murkoff, and Hathaway, *What to Expect*, 222.

21. Eve Kosofsky Sedgwick, "How to Bring Your Kids up Gay," *Social Text* 29 (1991): 161.

"'William's Doll' and Me" by Karl Bryant

1. Green had begun his work with gender-nonconforming children while still a medical student at Johns Hopkins University in the 1950s under the mentorship of John Money. Money was well known at the time and remains (in)famous for his work on intersex infants and children. Through Money, Green found his first gender-nonconforming child to study as part of a year-long student research project. Green and Money went on to publish work together throughout the 1960s, thus helping to lay the foundation for the development of a niche subspecialty on childhood gender variance within psychology and psychiatry. At the time, this work was largely motivated by an interest in understanding psychosexual development and by the possibility of preventing a set of nonnormative adult sexual orientation and gender identity outcomes, especially transsexuality.

2. Charlotte Zolotow, *William's Doll* (New York: Harper and Row, 1972).

3. Lenore J. Weitzman, Deborah Eifler, Elizabeth Hokada, and Catherine Ross, "Sex-Role Socialization in Picture Books for Preschool Children," *American Journal of Sociology* 77, no. 6 (1972): 1125–50.

4. Examples of the books I looked at include John Beatty and Patricia Beatty, *Master Rosalind* (New York: Morrow, 1974); Carol H. Behrman, *Catch a Dancing Star* (Minneapolis: Dillon, 1975); Tomie De Paola, *Oliver Button Is a Sissy* (New York: Harcourt Brace Jovanovich, 1979); Louise Fitzhugh, *Nobody's Family Is Going to Change* (New York: Farrar, Straus, and Giroux, 1974); Norma Klein, *Tomboy* (New York: Four Winds, 1978); Elizabeth Levy, *The Tryouts* (New York: Four Winds, 1979); Ben Shecter, *Hester the Jester* (New York: Harper and Row, 1977); Mary W. Sullivan, *What's This about Pete?* (Nashville, Tenn.: Nelson, 1976); Miriam Young, *No Place for Mitty* (New York: Four Winds, 1976). In total, I examined twenty-nine children's books.

5. See, e.g., Patricia Beatty, *By Crumbs, It's Mine!* (New York: Morrow, 1976); Moses L. Howard, *The Ostrich Chase* (New York: Holt, Rinehart, and Winston, 1974).

6. See, e.g., Beatty and Beatty, *Master Rosalind*; Julia First, *Flat on My Face* (Englewood Cliffs, N.J.: Prentice-Hall, 1974); Mildred Lawrence, *Touchmark* (New York: Harcourt Brace Jovanovich, 1975).

7. See, e.g., Howard, *Ostrich Chase*; Lawrence, *Touchmark*.

8. Marcia L. Simon, *A Special Gift* (New York: Harcourt Brace Jovanovich, 1978), 24.

9. De Paola, *Oliver Button Is a Sissy*, 20.

10. See, e.g., Elizabeth Winthrop, *Tough Eddie* (New York: Dutton, 1985); Zolotow, *William's Doll*.

11. William H. Hooks, *Doug Meets the Nutcracker* (New York: Warne, 1977), 72.

12. Klein, *Tomboy*.

"Free to Be on West 80th Street"
by Dorothy Pitman Hughes

1. Gloria Steinem, "The City Politic: A Racial Walking Tour," *New York*, February 24, 1969, 6–7; Gloria Steinem, "The City Politic: Room at the Bottom, Boredom at the Top," *New York*, June 30, 1969, 10–11.

"Epilogue" by Laura L. Lovett

1. Marlo Thomas and Christopher Cerf, eds., *Free to Be . . . a Family* (New York: Bantam, 1987). See also Letty Cottin Pogrebin, *Family Politics: Love and Power on an Intimate Frontier* (New York: McGraw-Hill, 1983).

2. Natasha Zaretsky, *No Direction Home: The American Family and the Fear of National Decline, 1968–1980* (Chapel Hill: University of North Carolina Press, 2007); Laura L. Lovett, *Conceiving the Future: Pronatalism, Reproduction, and the Family in the United States, 1890–1938* (Chapel Hill: University of North Carolina Press, 2007); Susan Faludi, *Backlash: The Undeclared War against American Women* (New York: Crown, 1991).

3. Stephanie Coontz, *The Way We Never Were: American Families and the Nostalgia Trap* (New York: Basic Books, 1992).

4. Elaine Tyler May, *Homeward Bound: American Families in the Cold War Era* (New York: Basic Books, 1990); Jessica Weiss, *To Have and to Hold: Marriage, the Baby Boom, and Social Change* (Chicago: University of Chicago Press, 2000).

5. Annelise Orleck and Lisa Gayle Hazirjian, eds., *The War on Poverty: A New*

Grassroots History, 1964–1980 (Athens: University of Georgia Press, 2011), especially Laurie B. Green, "Saving Babies in Memphis: The Politics of Race, Health,
and Hunger during the War on Poverty"; *The Negro Family: The Case for National
Action* (Washington, D.C.: Office of Policy Planning and Research, U.S. Department of Labor, 1965). For the relationship between the Moynihan Report and
the family values debate, see Judith Stacey, *In the Name of the Family: Rethinking
Family Values in the Postmodern Age* (Boston: Beacon, 1997), 5.

6. "Free to Be a Family Memos" Folder, Ms. Foundation Papers, Sophia Smith
Collection, Smith College Library, Northampton, Mass.

7. Letty Cottin Pogrebin, "Carnegie/Ms. Foundation Record Project," 2, in
ibid.

8. Letty Cottin Pogrebin, "A Note to Parents, Teachers and Other Grown-Up
Friends," in *Free to Be . . . a Family*, ed. Thomas and Cerf.

9. http://www.freetobeme.com/content.xjp?id=429 (accessed October 9,
2011).

10. http://www.free-to-be.net/ (accessed October 9, 2011).

11. To meet the requirements for abstinence education federal funds, this
organization had pledged to teach that "sex outside of marriage causes psychological and physical harm" and that "children born to unmarried parents
inflict harm on their parents and on society." Both of these statements were
in violation of California law at the time. See Margaret Crosby and Norma Jo
Waxman, "Close to Home: Sex Mis-Education in Schools," *ACLU of Northern
California Newsletter*, http://www.aclunc.org/news/opinions/close_to_home_
sex_mis-education_in_schools.html?ht= (accessed October 9, 2011).

12. Stacey, *In the Name of the Family.*

"Appendix: The Songs, Stories, and Skits of
Free to Be . . . You and Me: A Content Overview,"
by Lori Rotskoff and Laura L. Lovett

1. Gloria Auerbach, *The Woman Runner: Free to Be the Complete Athlete* (New
York: Simon and Schuster, 1984), 5.

2. Judith Stadtman Tucker, "Mommies Are People: Revisiting Free to Be . . .
You and Me," June 2007, http://www.mothersmovement.org/features/07/06/
f2b_prn.html (accessed March 11, 2012).

3. Pat Mainardi, "The Politics of Housework," reprinted in *Sisterhood Is Powerful*, ed. Robin Morgan (New York: Vintage, 1970), 506.

4. Tucker, "Mommies are People."

5. Carol Hall offers a personal account of the development of this song in her contribution to this book.

6. Tucker offers a critical interpretation of this poem and its accompanying illustration in "Mommies Are People."

7. Shelley Miller, telephone conversation with Lori Rotskoff, February 2, 2012.

About the Contributors

ALAN ALDA has earned international recognition as an actor, writer, and director. He has the distinction of being nominated for an Oscar (*The Aviator*), a Tony (*Glengarry Glen Ross*), and an Emmy (*The West Wing*), as well as writing a best-selling book (*Never Have Your Dog Stuffed*), all in the same year, 2005. He portrayed Hawkeye Pierce on M*A*S*H before going on to appear most recently on ER, 30 Rock, and The Big C. Alda hosted the award-winning PBS series *Scientific American Frontiers* for eleven years. He is the author of a play, *Radiance: The Passion of Marie Curie*, which had its world premiere at the Geffen Playhouse in Los Angeles in 2011. In all, he has received thirty-two nominations and won six Emmys for acting, writing, and directing. He has won the Director's Guild Award three times, and in 1994 he was inducted into the Television Hall of Fame.

LAURA BRIGGS is a scholar of reproductive politics in a transnational context, focusing primarily on the United States and Latin America. She holds a doctorate from Brown University. She is the author of *Reproducing Empire: Race, Sex, Science, and U.S. Imperialism in Puerto Rico* (2002); coeditor, with Diana Marre, of *International Adoption: Global Inequalities and the Circulation of Children* (2009); and author of *Somebody's Children: The Politics of Transracial and Transnational Adoption* (2012). She has written more than a dozen articles on topics including birth control, histories of activism, science fiction, and welfare politics. She recently became chair of Women, Gender, and Sexuality Studies at the University of Massachusetts after fourteen years at the University of Arizona, where she was head of Gender and Women's Studies and associate dean.

KARL BRYANT is assistant professor of sociology and women's studies at the State University of New York at New Paltz. He received a doctorate from the University of California, Santa Barbara. His research examines the overlapping areas of gender, sexuality, childhood studies, science studies, and the sociology of knowledge. His previous work has included a study of nonsexist children's stories published in the 1970s and 1980s, on which he draws for his essay in this volume. Bryant is completing a book-length history of the psychiatric diagnosis of gender identity disorder as applied to children. His most recent project examines the category of transgender childhood as a new form of social identity, including advocacy work on behalf of and media reports about transgender and gender-variant children.

BECKY FRIEDMAN is a staff writer and story editor for Out of the Blue Enterprises, a children's content development, production, licensing, and merchandising company. Friedman has written for the Emmy-nominated PBS literacy show *Super Why!* and is currently writing and story editing for *Daniel Tiger's Neighborhood*, an animated show for preschoolers based on the legacy of Fred Rogers that will premiere on PBS in the fall of 2012. In addition, she coordinates a monthly writers' group for Women in Children's Media. She holds a bachelor's degree from Tufts University and resides in Brooklyn, New York.

NANCY GRUVER is the founder and CEO of New Moon Girls (newmoon.com), an author, and a public speaker on contemporary issues related to girls. She is the mother of twin daughters and lives in Emeryville, California.

CAROL HALL wrote music and lyrics for the Tony-winning *The Best Little Whorehouse in Texas* and contributed songs to *Sesame Street, A . . . My Name Is Alice,* and *Free to Be . . . You and Me.* She wrote the off-Broadway musical *To Whom It May Concern* and the score for the musical *Max and Ruby.* Her work has won Grammy, Emmy, Drama Desk, and Peabody Awards, as well as the Johnny Mercer Award, acknowledging her contribution to American popular song. She also won an ASCAP Most-Performed Country Song Award for Dolly Parton's recording of "Hard Candy Christmas." Recently, she wrote lyrics for a musical of Truman Capote's *A Christmas Memory.* Barbra Streisand, Tony Bennett, Barbara Cook, Ann-Margret, and Big Bird, among others, have performed her songs.

CAROLE HART is an award-winning television and film producer/writer. She began her career working with her partner and husband, Bruce Hart, as one of the original writers of *Sesame Street,* for which she won her first Emmy. With Marlo Thomas, she coproduced the *Free to Be . . . You and Me* album and was instrumental in turning it into a book and television special. Her credits also include movies made for television (*Sooner or Later, Leap of Faith*); an Emmy-winning NBC series for adolescents, *Hot Hero Sandwich*; and a mixed-media documentary for the Lifetime Channel, *Our Heroes, Ourselves.* She recently produced and directed an award-winning feature documentary, *For the Next 7 Generations*, about the formation and journey of the International Council of Thirteen Indigenous Grandmothers, a group of medicine women and shamans from around the world who are working to find a path to a sustainable planet.

DOROTHY PITMAN HUGHES is a lifelong social justice activist and children's welfare advocate. During the 1960s and 1970s, she helped to create community-controlled resources that not only offered child care services but also provided job training, educational resources, and housing and food resources on Manhattan's Upper West Side. Known for her skill at community-based organizing, Hughes befriended Gloria Steinem during the late 1960s, and they began speaking together across the country on the importance of child care and of racial and socioeconomic equity in the women's movement. Hughes currently lives in Jacksonville, Florida, where she organizes an economic empowerment and community gardens project for local residents.

JOE KELLY is a frequent speaker and the author of many books and articles on fatherhood. His most recent position was fathering educator at the Emily Program, an eating disorders treatment agency in Minnesota and Seattle. He is the father of twin daughters and lives in Emeryville, California.

CHERYL KILODAVIS is a published author, strategic marketer, and social entrepreneur. She holds a bachelor's degree from the University of the Pacific and an M.B.A. from Seattle University. She is the author of *My Princess Boy* (2011), a children's book with a strong antibullying message. Originally written to explain her younger son's uniqueness to teachers and fellow students, the book now represents a broader movement of acceptance for every child. Currently, Kilodavis writes at www.myprincessboy.com and consults at www.kdtalent.com. She is also the author of *My Princess Boy Has a Champion* (2012).

DIONNE GORDON KIRSCHNER holds a bachelor's degree from UCLA. She worked for a year at the Creative Artists Agency before moving on to a successful career in television production. Her credits include the pilot and first year of the ABC series *My Wife and Kids*, starring Damon Wayans; four seasons of *Less Than Perfect*, with Andy Dick and Eric Roberts, for ABC; and the pilot and two seasons of CBS's *Gary Unmarried*, starring Jay Mohr. She has also worked on the children's show *Bucket and Skinner's Epic Adventures* for Nickelodeon. She lives in Los Angeles with her husband and their two sons.

FRANCINE KLAGSBRUN, editor of the volume *Free to Be . . . You and Me*, is the author of more than a dozen books, including *Mixed Feelings: Love, Hate, Rivalry, and Reconciliation among Brothers and Sisters* (1992). Her most recent book, *The Fourth Commandment: Remember the Sabbath Day* (2002), was a finalist for the National Jewish Book Award. She also edited *The First Ms. Reader* (1973). Her column "Thinking Aloud" appears monthly in the *Jewish Week*. She has also been a columnist for *Moment* Magazine and has contributed to the *New York Times*, the *Boston Globe*, and *Newsweek*. Klagsbrun holds bachelor's and master's degrees from Brooklyn College and the Institute of Fine Arts, and received an honorary doctorate in Hebrew literature from the Jewish Theological Seminary. She was a member of the Commission for the Study of Women in the Rabbinate and was at the forefront of the struggle to have women ordained as rabbis in the Conservative movement. She is currently working on a biography of Golda Meir.

STEPHEN LAWRENCE, a composer based in New York City, has written more than 250 songs and scores for *Sesame Street*, resulting in three shared Emmy Awards for Outstanding Achievement in Music Direction and Composition. He was the musical director of *Free to Be . . . You and Me*, composing the title song and many other songs from the landmark children's album and television special. Lawrence also composed the gold single "You Take My Breath Away" and the score for the film *Bang the Drum Slowly*. His other credits include the cult horror classic *Alice, Sweet Alice*, which won the music award at the Paris Festival of Fantasy and Science Fiction; the songs and score for the live-action movie musical *Red Riding Hood*; and music for the HBO animated musical *The Tale of Peter Rabbit*.

LAURA L. LOVETT is an associate professor of history at the University of Massachusetts, Amherst. She holds a doctorate from the University of California, Berkeley. Her work focuses on the history of women and the history of childhood and youth in the United States during the twentieth century. She is the author of *Conceiving the Future: Pronatalism, Reproduction, and the Family in the United States, 1890–1938* (2007) as well as scholarly articles in journals such as the *Public Historian*; the *Journal of Health Politics, Policy, and Law*; *Social Politics*; and *American Indian Quarterly*. She is a founding editor of the *Journal of the History of Childhood and Youth*.

COURTNEY E. MARTIN is an author, blogger, and speaker. Her most recent book is *Project Rebirth: Survival and the Strength of the Human Spirit from 9/11 Survivors* (2011). She is also the author of *Do It Anyway: The New Generation of Activists* (2010) and *Perfect Girls, Starving Daughters: How the Quest for Perfection Is Harming Young Women* (2007). She is editor emeritus at Feministing.com and a fellow at Dowser.com. Martin has appeared on *The Today Show*, *Good Morning America*, MSNBC, and *The O'Reilly Factor*. She is the recipient of the Elie Wiesel

Prize in Ethics, has held a residency at the Rockefeller Foundation's Bellagio Centre, and is a TED speaker. More information about her work is available at www.courtneyemartin.com.

KARIN A. MARTIN is a professor of sociology at the University of Michigan. She holds a doctorate from the University of California at Berkeley, and her research focuses on gender and sexuality, particularly in childhood. She is the author of *Puberty, Sexuality, and the Self: Boys and Girls at Adolescence* (1996). Her research has appeared in a variety of journals, including the *American Sociological Review*, *Gender and Society*, the *Journal of Family Issues*, and *Sex Roles*. She is currently examining children's participation and understandings in conversations with their parents about where babies come from.

TAYLOE MCDONALD is an accomplished artist and the executive director of Art with a Heart in Healthcare in Jacksonville, Florida. She partners with neuroscientists to research how experiencing art changes the brain. She explores the curious intersection of art and neuroscience on her blog, Artlab (http://tayloe.posterous.com/).

TREY MCINTYRE is a dancer and choreographer who has received grants from the National Endowment for the Arts and other foundations. After working at the American Ballet Theater, the New York City Ballet, and other companies, he founded the Trey McIntyre Dance Project, based in Boise, Idaho, in 2008. He has been selected to choreograph a dance piece to the original music from *Free to Be . . . You and Me*, which will premiere in 2012. More information about his dance company can be found at www.treymcintyre.com.

PEGGY ORENSTEIN is the author of numerous books, most recently *Cinderella Ate My Daughter: Dispatches from the Front Lines of the New Girlie-Girl Culture* (2011). Her previous books include the best-selling memoir, *Waiting for Daisy* (2007); *Flux: Women on Sex, Work, Kids, Love, and Life in a Half-Changed World* (2000); and *Schoolgirls: Young Women, Self-Esteem, and the Confidence Gap* (1994). A contributing writer for the *New York Times Magazine*, Orenstein has also written for the *Los Angeles Times*, *USA Today*, *Vogue*, *Elle*, *Discover*, *More*, *Mother Jones*, *Salon*, *O: The Oprah Magazine*, and the *New Yorker* and has contributed commentaries to NPR's *All Things Considered*. She has been featured on *Nightline*, *Good Morning America*, *The Today Show*, NPR's *Fresh Air* and *Morning Edition*, and the CBC's *As It Happens*. Her work has been honored by the Commonwealth Club of California, the National Women's Political Caucus of California, the

Planned Parenthood Federation of America, and the Asian Cultural Council. Orenstein, a graduate of Oberlin College, lives in the San Francisco Bay Area with her husband and their daughter.

LESLIE PARIS is associate professor of history at the University of British Columbia in Vancouver, Canada. She holds a doctorate from the University of Michigan. Her research focuses on American children's history, especially the intersection of adult ideologies of childhood and children's own experiences. She is the author of *Children's Nature: The Rise of the American Summer Camp* (2008), coauthor of *A Paradise for Boys and Girls: Adirondack Summer Camps* (2006), and coeditor of *Lost Kids: Vulnerable Children and Youth in Twentieth-Century Canada and the United States* (2009) and the two-volume *Girls' History and Culture Reader* (2011). She has also published on such topics as dollhouses, Skipper dolls, and age as a category of historical analysis. She is currently writing a history of American childhood between 1965 and 1980.

MIRIAM PESKOWITZ is the coauthor of the international and *New York Times* best-selling book *The Daring Book for Girls* (2007) and its follow-up, *The Double-Daring Book for Girls* (2009). She also wrote *The Truth behind the Mommy Wars: Who Decides What Makes a Good Mother* (2005) and *Spinning Fantasies: Rabbis, Gender, and History* (1997). She is coeditor with Laura Levitt of the classic feminist Jewish studies anthology, *Judaism since Gender* (1997). She also hosted the PBS special *Daring Kids with Miriam Peskowitz*.

DEESHA PHILYAW is a freelance writer whose work has been published in *Essence*, *Bitch*, and *Wondertime* magazines and the *Washington Post*. Her writing has also been featured in several anthologies, including *Literary Mama: Reading for the Maternally Inclined* (2005) and *Just Like a Girl: A Manifesta!* (2008). She is an adjunct writing instructor in Chatham University's master's of professional writing program. She is the coauthor of the forthcoming *Co-Parenting 101: Advice from a Formerly Married Couple on Parenting across Two Households* and a cofounder of CoParenting101.org. Philyaw holds a bachelor's degree from Yale University and a master's from Manhattanville College. She lives in Pittsburgh and is the mother of two daughters and two stepdaughters.

ABIGAIL POGREBIN, a Yale graduate and a former *60 Minutes* producer, is the author of *Stars of David: Prominent Jews Talk about Being Jewish* (2005), which is currently being adapted for an Off-Broadway musical production; *One and the*

Same (2009); and the Kindle single *Showstopper* (2011). She has written for numerous publications, including *New York* Magazine, *Harper's Bazaar*, the *Daily Beast*, *Salon*, and the *Huffington Post*, and she moderates the interview series "What Everyone's Talking About" at the JCC in Manhattan. She lives in New York City with her husband and two children.

LETTY COTTIN POGREBIN, a writer, editor, lecturer, and social justice activist, is the author of nine books, including a novel, *Three Daughters* (2002), and two acclaimed memoirs, *Deborah, Golda, and Me: Being Female and Jewish in America* (1991), and *Getting Over Getting Older* (1996). Her 1980 book, *Growing Up Free*, a guide to nonsexist child rearing, has been taught at universities around the country. She edited the anthology *Stories for Free Children* (1982) and served as the editorial consultant on *Free to Be . . . You and Me*. After graduating from Brandeis University, Pogrebin became one of the founding editors of *Ms.* Magazine, where she worked for seventeen years. Her essays and op-eds have appeared in *Ms.*, the *New York Times*, the *Washington Post*, the *Los Angeles Times*, the *Nation*, and the *Huffington Post*, among other publications. Pogrebin also cofounded the National Women's Political Caucus, the Ms. Foundation for Women, and the Free to Be Foundation. She is a past president of Americans for Peace Now and served two terms as president of the Authors Guild. Her honors include a Yale University Poynter Fellowship in journalism, a "Notable American Award," and four fellowships at the MacDowell Colony for the Arts. Pogrebin lives in New York City with her husband; they have three children and six grandchildren.

ROBIN POGREBIN is an arts and culture reporter for the *New York Times*. She is a graduate of Yale University and was previously an associate producer for Peter Jennings's documentary unit at ABC News and a staff reporter for the *New York Times*. Pogrebin's articles also run regularly in the *International Herald Tribune*, and she has occasionally done freelance pieces for *New York*, *Vogue*, and *Departures* magazines. She lives in New York City with her husband and two children.

PATRICE QUINN is a singer and actress who has performed on film, on television, and in the theater with some of the world's finest musicians. As the founder of ArtsExpand, a nonprofit organization that connects arts professionals with at-risk youth for the enrichment of the entire community of Los Angeles, she has taught acting at the Los Angeles County High School for the Arts. She lives in Los Angeles.

LORI ROTSKOFF is a cultural historian, writer, and teacher. She has taught at Yale University and Sarah Lawrence College and currently teaches classes for adults at the Barnard Center for Research on Women, where she has worked since 2005. She holds a bachelor's degree from Northwestern University and a doctorate from Yale University. Her previous book, *Love on the Rocks: Men, Women, and Alcohol in Post–World War II America* (2002), was named an Outstanding Academic Title by the American Library Association. Her book reviews have appeared in *Brain, Child: The Magazine for Thinking Mothers, Reviews in American History*, the *Chicago Tribune*, and the *Women's Review of Books*. She has received fellowships and research grants from the Woodrow Wilson Foundation, the American Historical Society, the Smith College Library Archives, and the Schlesinger Library at the Radcliffe Institute for Advanced Study. She lives in Larchmont, New York, with her husband and two sons.

DEBORAH SIEGEL holds a doctorate from the University of Wisconsin and is the author of *Sisterhood, Interrupted: From Radical Women to Grrls Gone Wild* (2007), coeditor of the literary anthology *Only Child* (2006), creator of the Girl w/Pen blog, and a founding partner of She Writes, the largest online community of women who write. Her writing on women, contemporary families, sex, popular culture, and the unfinished business of feminism across generations has appeared in venues including CNN.com, the *Washington Post*, the *Guardian, Ms.*, and *More*. She serves on the board of the Council on Contemporary Families and currently works with the OpEd Project, a social venture designed to broaden the range of voices that are heard in public debate, especially women's. She blogs at the Pink and Blue Diaries about gender, parenthood, writing, and life.

JEREMY ADAM SMITH is the author of *The Daddy Shift: How Breadwinning Moms, Stay-at-Home Dads, and Shared Parenting Are Transforming the American Family* (2009), coeditor of *Rad Dad: Dispatches from the Frontiers of Fatherhood* (2011), and founder of the blog Daddy Dialectic (daddy-dialectic.blogspot.com). He was a 2010–11 John S. Knight Journalism Fellow at Stanford University and now serves as web editor for the University of California, Berkeley, Greater Good Science Center.

BARBARA SPRUNG is codirector of the Educational Equity Center at FHI 360. In 1972, she founded the Nonsexist Child Development Project for the Women's Action Alliance, and she directed the project until 1978. From 1982 to 2004, she was cofounder and codirector of Educational Equity Concepts, which developed programs and materials to create equal opportunity for all children regardless of gender, race, disability, or level of family income. She holds a bachelor's degree from Sarah Lawrence College and a master's from the Bank Street College of Education, and she is a graduate of the Institute for Not-for-Profit Management, Columbia University. She is the author of *Nonsexist Education for Young Children: A Practical Guide* (1975), *Perspectives on Nonsexist Education* (1978), and numerous articles and curriculum guides. Most recently, she coauthored *The Anti-Bullying and Teasing Book for Preschool Classrooms* (2005) and *Supporting Boys' Learning: Strategies for Teacher Practice, Pre-K–Grade 3* (2010).

GLORIA STEINEM is a writer, lecturer, editor, and feminist activist. She travels in the United States and other countries as an organizer and is a frequent media spokeswoman on issues of equality. Her books include the best sellers *Revolution from Within: A Book of Self-Esteem, Outrageous Acts, and Everyday Rebellions* (1992), *Moving beyond Words* (1994), and *Marilyn: Norma Jean* (1997), on the life of Marilyn Monroe. She cofounded *Ms.* Magazine, *New York* Magazine, the *Ms.* Foundation for Women, and the Women's Media Center.

MARLO THOMAS is an award-winning actress, author, and activist. She has been honored with four Emmy Awards, a Peabody, a Golden Globe, and a Grammy and has been inducted into the Broadcasting Hall of Fame. She conceived, produced, and starred in television's *That Girl* (1966–71), which broke new ground for independent women. Her pioneering spirit continued with her creation of *Free to Be . . . You and Me.* She has remained a constant presence on television and in Broadway and Off-Broadway theater.

She cofounded the *Ms.* Foundation for Women and the Free to Be Foundation and is the national outreach director for St. Jude Children's Research Hospital. Her activism has been honored with numerous awards, including the ACLU's Thomas Paine Award, the William Kunstler Racial Justice Award, and the American Cancer Society's Humanitarian Award.

Her six books, all *New York Times* best sellers, include *Free to Be . . . You and Me* (1972); *Free to Be . . . a Family* (1987); *The Right Words at the Right Time,* 2 vols. (2002, 2006); *Thanks and Giving: All Year Long* (2004), which also became a Grammy-winning CD; and her memoir, *Growing Up Laughing* (2010). In 2010, she launched a website, MarloThomas.com, and she now serves as editor-at-large of the *Huffington Post*'s Women's Page. She lives in New York with her husband, Phil Donahue.

Acknowledgments

It is a pleasure to acknowledge many people who helped us bring this book to fruition. First, we thank all of our contributors for writing the thoughtful essays that comprise this volume. We would not have been able to document this history without input from the original *Free to Be* collaborators, and we are very grateful to them for recording their stories here.

We thank Marlo Thomas for her invaluable support and dedication to chronicling *Free to Be*'s history. She graciously provided access to archives, shared photographs from her personal collection, offered many helpful suggestions, and wrote a wonderful prologue. Thanks also to Francesca Dolce for aiding our research and to Amy Novak for attending to many details in the final months.

We are indebted to Letty Cottin Pogrebin for sharing her knowledge and insight with warmth and generosity and for encouraging us at every step along the way. Carole Hart and Carol Hall offered suggestions and clarified important details as we revised our work.

Our agent, Cecelia Cancellaro, had faith in our project from the moment we contacted her, and we have benefited from her sound advice and support ever since.

Our trusted editor at the University of North Carolina Press, Chuck Grench, expertly shepherded us through the thickets of the publication process. Many others at UNC Press also supported our work and kept us on track, including Sara Jo Cohen, Paul Betz, Ellen Bush, Beth Lassiter, and Dino Battista.

As we researched, edited, and revised this volume, we benefited tremendously from the perceptive comments and incisive suggestions of our external reviewers, Amy Erdman Farrell and Christina Baker Kline. We were fortunate indeed to receive their discerning remarks at several important junctures along the way.

We are also grateful to those who provided photographs or permission to reproduce images, including Thom Loubet of the Free to Be Foundation, Bettye Lane, the Sophia Smith Collection, Abigail Pogrebin, and Rita Waterman.

We benefited from many comments we received from fellow panelists and audiences at the Society for the History of Childhood and Youth conferences in 2009 and 2011. In addition, we appreciate the feedback we receive from our students, who remind us why projects like this are important to pursue in the first place.

From Laura Lovett: I thank Jessica Weiss and her copanelists at the American Studies Association as well as the first UMass ISHA Writing Group, whose support and critiques were invaluable. Marla Miller's work on the Women's Action Alliance materials in the Sophia Smith Collection, as well as the support, knowledge, and good humor of Sherrill Redmon, Maida Goodwin, Karen Kukil, Susan Barker, and Amy Hague at Sophia Smith have made this research possible. I also thank Deb Meem and other scholars at the University of Cincinnati for their incisive comments on the project. Bengt Sandin of the Tema Barn in the Department of Thematic Studies at the University of Linköping introduced me to students who helped me think about the international impact of this project. Thanks also go to the scholars at the Five Colleges Women's Studies Research Center, who appreciated the importance of this project and who made my time there memorable. As always, my coeditors at the *Journal of the History of Childhood and Youth*, Karen Sánchez-Eppler, Alice Hearst, Brian Bunk, and Martha Saxton, made thinking about the importance of children an enjoyable process. I could not have undertaken this work without generous aid from the College of Humanities and Fine Arts at the University of Massachusetts, Amherst, Department of History or the support and resources of the Leslie Center for the Humanities at Dartmouth College, especially Adrian Randolph, Colleen Boggs, and Annabel Martín and the Women's and Gender Studies Program. I am grateful as always for the support of my daughters and spouse, who help me understand the importance of feminist parenting.

From Lori Rotskoff: I thank the Sophia Smith Collection for awarding me a research travel grant and the Schlesinger Library at the Radcliffe Institute for a research support grant. For helpful comments on earlier drafts of my work, which I presented at annual meetings of the Organization of American Historians, the Berkshire Conference on Women's History, the Society for the History of Childhood and Youth, and the Sarah Lawrence College Women's History Conference, I thank Kirsten Swinth, Amy Farrell, Molly Ladd-Taylor, Heather Munro Prescott, Elspeth Brown, and Uta Poiger. I'm also grateful to the Larchmont Historical Society for inviting me to speak about my work at an earlier stage. Thanks also to Ilana Trachtman, Shelley Miller, and Mary Rodgers for sharing valuable insights.

Heather Hewett has been an exceptional writing partner, colleague, and friend, and I'm buoyed by her support at every turn. I'm also grateful to Deborah Siegel for years of inspiration, and to Patty Horing for providing pointed feedback on many drafts. I am fortunate to live and work surrounded by wonderful friends who bolstered me with encouragement, happy distractions, and timely carpool rescues during the time I spent working on this project. Last but certainly not least, I'm blessed to share my life every day with Michael, Benji, and Eli. I thank them and my entire family for their patience, love, good humor, and unwavering support.

Copyright Credits for
Contributions to the Book

Index

Bullying: and gender roles, 155–56, 159, 277 (n. 2); and gender-nonconforming behavior, 203, 251, 255

Burton, Gabrielle, 130

Buss, Dale, 125

Butler, Shelley, 175

Carbine, Pat, and *Free to Be*, 31

Careers: and balance of motherhood, 23–24, 65, 146–49, 151–52, 158, 165, 218, 251; and *Free to Be* series, 96, 119–20, 126, 128, 274; and gender equality, 100–101, 118; and board games, 112; child's play as influential for, 114, 117–22, 123; and balance of fatherhood, 159, 165; and coparenting, 168. *See also* Workplace equity

Carla, Lea, 232

Carnegie Council on Children, 16, 258

Cassidy, Jack, 128, 267

Catalyst, 148

Cavett, Dick, 266

Ceballos, Jacqueline, 121

Cerf, Christopher, 256, 259

Channing, Carol, performance of "Housework," 129, 132, 173, 190, 247, 269

Chauvinism, 101–2, 105, 109

Chicago International Film Festival, 127

Children and childhood: and feminism, 2, 4–5, 82, 83–85, 88–89, 90, 278 (n. 6); and children's commitment to gender equality, 2, 92–97, 98, 99–110, 134, 220, 285 (n. 17); *Free to Be* series' representations of, 7, 36, 68; *Free to Be* series' focus on, 62, 63, 68, 81, 83, 86; and children's culture of 1970s, 81, 82, 83, 91, 111; types of play, 115; and children's culture of 2000s, 174, 187–88

Children's Book Council, 84

Children's literature: and gender roles, 14–15, 16, 38–39, 44, 45, 66–67, 85–86, 201; sexism in, 16, 84; *Free to Be* tele-

vision special's dramatization of, 30; for *Free to Be* album, 41–43; and racial stereotypes, 42, 86, 113; gender stereotypes in, 71, 72–73, 74, 85, 117, 122, 125, 143–44, 201–2, 254; and visibility as measure of gendered power, 84; and "Cop-Out" genre, 85–86; and nonsexist literature boom, 202; gender-nonconforming behavior in, 202–4; and racial equality, 210

Children's Television Workshop, 35

Christian Right, 133

"Circle of Friends" (Hart and Lawrence), and *Free to Be* television special, 39, 265–66

Citizenship, ideals of, 28

Civil rights movement: and *Free to Be* series' message, 2, 29, 235; and children's culture, 82; and activism, 229, 232, 237; backlash against, 256

Clifton, Lucille, 29, 38, 69–70, 259, 273–74

Clinton, Bill, 259

Clinton, Hillary, 66

Cold War, 260

Congress of Racial Equality (CORE), 229, 232

Consciousness-raising groups, 5, 83, 86, 231

Conservative social values: and educational textbooks, 86; and nonsexist child-rearing movement, 124, 132–33; and gays and lesbians as parents, 161; and families, 256–57; and idea of freedom, 261

Consumer products, and gender roles, 2, 46, 185–90

Coolidge, Rita, 39, 266

The Cosby Show (television show), 237, 254

Culture wars, 86, 262

Curvan, Caroline Ranald, 106–7, 285 (n. 34)

Danish, Barbara, 86

The Daring Book for Girls (Peskowitz), 196–98

and motherhood, 5, 277–78 (n. 5); and Thomas, 27, 83, 86; and *Free to Be* album, 30, 35, 279 (n. 6); and humanistic psychology, 32–33, 279–80 (n. 11); and Alda, 60–61; and gender roles, 64, 138, 139, 142, 143, 173–74, 180–81, 241, 265; and personal freedom, 65; and *Free to Be* series' message, 81, 82, 91, 127, 130–31, 132, 138, 151–53, 157, 173, 198, 240, 268; and children's commitment to gender equality, 92–97, 104–5; popular expressions of, 93, 284 (n. 3); and Billie Jean King, 98–99; toys on agenda of, 112–13, 117–18; third-wave, 139; family values of, 165–72; post-secondwave, 174; and cultural change, 241; backlash against, 256; and positive psychology, 279 (n. 11)

Feminist Press, 86

Feminists on Children's Media, 84, 85

"The Field" (Roiphe), 29

Fine, Cordelia, 145

The First Ms. Reader, 63, 64

Fisher-Price, 189

Flack, Roberta, 57, 207, 210, 212, 238, 274

Florey-Tighe, Viola, 288 (n. 32)

Flowers, Wayland, 38, 265

Focus on the Family, 133, 257

Freedom. *See* Personal freedom

Free to Be (album): Thomas's conception of, 1, 4, 14–16, 19–20, 27, 35, 41–42, 48, 49, 59, 68, 81, 83, 110, 128, 133, 172, 201–2, 231; make-believe world of, 6; memories of, 13, 173, 174, 191, 193–94, 215–16, 220, 222, 223, 242–43; testing on children, 16–17, 43; success of, 17, 38, 43, 58, 81, 127; collaborators on, 27, 28, 34, 35–38, 41–43, 56–58, 113; African American performers on, 29; release of, 35, 38; recording of, 37–38; children's literature for, 41–42, 83; toys featured in, 113; distribution of, 122; and Public Action Coalition on Toys award,

125; Grammy nomination for, 127, 280 (n. 2); careers featured in, 128; reviews of, 128–29. *See also specific songs*

Free to Be (book): creation of, 1, 17, 34, 38, 43–44, 63; inspiration of, 6; Steinem's preface to, 9, 31; memories of, 13; children's perspectives included in, 29; sheet music in, 29, 131; thirty-fifth anniversary edition of, 39–40; Klagsbrun as editor of, 43, 63; success of, 44, 81; children's response to, 66; careers featured in, 120; distribution of, 122; and Public Action Coalition on Toys award, 125; reviews of, 130–31; American Library Association Award for, 280 (n. 2)

"Free to Be" (song; Hart and Lawrence): writing of, 16, 37, 56; messages of, 142, 189, 267; new lyrics for, 152–53; memories of, 194, 222, 240, 245–46

Free to Be (television special): creation of, 1, 17, 34, 38; inspiration of, 6; stage version for children, 13, 18, 61, 185; screening for TV executives, 17–18; Emmy Award for, 18, 38, 44, 127, 280 (n. 2); reviews of, 18, 132; African American performers on, 29; airing of, 29–30, 158, 240; production of, 43; success of, 81, 82, 134; controversies over "William's Doll," 89–90; careers featured in, 119–20; Peabody Award for, 127, 280 (n. 2); controversies over "Housework" sketch, 130, 289 (n. 7); memories of, 194; and West 80th Street Day Care Center, 231, 237–38

Free to Be . . . a Family, 69, 256–60

Free to Be Foundation, 243

Free to Be . . . You and Me series: and gender roles, 1, 2, 15, 21–23, 42–43, 49, 58, 83, 87, 88–89, 90, 127, 144, 145, 155, 162, 180, 189, 190, 198, 199, 200–201, 203, 205, 218, 220, 240–41, 252, 255, 256; and social equality, 1, 2–3, 29, 34, 45, 48, 86, 90, 231, 233,

262; diversity endorsed by, 1, 82, 220; fortieth anniversary of, 3–4, 7, 13; historical analysis of, 3–6, 8, 82; production of, 4, 5–6; backlashes to, 4, 45, 58, 69, 77; and personal freedom, 5, 6, 8, 16, 27, 31, 32, 33, 39, 56, 65, 82, 83, 90–91, 104, 110, 133, 144, 151–52, 159, 186, 194, 196, 198, 214, 216, 217, 228, 232, 235–39, 244, 245–50, 254, 267; and nonsexist child-rearing movement, 5, 7, 49, 50–52, 131, 240; as classic, 6–7, 10; attitude toward children, 7, 36, 68; and parenting advice manuals, 7, 173, 174, 175; cultural impact of, 7–8, 9, 18–19, 34, 38, 39–40, 44–45, 58, 61, 68–69, 83, 151, 200, 235, 240, 262; responses to, 8, 21–22, 44, 127–34; interpretations of, 8–9, 19, 243–44; as cross-generational touchstone, 13, 61, 90, 151; and humanistic psychology, 31–33; and fatherhood, 49, 51, 120, 154–55, 157–58, 159, 194, 201, 205; children as focus of, 62, 63, 68, 81, 83, 86; and fairness, 66–67; and feminism, 81, 82, 91, 127, 130–31, 132, 138, 151–53, 157, 173, 198, 240, 268; generational cohort of, 81, 142; success of, 81–82, 86, 95, 127, 134, 282 (n. 24); careers featured in, 96, 119–20, 126, 128, 274; and children's commitment to gender equality, 108–9; toys featured in, 113–14; and Women's Action Alliance, 122–23; Dobson on, 125; and mass media, 127–32, 269–70; memories of, 146–53, 160–64, 166, 167–68

Freud, Sigmund, 64, 115
Freudian psychoanalysis, 32, 279 (n. 11)
Friedan, Betty, 3, 32, 119, 279–80 (n. 11)
Friedman, Becky, 8

Gardner, Herb, 15, 16, 36
Gays and lesbians: as parents, 157–58, 159, 160–64. See also Homosexuality

Gender difference, issues of, 8, 116, 251–52, 254–55
Gender equality: children's commitment to, 2, 92–97, 98, 99–110, 134, 220, 285 (n. 17); and Title IX, 47, 57, 95, 97; and "Click" moments, 62, 65, 102, 103; and self-actualization, 82; and Billie Jean King, 98
Gender identities: as socially constructed, 83–84, 116, 181, 189; children's awareness of, 145; and gender identity disorder in children, 180; and childhood gender variance, 199–200, 292 (n. 1)
Gender impermanence, 189
Gender roles: *Free to Be* series' perspective on, 1, 2, 15, 21–23, 42–43, 49, 58, 83, 87, 88–89, 90, 127, 144, 145, 155, 162, 180, 189, 190, 198, 199, 200–201, 203, 205, 218, 220, 240–41, 252, 255, 256; and toys, 2, 46, 72–73, 75–77, 89, 109, 111, 113–14, 122–23, 177, 180–81, 186–89; and consumer products, 2, 46, 185–90; and workplace equity, 5, 45–46, 49–53, 55, 100, 118–19, 159; cultural priorities of, 8; and children's literature, 14–15, 16, 41–42, 44, 45, 66–67, 85–86, 201; in post–World War II era, 28; and self-actualization, 32; socialization influencing, 42, 83, 87, 90, 113, 115, 116, 124, 125, 127, 137–39, 181, 189, 265; Letty Cottin Pogrebin on, 45–48, 116, 124; and social equality, 62, 63, 64, 205, 242; and gender stereotypes, 64, 71–73, 89, 117, 118–19; and feminism, 64, 138, 139, 142, 143, 173–74, 180–81, 241, 265; and homosexuality, 75, 90, 123–24, 125, 133, 155; personal freedom in, 75, 196–98; and power relations, 88, 96; studies of, 114–17, 200, 292 (n. 1); parents' influence on, 116, 160–61; parents' experiences of, 137–45, 160–64, 173–74, 290 (n. 3); and bullying, 155–56, 159, 277

(n. 2); and gender-neutral parenting, 174–79, 291 (n. 3); and gender-
nonconforming behavior, 176–78,
199–201, 202, 203, 204–6, 251–52,
254–55, 292 (n. 1); and hip-hop,
219–20; and "Housework," 269–70;
and "The Sun and the Moon," 273
Gender stereotypes: alternatives to,
1, 19, 97; and *Free to Be* television
special, 17–18, 43, 64–65; and *Free to
Be* album, 36, 56, 83, 200–201, 224–25;
and Letty Cottin Pogrebin, 42–43,
71, 113; and gender roles, 64, 71–73,
89, 117, 118–19; in education, 71–75,
86, 195–96; and toys, 112–13, 120–22,
125–26, 175; and gender-neutral
parenting, 175; and *That Girl*, 226;
continued influence of, 262
General Mills Corporation, 106
GI Bill of Rights, 28
Gilligan, Carol, 170
Gilman, Susan Jane, 81
Gimpel, Erica, 238
Ginsburg, Ruth Bader, 66
"Girl Land" (Rodgers and Hart), 128,
267–68
Girls Inc., 139
"Glad to Have a Friend Like You" (Hall):
messages of, 22, 189, 268; writing of,
55; toys featured in, 114, 268
Goldberg, Whoopi, 259–60
Goodman, Ellen, 122
Gordone, Leah-Carla, 238
Gould, Lois, 144, 290 (n. 2)
Green, Constance, 85
Green, Richard, 200, 292 (n. 1)
Greenberg, Selma, 74–75
Greenburg, Dan, 32, 59, 114, 167, 266
Greever, Anne Gordon, 132
Grier, Rosey, performance of "It's All
Right to Cry," 37, 55, 57, 67, 99, 132,
185, 238, 270
Growing Up Laughing (Thomas), 27
Gruver, Nancy, 7
Gustavson, Fran, 122

Hall, Carol: origins of lyrics, 4, 16; as
songwriter for *Free to Be* album,
35–36, 37, 49–53, 55, 114, 268, 270,
271–72; career as composer, 288
(n. 36)
Harnick, Sheldon, collaboration on
Free to Be album, 15, 36, 64, 82,
129–30, 269
Hart, Bruce: creation of title, 16, 37;
as *Sesame Street* contributor, 35; as
composer for *Free to Be* album, 36,
37, 56, 267; as composer for *Free to Be*
television special, 39; death of, 40
Hart, Carole: as coproducer of *Free to Be*,
1, 4, 15, 34, 36–40, 42, 43, 56, 68; as
Sesame Street contributor, 15, 35; as
television writer, 28
Hathaway, Sandra, 179
"Helping" (Silverstein): writing of, 36;
Smothers's performance of, 37, 269;
messages of, 268–69
Heterosexuality, 90, 123, 124, 126, 160,
179, 204
Hip-hop, 218–20, 221
Hokada, Elizabeth, 281 (n. 14)
Holgate, 114
Hollywood Reporter, 132
Homophobia, 67, 68, 124, 126, 161
Homosexuality: and gender roles, 75,
90, 123–24, 125, 133, 155; and parent-
ing advice manuals, 178–79, 180. *See
also* Gays and lesbians
Horing, Patricia Lewy, 99
"Housework" (Harnick): criticism of, 64,
129–30, 270, 289 (n. 7); messages of,
82, 269–70; Channing's performance
of, 129, 132, 173, 190, 247, 269; memo-
ries of, 173
Hughes, Dorothy Pitman, 234
Humanistic psychology, 31–33, 279–80
(n. 11)

Ideal Toy Corporation, 125
Institute for Child Welfare, University
of Minnesota, 115

Instructo, 119

Iowa Child Research Station, 115

"It's All Right to Cry" (Hall): memories of, 13; writing of, 16, 37, 55, 57; Grier's performance of, 37, 55, 57, 67, 99, 132, 185, 238, 270; messages of, 270

Jacklin, Carol, 116

Jackson, Michael: and *Free to Be* television special, 8, 45, 57, 67, 207, 210, 212, 238, 274; skin changes of, 207–8, 212, 213, 275; death of, 209; and personal freedom, 214

J. Crew, 180

Jews and Judaism: and feminism, 63; and rituals for infants, 141–42

Jones, Shirley, 267

Jorgensen, Christine, 129

Jowitt, Deborah, 128–29

Kelly, Joe, 7

Keyser, Janis, 175

Kilodavis, Cheryl, *My Princess Boy*, 251–52, 254–55

King, Billie Jean, 98–99

King, Carole, 30

Kingsley, Emily, 259

Kirschner, Dionne, 4, 14–15, 17, 19–20

Klagsbrun, Francine, 4, 43, 63

Kleban, Ed, 57

Kratz, Deb, 175

Kristofferson, Kris, 39, 266

"Ladies First" (Silverstein): writing of, 16; and *Free to Be* album, 36, 87, 270; and *Free to Be* book, 66, 87, 270; and gender roles, 87–88, 232, 268; and metaphors of circle, 266; and *Free to Be* television special, 270; messages of, 271

Ladies' Home Journal, 82

Lady Gaga, 181

Lane, Bettye, 121

Laron, Elaine, 29, 58, 273

Lauer, Andrea, 243

Lawrence, Stephen: on musical arrangements, 4, 57, 58; as composer for *Free to Be* album, 16, 35, 37, 39, 56–58, 267, 274; as *Sesame Street* composer, 56

Lazarre, Jane, 277 (n. 5)

Leach, Penelope, 176

Lennon, John, 234

Leonard, John, 18

Lesbians. *See* Gays and lesbians

"Let's Hear It for Babies" (Kleban), 38, 57, 58, 265

Levittown, N.Y., 28, 279 (n. 4)

"Like Me" (Kingsley), 259

Lindsay, John, 230

Lipton, James, 58

Little Miss Muffet Fights Back (Feminists on Children's Media), 84

Lollipop Power, 86

Lovett, Laura L., 18, 132–33

Maccoby, Eleanor, 116

Magnetel games, 121

Mainardi, Pat, 269

Marriage: and *That Girl*, 27, 41, 83; in post–World War II era, 27–28; and divorce, 29, 131, 257; changes in, 158–59; interracial, 234; challenges of, 248–50; same-sex, 261–62; median age at first, 278 (n. 2)

Martin, Karin A., 7

Marvin, Delethia, 232

Maslow, Abraham, 32–33

Mass media: and gender stereotypes, 8, 143, 155; Letty Cottin Pogrebin on, 105–6; and children's commitment to gender equality, 105–8; and toy advertising, 106–7; creativity featured on television shows, 114; and family structure, 118–19; and *Free to Be* series, 127–32, 269–70; and race, 209, 211–13, 214; and family values debate, 261

Matchbox cars, 121

Maury, Inez, 86

McBride, Kari, 163
McGraw-Hill, 43
McGraw-Hill Films, 30
McIntyre, Trey, 8
Meyers, Jonathan Tipton, 232, 238
Middle-class identity, 33
Miles, Betty, 16, 37, 263
Miller, Shelley, 57, 274
Milton Bradley, 114, 119
Money, John, 292 (n. 1)
Monopoly Pink Boutique edition, 188
Morgan, Robin, 3
Morse, Bobby, 267
Motherhood: and feminism, 5, 277–78 (n. 5); balance of, 23–24, 65, 146–49, 151–52, 158, 165, 218, 251; and coparenting, 165–72. *See also* Fatherhood
Moynihan, Daniel Patrick, 257
Ms. Foundation for Women, 30, 31, 34
Ms. magazine: journalism of, 4; founding of, 16, 41, 49; and *Free to Be* album, 30, 38, 129–30, 133; and gender stereotypes, 42, 62; "Stories for Free Children," 42, 68, 75, 95, 111, 275, 288 (n. 32); and *Free to Be* book, 63, 131; and Wonder Woman image, 67; and children's culture, 82, 94–95, 111; children's letters to, 92, 93, 94–95, 96, 99–100, 101, 102–3, 104, 107–8, 109, 284 (n. 1); as voice of popular feminism, 93; and Billie Jean King, 98–99; "What It's Like to Be Me" feature, 103; "Toys for Free Children," 111, 117, 122; and nonsexist child-rearing movement, 113; profitability of, 282 (n. 24)
Multiculturalism, 42, 288 (n. 32)
Murkoff, Heidi, 179
Murphy Brown (television show), 261
"My Dog Is a Plumber" (Greenburg), 59, 114, 266
My Princess Boy (Kilodavis), 251–52, 254–55

Nabisco, 121
Nader, Ralph, 125
Nas, 218–19, 220
National Association for Female Executives, 122
National Conference of Christians and Jews, 127
National Education Association, 127
National Organization for Women (NOW), 84, 120–22, 279–80 (n. 11)
National Women's Agenda, 118
Neuroplasticity, 189
Neuroscience, 138
Newbery Award, 84
New Direction for Life Ministries, 260
New Moon Girls, 170–72
New Right, 86
New Seekers, 222, 267
New York City High School Arts Festival, 127
New York City marathon, 264
New Yorker, 131
New York Times, 127, 128, 130
Nonsexist Child Development Project (NSCD), 71, 73–74, 113, 116–19
Nonsexist child-rearing movement: *Free to Be* series' role in, 5, 7, 49, 50–52, 131, 240; and Letty Cottin Pogrebin, 42, 114–15, 175; and feminism, 82; development of, 93; and mass media advertising, 107; and gender equality, 109; and *Ms.* magazine, 113; and diversity, 119, 126; and homosexuality, 123–24; criticism of, 124–25, 132–33
Non-Sexist Education for Young Children, 119
"No One Else" (Laron), 29
Nordstrom, Ursula, 15

Occupy resistance movement, 235
Ode Records, 30
Ogata, Amy, 114
Ono, Yoko, 234
O'Reilly, Jane, 62, 63, 64

Orenstein, Peggy, 7
Oxnard Press-Courier, 130
Ozick, Cynthia, 64

"The Pain and the Great One" (Blume), 29
Paltrow, Gwyneth, 58
Parenting advice manuals: *Free to Be* series' influence on, 7, 173, 174, 175; and gender-neutral child rearing, 174–79, 180
Parents and parenting: and appeal of *Free to Be* album, 36; roles of, 45, 61, 65, 77, 148–49, 157, 158; and mass media, 105–6; and toy selection, 112–13, 114, 116; Dobson on, 124–25, 133; and gender roles of children, 137–45, 160–64, 173–74, 290 (n. 3); gays and lesbians as, 157–58, 159, 160–64; and coparenting, 165–72, 181, 218; and gender-neutral parenting advice, 174–79, 180; and children's self-actualization, 199; and racial equality, 210–11, 213–14. *See also* Families; Fatherhood; Motherhood; Nonsexist child-rearing movement
"Parents Are People" (Hall): memories of, 1, 167–68, 215, 220; message from, 3, 22, 65, 96, 204, 217–18, 231; in *Free to Be* television special, 18, 119–20, 271–72; writing of, 50–53, 55; Thomas's performance of, 57; Belafonte's performance of, 57, 271–72; careers featured in, 119–20, 126; reviews of, 129
Parents for Responsibility in the Toy Industry, 120–21
Paris, Leslie, 134, 278 (n. 6), 279 (n. 6)
Parker, Steven, 176, 178
Parten, Mildred, 115
Peabody Award, 18
Personal freedom: *Free to Be* series' emphasis on, 5, 6, 8, 16, 27, 31, 32, 33, 39, 56, 65, 82, 83, 90–91, 104, 110, 133, 144, 151–52, 159, 186, 194, 196, 198,

214, 216, 217, 228, 232, 235–39, 244, 245–50, 254, 267; children's conceptions of, 33, 91, 194, 216–17, 280 (n. 12); in gender roles, 75, 196–98; and gender stereotypes, 117
Personal is political claim, 5
Peskowitz, Miriam, *The Daring Book for Girls*, 196–98
Petoskey News Review, 132
Philyaw, Deesha, 7–8
Pinchbeck, Daniel, 29
Playskool, 117–18
Pogrebin, Abigail, 7, 43, 106
Pogrebin, Bert, 146
Pogrebin, David, 43, 106
Pogrebin, Letty Cottin: and activism, 4, 48; and *Ms.* magazine, 16, 41, 68, 111, 114, 122, 146; and children's literature for *Free to Be* album, 16, 41–43; as book publicist, 28; collaboration on *Free to Be* series, 31, 44, 242; and Maslow, 33; and nonsexist child rearing, 42, 114–15, 175; and gender stereotypes, 42–43, 71, 113; on political correctness, 43–44, 45; on gender roles, 45–48, 116, 124; on mass media, 105–6, 107; on toys, 111–14, 117, 122, 126; balance of motherhood, 146–47, 151; collaboration on *Free to Be . . . a Family*, 256, 258–59
Pogrebin, Robin, 7, 43, 106
Popenoe, Paul, 124
Pratt, Carolyn, 114
Prince, 208, 209
PTA committees, 5
Public Action Coalition on Toys (PACT), 125

Quayle, Dan, 261
Quinn, Patrice Pitman, 231–32

Race and racism, reflections on, 208, 209–14
Racial discrimination: in post–World War II era, 28, 210, 214; in hous-

ing, 28–29, 279 (n. 4); and personal freedom, 90; *Free to Be* series not addressing, 220

Racial equality: and *Free to Be* television special, 18, 43, 265; and *Free to Be* series, 29, 232, 237–38, 259; children's commitment to, 103; and *Free to Be* book, 120; and parents and parenting, 210–11, 213–14

Racial stereotypes: alternatives to, 1; and children's literature, 42, 86, 113; in educational materials, 73, 74, 119, 288 (n. 32); and toys, 113, 119

Racial terrorism, 209–10, 214

Raposo, Joe, 35

Reagan, Ronald, 259

Really Rosie (album), 30

Really Rosie (television production), 30

Redbook, 82

Redstockings, 269

Reiner, Carl, 15, 36

Religion, 8, 63, 141–42, 179, 190, 192, 245, 246–50, 252, 260

Reproductive freedom, 5

Ressner, Phil, 266–67

Reynolds, Peter, 39

Rich, Adrienne, 277–78 (n. 5)

Richards, Renee, 129

Richlands New Press, 132

Riggs, Bobby, 98–99

Riggs-King tennis match, 98–99

Right: Christian Right, 133; New Right, 133. *See also* Conservative social values

Rockwell, Julius, 114

Rodgers, Mary, 28, 36, 87, 267, 270–71

Rodgers, Richard, 50

Rogers, Fred, 227–28

Roiphe, Anne, 29

Rosemond, John, 177

Ross, Catherine, 281 (n. 14)

Ross, Diana, 57, 238, 274

Ross, Edward A., 115

Rotskoff, Lori, 18

Same-sex marriage, 261–62

Sears, R. R., 115–16

Seattle Daily Times, 132

Sedgwick, Eve Kosofsky, 179

Seeger, Pete, 238

Self-actualization, 32–33, 82, 91, 199

Self-help literature, 83

Sendak, Maurice, 30

Serbin, Lisa, 75

Sesame Street, 15, 35, 56

Sexism: in children's literature, 16, 84; and *Free to Be* series' message, 65, 87; in mass media, 105; and toys, 111–13, 120–21, 122; and consciousness-raising groups, 231

Sexuality, contemporary concern over, 262

Sharenow, Arthur, 100

Sharenow, Judith, 100

Shukat, Scott, 35

Siegel, Deborah, 7

Silverstein, Shel: collaboration on *Free to Be* album, 15, 16, 36, 87, 268–69; as children's author, 36, 269

Single women, *That Girl* on, 27, 41, 83

"Sisters and Brothers": recording of, 37–38; on *Free to Be* television special, 39, 272–73; messages of, 232, 236, 237, 272; and metaphors of circle, 266

Sitea, Linda, 29, 131

Slavery, 235–36, 257

Smith, Jeremy Adam, 7

Smothers, Tom, performance on *Free to Be* album, 37, 269

Social equality: *Free to Be* series' commitment to, 1, 2–3, 29, 34, 45, 48, 86, 90, 231, 233, 262; issues of, 8, 61, 62; and *Free to Be* album, 27; and Alda, 60–61; and gender roles, 62, 63, 64, 205, 242

Social expectations, 1

Social psychology, 115

Socioeconomic status: and self-actualization, 33; and children's

Wal-Mart, 188
Walters, Barbara, 241
Walton, Tony, 38
Warner, Judith, 197
War on Poverty, 257
Warwick, Dionne, 58, 273
Washington Post, 130
Watson, James, 115
"We and They" (Clifton), 69–70
Weitzman, Lenore J., 281 (n. 14)
Welfare programs, 257, 259–60
West 8oth Street Day Care Center,
    229–33, 234, 235, 236–38
West Side Community Alliance, 234
"What Shall I Be?" (board game), 112
"What Shall I Wear?" (board game), 112,
    286 (n. 3)
"When I Grow Up" (educational game),
    117
"When We Grow Up" (Miller and Law-
    rence): cultural impact of, 8, 22; and
    Free to Be television special, 8, 57, 67,
    207, 212, 274; and *Free to Be* album,
    57, 274; message of, 212, 255
White women, employment of, 28
Williams, Dar, 162
Williams, Jay, 167, 282 (n. 27)
"William's Doll" (Harnick and Rodgers):
    memories of, 1, 13, 143, 154–55, 157,
    159, 194, 204, 243; and normative
    masculinity of fatherhood, 7, 89, 113,

122, 154, 201, 204, 206, 275; contro-
    versies over, 18, 67–68, 89–90, 124,
    132; inspiration for, 36; and gender
    stereotypes, 89, 91, 201, 204, 205–6,
    224–25, 275; toys featured in, 113;
    and Women's Action Alliance poster,
    122–23; and metaphors of circle, 265
Women on Words and Images, 84, 85
Women's Action Alliance (WAA), 71–72,
    73, 113, 116, 118, 122
Women's liberation movement: and
    Free to Be series' message, 2, 4, 45,
    65; and *Really Rosie*, 30. *See also*
    Feminism
Working mothers: balance of, 23–24, 45,
    218; workplace equity for, 45, 148; in
    children's literature, 86; and career
    options, 118; and *Free to Be* series,
    120; and child care services, 229–30,
    231, 234
Workplace equity: and gender roles, 5,
    45–46, 49–53, 55, 100, 118–19, 159; in
    post–World War II era, 28; and equal
    pay for women, 45, 61, 97; for work-
    ing mothers, 45, 148
Writers' Guild, 84

"Zachary's Divorce" (Sitea), 29, 131
Zolotow, Charlotte, *William's Doll*, 15, 36,
    89, 175, 201, 202, 205, 206, 275, 283
    (n. 28)